Manrique

D0823238

Vocabulary
Power Plus for
College and Career Readiness

By Daniel A. Reed
Edited by Paul Moliken

Vocabulary

Prestwick House

P.O. Box 658 • Clayton, DE 19938
(800) 932-4593 • www.prestwickhouse.com

ISBN   978-1-62019-1453

Copyright ©2014 by Prestwick House, Inc. *Revised July, 2015.*
All rights reserved. No portion may be reproduced without permission in writing from the publisher.

Vocabulary Power Plus for College and Career Readiness

• Table of Contents •

Vocabulary Power Plus for College and Career Readiness

LEVEL TWELVE

·Introduction·

VOCABULARY POWER PLUS FOR COLLEGE AND CAREER READINESS combines classroom-tested vocabulary drills with reading and writing exercises designed to foster the English and language arts skills essential for college and career success, with the added advantage of successfully preparing students for both the Scholastic Assessment Test and the American College Testing assessment.

Although *Vocabulary Power Plus* is a proven resource for college-bound students, it is guaranteed to increase vocabulary, improve grammar, enhance writing, and boost critical reading skills for students at all levels of learning.

Critical Reading exercises include lengthy passages and detailed, evidence-based, two-part questions designed to promote understanding and eliminate multiple-choice guessing. We include SAT- and ACT-style grammar and writing exercises and have placed the vocabulary words in non-alphabetical sequence, distributed by part-of-speech.

Coupled with words-in-context exercises, inferences cultivate comprehensive word discernment by prompting students to create contexts for words, instead of simply memorizing definitions. Related words-in-context exercises forge connections among words, ensuring retention for both knowledge and fluency, and nuance exercises instill active inference habits to discern not just adequate words for contexts, but the best words in a specific context.

The writing exercises in *Vocabulary Power Plus* are process-oriented and adaptable to individual classroom lesson plans. Our rubrics combine the fundamentals of the essay-scoring criteria for both the SAT and ACT optional writing portions, with emphasis on organization, development, sentence formation, and word choice. This objective scoring opportunity helps students develop a concrete understanding of the writing process and develop a personal approach to punctual, reactive writing.

We hope that you find the *Vocabulary Power Plus for College and Career Readiness* series to be an effective tool for teaching new words, and an exceptional tool for preparing for assessments.

Strategies for Completing Activities

Roots, Prefixes, and Suffixes

A knowledge of roots, prefixes, and suffixes can give readers the ability to view unfamiliar words as mere puzzles that require only a few simple steps to solve. For the person interested in the history of words, this knowledge provides the ability to track word origin and evolution. For those who seek to improve vocabulary, the knowledge creates a sure and lifelong method; however, there are two points to remember:

1. Some words have evolved through usage, so present definitions might differ from what you infer through an examination of the roots and prefixes. The word *abstruse*, for example, contains the prefix *ab–* (away) and the root *trudere* (to thrust), and literally means "to thrust away." Today, *abstruse* is used to describe something that is hard to understand.

2. Certain roots do not apply to all words that use the same form. If you know that the root *vin* means "to conquer," then you would be correct in concluding that the word *invincible* means "incapable of being conquered"; however, if you tried to apply the same root meaning to *vindicate* or *vindictive*, you would be incorrect. When analyzing unfamiliar words, check for other possible roots if your inferred meaning does not fit the context.

Despite these considerations, a knowledge of roots and prefixes is one of the best ways to build a powerful vocabulary.

Critical Reading

Reading questions generally fall into several categories.

1. Identifying the main idea or the author's purpose. *What is this selection about?*

In some passages, the author's purpose will be easy to identify because the one or two ideas leap from the text; however, other passages might not be so easily analyzed, especially if they include convoluted sentences. Inverted sentences (subject at the end of the sentence) and elliptical sentences (words missing) will also increase the difficulty of the passages, but all these obstacles can be overcome if readers take one sentence at a time and recast it in their own words. Consider the following sentence:

> These writers either jot down their thoughts bit by bit, in short, ambiguous, and paradoxical sentences, which apparently mean much more than they say—of this kind of writing Schelling's treatises on natural philosophy are a splendid instance; or else they hold forth with a deluge of words and the most intolerable diffusiveness, as though no end of fuss were necessary to make the reader understand the deep meaning of their sentences, whereas it is some quite simple if not actually trivial idea, examples of which may be found in plenty in the popular works of Fichte, and the philosophical manuals of a hundred other miserable dunces.

If we edit out some of the words, the main point of this sentence is obvious.

> These writers either jot down their thoughts bit by bit, in short, ambiguous, and paradoxical sentences, which apparently mean much more than they say—of this kind of writing Schelling's treatises on natural philosophy are a splendid instance; or else they hold forth with a deluge of words and the most intolerable diffusiveness, as though n[it]d of fuss were necessary to make the reader understand the deep meaning of their sentences, whereas it is som[a]quite simple if not actually trivial idea, examples of which may be found in plenty in the popular works of Fichte, and the philosophical manuals of a hundred other miserable dunces.

Some sentences need only a few deletions for clarification, but others require major recasting and additions; they must be read carefully and put into the reader's own words.

> Some in their discourse desire rather commendation of wit, in being able to hold all arguments, than of judgment, in discerning what is true; as if it were a praise to know what might be said, and not what should be thought.

After studying it, a reader might recast the sentence as follows:

> In conversation, some people desire praise for their abilities to maintain the conversation rather than their abilities to identify what is true or false, as though it were better to sound good than to know what is truth or fiction.

2. Identifying the stated or implied meaning. *What is the author stating or suggesting?*

The literal meaning of a text does not always correspond with the intended meaning. To understand a passage fully, readers must determine which meaning—if there is more than one—is the intended meaning of the passage. Consider the following sentence:

> If his notice was sought, an expression of courtesy and interest gleamed out upon his features; proving that there was light within him and that it was only the outward medium of the intellectual lamp that obstructed the rays in their passage.

Interpreted literally, this Nathaniel Hawthorne metaphor suggests that a light-generating lamp exists inside the human body. Since this is impossible, the reader must look to the metaphoric meaning of the passage to understand it properly. In the metaphor, Hawthorne refers to the human mind—consciousness—as a lamp that emits light, and other people cannot always see the lamp because the outside "medium"—the human body—sometimes blocks it.

3. Identifying the tone or mood of the selection. *What feeling does the text evoke?*

To answer these types of questions, readers must look closely at individual words and their connotations; for example, the words *stubborn* and *firm* have almost the same definition, but a writer who describes a character as *stubborn* rather than *firm* is probably suggesting something negative about the character.

Vocabulary Power Plus for College and Career Readiness includes evidence-based follow-up questions in every critical reading lesson, as prescribed by the Partnership for Assessment of Readiness for College and Careers (PARCC) consortium, and will be used in the 2016 revision of the SAT. These questions prompt for the contextual evidence that students use to answer the primary questions.

Writing

The optional writing portions on the two major assessment tests allow approximately 30 minutes for the composition of a well-organized, fully developed essay. Writing a satisfactory essay in this limited time requires facility in determining a thesis, organizing ideas, and producing adequate examples to support the ideas.

These fundamentals are equally important for success on the Smarter Balanced Assessment Consortium ELA Performance Task, which includes a substantial essay writing assignment based on provided source texts.

Such a time-limited essay might lack the perfection and depth that weeks of proofreading and editing provide research papers. Process is undoubtedly of primary importance, but students must consider the time constraints of both reality and those of the assessments they elect to complete. Completion of the essay is just as important as organization, development, and language use.

The thesis, the organization of ideas, and the support make the framework of a good essay. Before the actual writing begins, writers must create a mental outline by establishing a thesis, or main idea, and one or more specific supporting ideas (the number of ideas will depend on the length and content of the essay). Supporting ideas should not be overcomplicated; they are simply ideas that justify or explain the thesis. The writer must introduce and explain each supporting idea, and the resultant supporting paragraph should answer the *Why?* or *Who cares?* questions that the thesis may evoke.

Once the thesis and supporting ideas are identified, writers must determine the order in which the ideas will appear in the essay. A good introduction usually explains the thesis and briefly introduces the supporting ideas. Explanation of the supporting ideas should follow, with each idea in its own paragraph. The final paragraph, the conclusion, usually restates the thesis or summarizes the main ideas of the essay.

Adhering to the mental outline when the writing begins will help the writer organize and develop the essay. Using the Organization and Development scoring guides to evaluate practice essays will help to reinforce the process skills. The Word Choice and Sentence Formation scoring guides will help to strengthen language skills—the vital counterpart to essay organization and development.

Vocabulary Power Plus for College and Career Readiness includes two styles of writing prompts. SAT-style writing prompts feature general subjects such as art, history, literature, or politics. ACT-style writing prompts involve subjects specifically relevant to high school students. Both styles of writing prompts require students to assume a point of view and support it with examples and reasoning.

Pronunciation Guide

a	—	track
ā	—	mate
ä	—	father
â	—	care
e	—	pet
ē	—	be
i	—	bit
ī	—	bite
o	—	job
ō	—	wrote
ô	—	port, fought
o͞o	—	proof
o͝o	—	full
u	—	pun
ū	—	you
û	—	purr
ə	—	about, system, supper, circus
oi	—	toy
îr	—	steer

Word List

Lesson 1
arable
camaraderie
desiccate
equanimity
frangible
interminable
litany
lugubrious
moratorium
replete
truncate
ubiquitous
vernacular
wrenching
zealous

Lesson 2
brigand
carte blanche
contemptuous
cosmopolitan
donnybrook
incantation
interlocutor
metamorphosis
nomenclature
nonchalant
procrustean
rife
sophistry
stygian
vestige

Lesson 3
abstemious
archaic
arrogate
atelier
axiom
dulcet
expurgate
iniquity
patronizing
pellucid
peremptory
perspicacious
scapegoat
talisman
vacillate

Lesson 4
apocryphal
catharsis
crepuscular
efficacious
estrange
internecine
intrinsic
inundate
kudos
maxim
putrid
revere
risible
servile
sybaritic

Lesson 5
anomaly
compendium
comprise
consternation
coterie
disconcert
eidetic
expiate
flippancy
foist
incongruous
innocuous
plethora
preamble
vitriolic

Lesson 6
accoutrement
antediluvian
contrive
haughty
hubris
imbroglio
peregrination
platitude
prognosticate
quotidian
sanctimonious
scullion
sectarian
stringent
venerate

Word List

Lesson 7
anecdote
churlish
coeval
cogent
convoluted
dilatory
entreat
gibberish
incumbent
inimical
livid
lurid
nexus
promulgate
staid

Lesson 8
aleatory
allay
ameliorate
asperity
exegesis
inveigh
lionize
otiose
pander
profligate
puerile
recalcitrant
renunciation
unimpeachable
vitiate

Lesson 9
benign
blithe
bumpkin
corroborate
culpable
frenetic
hortatory
indecorous
orotund
penultimate
pervasive
provocative
recrimination
soporific
toady

Lesson 10
circuitous
circumlocution
deprecate
indolent
largesse
luminous
majordomo
perambulate
perquisite
polemical
probity
tacit
timorous
untenable
veneer

Lesson 11
bulwark
canard
cortege
crescendo
demotic
disingenuous
dogged
etymology
impresario
intransigent
malaise
requisite
simian
solecism
wont

Lesson 12
assiduous
bellicose
compunction
condescending
epiphany
panacea
physiognomy
propensity
pulchritude
revel
rhapsodize
sepulcher
umbrage
voluble
wizened

Word List

Lesson 13
analgesic
conflagration
discretionary
draconian
florid
flummox
fractious
histrionics
implicate
moribund
noisome
punctilious
turpitude
unpalatable
veritable

Lesson 14
artisan
boondoggle
curmudgeon
fiduciary
inculcate
indiscernible
moiety
opprobrium
phlegmatic
potentate
protégé
reciprocate
repugnant
tenable
virulent

Lesson 15
appellation
autonomy
chthonian
coagulate
extirpate
gustatory
jurisprudence
malevolent
misanthrope
peripatetic
prominent
puissance
scion
supercilious
tutelary

Lesson 16
arcane
bourgeois
exculpate
indefeasible
matriculate
mercurial
nascent
paladin
salubrious
sine qua non
squelch
tangential
trenchant
tyro
vicissitude ·

Lesson 17
alimentary
ascetic
attenuate
attribute
celerity
congenital
depravity
discourse
encomium
ethereal
megalomania
mutable
primordial
remuneration
tactile

Lesson 18
cumulative
exhilaration
extricate
goad
impunity
lithe
poignant
propriety
pundit
satiate
superfluous
surfeit
trite
venial
vituperative

Word List

Lesson 19
abjure
dissipate
extant
fulsome
inchoate
inveterate
propitious
rescind
schism
spurious
stentorian
transient
tremulous
unwieldy
utilitarian

Lesson 20
acme
cerebral
conundrum
deleterious
discerning
echelon
hypocrisy
idyllic
malinger
nondescript
punitive
relegate
serendipity
soluble
waive

Lesson 21
abrogate
analects
anomie
apostasy
cognizant
extrinsic
factotum
febrile
magniloquent
outré
parity
propinquity
prosaic
supine
surreptitious

Lesson One

1. **camaraderie** (kä mə rä´ də rē, kä rä) *n.* rapport and goodwill
    The coach attributed the team's success to the *camaraderie* among the players.
    syn: friendship; amity   *ant: enmity; hostility*

2. **litany** (li´ tə nē) *n.* a long, repetitive, or dull account
    The dissatisfied customer read a *litany* of complaints to the company representative.

3. **wrenching** (rench´ ing) *adj.* causing mental or physical pain
    The *wrenching* photographs of the starving children prompted Mike to send a donation.
    syn: distressing; agonizing   *ant: pleasant; comforting*

4. **arable** (ar´ ə bəl) *adj.* suitable for cultivation of land
    Death Valley and the Badlands are both characterized by their lack of *arable* soil.
    syn: fertile; fecund   *ant: barren; infertile*

5. **desiccate** (des´ i kāt) *v.* to dry out; to remove moisture
    Janet *desiccates* flowers and then uses them to make wreaths.
    syn: dehydrate   *ant: moisten; dampen*

6. **vernacular** (vər nak´ yə lər) *n.* everyday language
    Using slang or *vernacular* in a formal term paper is usually inappropriate.

7. **replete** (ri plēt´) *adj.* full; abundant
    The anglers were happy to find their stream *replete* with trout.
    syn: abounding; rife   *ant: lacking; empty*

8. **moratorium** (môr ə tôr´ ē əm) *n.* a suspension of activity; an authorized delay
    The warring factions declared a *moratorium* on combat during the peace talks.
    syn: cessation; postponement   *ant: rush; continuation*

9. **ubiquitous** (yōō bik´ wi təs) *adj.* occurring or seeming to occur everywhere;
        omnipresent
    The camping trip was horrible; the mosquitoes were *ubiquitous* and hungry.
    syn: universal   *ant: nonexistent*

10. **frangible** (fran´ jə bəl) *adj.* fragile; easy to break
    Mom seldom removed the *frangible*, antique dishes from the cabinet.
    syn: delicate; breakable   *ant: sturdy; strong*

11. **lugubrious** (lə gōō′ brē əs) *adj.* mournful; gloomy
    The *lugubrious* funeral scene temporarily interrupted the comic tone of the play.
    syn: somber; depressing   *ant: joyful*

12. **equanimity** (ēk wə nim′ i tē) *n.* composure; calmness
    Oddly enough, the plaintiff recounted the story of her attack with perfect *equanimity*.
    syn: poise; sangfroid   *ant: anxiety; agitation*

13. **zealous** (zel′ əs) *adj.* fervent; fanatical
    The *zealous* gardener planted so many flowers that a number of them did not have
    the necessary space in which to grow.
    syn: passionate; enthusiastic   *ant: uninterested; indifferent*

14. **interminable** (in tûr′ mə nə bəl) *adj.* tiresome and long; seemingly endless
    The last few hours of school before the holiday vacation seemed *interminable*.
    syn: tedious   *ant: fleeting; limited*

15. **truncate** (trung′ kāt) *v.* to shorten
    The candidate *truncated* his campaign because of a family illness.
    syn: abridge; abbreviate   *ant: lengthen; increase*

Exercise I

Words in Context

From the list below, supply the words needed to complete the paragraph. Some words will not be used.

litany	truncate	lugubrious	camaraderie
equanimity	interminable	zealous	

1. Tony brushed the rain off his jacket as he walked through the glass doors to the school. It was a[n] _____ Saturday morning, so Tony was happy that the assessment test was not scheduled for a beautiful spring day. He sat down with his answer booklet, and the test proctor began the standard, twenty-minute _____ of instructions, as though the _____, four-hour test were not long enough without the elaborate directions. Tony, not at all nervous after having taken the test three times already, listened to the proctor with _____; however, some of the more _____ test-takers anxiously tapped their No. 2 pencils, eager to begin filling in the hundreds of tiny circles on their answer sheets.

From the list below, supply the words needed to complete the paragraph. Some words will not be used.

frangible	desiccate	arable	ubiquitous
replete	vernacular	zealous	

2. Abby had taken Spanish in high school, but she had trouble understanding the shopkeeper's _____. The little shop was _____ with the same type of things that tourists often needed, such as film, medicine, and long-distance phone cards; a shelf in front of the counter contained the hundreds of keychains, coffee mugs, old, _____ hard candies, and tee shirts _____ in every souvenir shop. A row of _____ vases and pottery on a shelf behind the counter caught Abby's eye, but she had actually come in to ask about the exotic plants growing in the _____ plot outside, behind the store.

From the list below, supply the words needed to complete the paragraph. Some words will not be used.

litany	truncate	camaraderie	wrenching
moratorium	arable	desiccate	

3. After the _____ on racing during a storm had been lifted and the track dried, spectators watched the _____ and ease among members of the pit crews as they made adjustments to cars in the minutes before drivers could return to the track. Despite the excitement in the air, the whole scene was depressing for Miles, a former driver who had to watch the race from the stands. The eight titanium pins holding his leg bones together never let him forget the _____ injury that had _____ his once-promising racing career.

Exercise II

Sentence Completion

Complete the sentence in a way that shows you understand the meaning of the italicized vocabulary word.

1. When Angie complained about having to do chores for her allowance, her dad began his usual *litany* about…

2. The *interminable* wait at the checkout line made Raymond decide…

3. The NCAA imposed a brief *moratorium* on Central University's football games when several athletes…

4. Giles tried to suppress his *wrenching* memories of…

5. When you pack the boxes for the move, put the *frangible* items…

6. Dirk began to question the *camaraderie* of his teammates when one of them…

7. It's difficult to maintain one's *equanimity* when…

8. Bill likes comic poems, but Sylvia prefers *lugubrious* ones that…

9. The pioneers *desiccated* some of the beef so that they…

10. Between innings, one of the *zealous* fans at the game…

11. The actor became frustrated when the *ubiquitous* tabloid reporters…

12. The cooler at the picnic was *replete* with…

13. Anita wanted a home with an *arable* yard where she…

14. Shelly used common *vernacular* to identify the animals, but the zoology professor wanted her to…

15. You will need to *truncate* your award speech if you find out…

Exercise III

Roots, Prefixes, and Suffixes

Study the entries and answer the questions that follow.

The prefix *ortho–* means "straight" or "correct."
The prefix *hetero–* means "different."
The prefix *homo–* means "same."
The roots *dogm* and *dox* mean "belief."
The root *gen* means "type."
The suffix *–logy* means "word."

1. Using *literal* translations as guidance, define the following words without using a dictionary.

    A. dogmatic   D. orthodox
    B. heterodox   E. doxology
    C. homogenous   F. heterogeneous

2. If *para–* means "beyond," then a *paradox* is something that is _____.

3. List as many words as you can think of that begin with the prefix *ortho–*.

4. What is *homogenized* milk?

5. Give an example of a *dogma*.

6. List as many words as you can think of that contain the root *gen*.

Exercise IV

Inference

Complete the sentence by inferring information about the italicized word from its context.

1. If you have *arable* ground on your property, then you might consider…

2. That is a *ubiquitous* species of tree, so don't be surprised if, during your vacation abroad, you…

3. If you are bored, and the weather is *lugubrious*, you might…

Exercise V

Writing

Here is a writing prompt similar to the one you will find on the writing portion of an assessment test.

Plan and write an essay based on the following statement:

> Books are the best type of the influence of the past, and perhaps we shall get at the truth—learn the amount of this influence more conveniently—by considering their value alone.

> –Ralph Waldo Emerson, "The American Scholar"

Assignment: In an essay, explain whether you agree or disagree with Emerson's suggestion that books are the best type of influence of the past. Include a comparison of books with other methods of gaining knowledge or understanding history, and explain why books do or do not have the value that they did in 1837, the year of Emerson's quote. Support your opinion using evidence from your reading, studies, observations, and experience.

Thesis: Write a *one-sentence* response to the above assignment. Make certain this single sentence offers a clear statement of your position.

Example: Although books are excellent tools for presenting history, continual advancements in practical technology are the best types of influences from the past.

_____

_____

Organizational Plan: List at least three subtopics you will use to support your main idea. This list is your outline.

1. _____

2. _____

3. _____

Draft: Following your outline, write a good first draft of your essay. Remember to support all of your points with examples, facts, references to reading, etc.

Review and Revise: Exchange essays with a classmate. Using the scoring guide for Organization on page 271, score your partner's essay (while he or she scores yours). Focus on the organizational plan and the use of language conventions. If necessary, rewrite your essay to improve the organizational plan and/or your use of language.

Exercise VI

English Practice

Identifying Sentence Errors

Identify the grammatical error in each of the following sentences. If the sentence contains no error, select answer choice E.

1. <u>Many individual's believe</u> that <u>if they</u> are polite to <u>their neighbors,</u> they
          (A)   (B)   (C)
    <u>can be impolite</u> to their families.   <u>No error</u>
           (D)   (E)

2. The <u>commonly known</u> expression <u>that "a dog is a man's</u> best friend" is
             (A)   (B)
    <u>frequently incorrect; all</u> a person has to do <u>is read</u> the newspaper.   <u>No error</u>
           (C)   (D)   (E)

3. <u>The home run</u> Hal <u>hit flew</u> out of the <u>stadium into</u> the parking lot,
       (A)   (B)   (C)
    and smashed the window of a <u>brand-new car.</u>   <u>No error</u>
                             (D)   (E)

4. Until one of the <u>members of the rival gangs propose</u> a <u>truce, there</u> will be no
                              (A)   (B)
    safety for <u>honest</u> citizens <u>of this city.</u>   <u>No error</u>
             (C)   (D)   (E)

5. No matter <u>how hard</u> Theresa <u>tries, she</u> cannot win the <u>approval of</u> her
              (A)   (B)   (C)
    <u>field hockey coach.</u>   <u>No error</u>
        (D)   (E)

Improving Sentences

The underlined portion of each sentence below contains some flaw. Select the answer choice that best corrects the flaw.

6. <u>Scientists think of the underwater world beneath the sea as a vast laboratory,</u> in
    which strange creatures do odd, unexplained things.
    A. Scientists think the underwater world beneath the sea is a vast laboratory
    B. Scientists think that the underwater world beneath the sea is a vast laboratory
    C. Scientists think of the underwater world as a vast laboratory
    D. A vast laboratory is how scientists view the underwater world beneath the sea
    E. Beneath the sea lies a vast laboratory

7. Ben Franklin was a statesman, politician, printer, author, philosopher, inventor, and Ambassador to France, <u>yet most people studying history in school only think of him as a man standing in a lightning storm with a kite and a key.</u>
   A. yet most people who only study history in school think of him as a man standing in a lightning storm with a kite and a key.
   B. yet most people in history think of him as a man standing in a lightning storm with a kite and a key.
   C. yet most people with only a tiny knowledge of high school history think of him as a man standing in a lightning storm with a kite and a key.
   D. yet most people in school only think of him as a man standing in a lightning storm with a kite and a key.
   E. yet most students think of him only as a man standing in a storm with a kite and a key.

8. "The reason I choose not to," said the potential customer to the car salesman, <u>"is because of the fact that you have not given me enough for my trade-in."</u>
   A. "Is due to the fact that you have not given me enough for my trade-in."
   B. "is because of you having not given me enough for my trade-in."
   C. "is because you have not given me enough for my trade-in."
   D. "is that you have not given me enough for my trade-in."
   E. "is because of the fact that you aren't giving me enough for my trade-in."

9. There is only one prerequisite for the <u>job; You must have a college degree in Physics.</u>
   A. job: you must have a college degree in physics.
   B. job, you must have a college degree in physics.
   C. job you must have a college degree in Physics.
   D. job; You must have a college degree in physics.
   E. job, and it is that a college degree in physics is necessary.

10. <u>Ever since he has devoted himself entirely to helping the homeless.</u>
   A. Ever since he has devoted himself entirely to helping the homeless, he has been happy.
   B. Ever since, he has devoted himself entirely to helping the homeless.
   C. He has devoted himself entirely to helping the homeless.
   D. Ever since he has entirely devoted himself to helping the homeless.
   E. Ever since he has devoted himself, entirely, to helping the homeless.

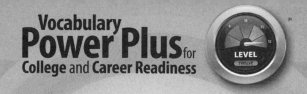
Lesson Two

1. **donnybrook** (don´ ē brook) *n.* a fight; an uproar
    During the last minute of the close championship game, a referee's foolish decision caused a *donnybrook* among the fans of both teams.
    syn: brawl; quarrel; altercation   *ant: agreement*

2. **interlocutor** (in tər lok´ yə tər) *n.* someone who participates in a conversation
    The delusional man wandered down the street, conversing with some invisible *interlocutor.*

3. **carte blanche** (kärt blänch) *n.* boundless authority; unlimited power to act
    The secret agent had *carte blanche* to complete the extremely vital mission.
    syn: license; sanction; free rein   *ant: restriction*

4. **rife** (rīf) *adj* abundant; prevalent
    Be careful while shopping, because that part of the city is *rife* with crime.
    syn: overflowing; rampant   *ant: lacking; limited*

5. **contemptuous** (kən temp´ chōō əs) *adj.* haughty; scornful
    The *contemptuous* bank loan officer was rude to the poorly dressed applicants.
    syn: arrogant; derisive   *ant: humble; polite*

6. **stygian** (sti´ jē ən) *adj.* dark and forbidding
    The *stygian* house, empty for decades, was often the source of unexplained phenomena.
    syn: shadowy   *ant: bright; illuminated*

7. **vestige** (ves´ tij) *n.* a trace or evidence of something that once existed
    The rich vein of coal is a *vestige* of Earth's lush, prehistoric forests.
    syn: remnant; hint

8. **nomenclature** (nō´ mən klā chər) *n.* a technical name or naming system in an
        art or science
    Students often spend hours memorizing the *nomenclature* of organic chemistry.
    syn: terminology

9. **incantation** (in kan tā´ shən) *n.* a chant; a recited magical spell
    The sorceress uttered a long *incantation* as she mixed the magic potion.
    syn: invocation

10. **metamorphosis** (met ə môr´ fə sis) *n.* a transformation or dramatic change
    That butterfly will experience a physical *metamorphosis* as it passes from the pupa stage to the adult stage.
    syn: mutation   *ant: stasis*

11. **nonchalant**   (non shə länt´)   *adj.*   unconcerned; indifferent
The *nonchalant* banker looked at the million-dollar check as though he saw one every day.
syn: detached; relaxed   *ant: excited; concerned; alarmed*

12. **procrustean**   (prō krus´ tē ən)   *adj.*   marked by a disregard for individual
        differences or circumstances
The *procrustean* teacher warned the class that he would accept no excuses for tardiness.
syn: ruthless; undiscriminating   *ant: sympathetic; compassionate*

13. **sophistry**   (sä´ fə strē)   *n.*   a deliberately deceptive or misleading argument
The TV talk-show host's convincing *sophistry* made his guests look foolish for disagreeing with him.
syn: chicanery; ruse   *ant: truth*

14. **cosmopolitan**   (koz mə pol´ i tən)   *adj.*   worldly; sophisticated
Brett longed to have the *cosmopolitan* lifestyle of an international investor.
syn: cultured   *ant: provincial*

15. **brigand**   (brig´ ənd)   *n.*   a robber or bandit
The stagecoach driver kept a nervous watch for *brigands* while transporting the heavy cash box.
syn: highwayman; outlaw

Exercise I

Words in Context

From the list below, supply the words needed to complete the paragraph. Some words will not be used.

donnybrook	**cosmopolitan**	**carte blanche**	**vestige**
procrustean	**incantation**	**metamorphosis**	

1. Mr. Trunk, the new manager, walked into his new, albeit antiquated, office. The only
    _____ of the former manager was a dusty hot rod calendar, three years out of
    date. Recruited for his _____ leadership style and general lack of compassion,
    Mr. Trunk promised the company president that production would experience a[n]
    _____ for the better before the end of the year. Trunk had _____ to
    change operations any way he saw fit, though he knew that his changes would not be
    taken lightly; his revisions of break and lunchtime policies nearly got him into a[n]
    _____ with angry workers, who felt that they had been wronged.

From the list below, supply the words needed to complete the paragraph. Some words will not be used.

rife	**nonchalant**	**donnybrook**	**interlocutor**
contemptuous	**nomenclature**	**brigand**	

2. The _____ sprang from the hedges, produced his saber, and ordered the
    obviously wealthy couple to surrender their valuables, but the couple's _____
    reaction to the threat bewildered the thief.
        "How _____ you aristocrats are," said the robber. "An outlaw threatens your
    lives, and you just stare with indifference?"
        "Yes, because they have nothing to fear. Lower your weapon, highwayman." The
    sudden voice of a new _____ startled the thief, but not as much as the sharp tip
    of the dagger jabbing into his shoulder blade. The thief dropped his sword, regreting he
    had not seen the watchman approaching from behind. To reduce the serious crime that
    had become _____ in the district, the government had recruited extra officers to
    patrol the cobblestone streets.

From the list below, supply the words needed to complete the paragraph. Some words will not be used.

stygian	**brigand**	**incantation**	**cosmopolitan**
carte blanche	**nomenclature**	**sophistry**	

3. In an effort to overcome the overwhelming boredom of his _____, stone-floored
    prison cell, Tobias exercised his knowledge by identifying each insect he saw by its
    Latin _____. The only alternative he had was to listen to the prisoner in the
    neighboring cell shout the same _____ that had failed to convince the judge that
    he was innocent. In several weeks, the repetitive daily rant began to sound like a[n]
    _____ to Tobias, perhaps a spell that would melt the bars of the noisy prisoner's
    cell. The two prisoners conversed occasionally. Tobias, a well-traveled, renowned
    explorer, related tales from his _____ life, but the conversation inevitably
    returned to the topic of the other man's wrongful imprisonment.

Exercise II

Sentence Completion

Complete the sentence in a way that shows you understand the meaning of the italicized vocabulary word.

1. A *donnybrook* erupted at the grocery store when…

2. The *stygian* cave made a good hideout for the outlaw because…

3. George was a great *interlocutor* in the debate because he…

4. The *brigands* plotted to…

5. The magician's *incantation* before the trick was designed to…

6. The lawn is *rife* with weeds this year because…

7. Try to remain *nonchalant* when…

8. Ian had *carte blanche* when using the family car because…

9. The *procrustean* bus driver refused to…

10. Paul experienced a total *metamorphosis* in his behavior after…

11. The *contemptuous* child wondered why none of his classmates…

12. Most people know that H_2O is the chemical *nomenclature* for…

13. Kelly thought herself too *cosmopolitan* to…

14. The cement foundation, overgrown with vines and littered with charred wood, is the only remaining *vestige* of…

15. The arch villain used *sophistry* to convince the hero to…

Exercise III

Roots, Prefixes, and Suffixes

Study the entries and answer the questions that follow.

The suffix –*escent* means "becoming" or "growing."
The prefix *ob*– means "toward" or "against."
The prefix *con*– means "totally" or "completely."
The root *val* means "strong" or "healthy."
The root *rub* means "red."
The roots *irid* and *iris* mean "rainbow" or "brightly colored."
The root *fac* means "to make."

1. Using *literal* translations as guidance, define the following words without using a dictionary.

A.	rubefacient	D.	convalescent
B.	iridescent	E.	iris
C.	rubescent	F.	valor

2. What do you think the musical term *crescendo* means?

3. List some of the deeds that a *valiant* knight might do.

4. List as many words as you can think of that contain the root *vul*.

Exercise IV

Inference

Complete the sentence by inferring information about the italicized word from its context.

1. If Nina behaved in a *nonchalant* manner when she saw her report card, then she probably…

2. The forest around the house is *rife* with poison ivy, so we should…

3. Mike used to be rebellious, but he experienced a *metamorphosis* that…

Critical Reading

Below is a reading passage followed by several multiple-choice questions. Carefully read the passage and choose the best answer for each of the questions.

Edward Sandford Martin (1856-1939) was a humor writer and one of the founders of Life Magazine. *The following passage is an excerpt from Martin's essay, "The Tyranny of Things." In it, Martin discusses how easily people become slaves to material goods, including even material things that are thought to be justifiably coveted, such as large homes.*

There was a story in the newspapers the other day about a Massachusetts minister who resigned his charge because someone had given his parish a fine house, and his parishioners wanted him to live in it. His salary was too small, he said, to admit of his living in a big house, and he would not do it. He was even deaf to the proposal that he should share the proposed tenement
5   with the sewing societies and clubs of his church, and when the matter came to a serious issue, he relinquished his charge and sought a new field of usefulness. The situation was an amusing instance of the embarrassment of riches. Let no one to whom restricted quarters may have grown irksome, and who covets larger dimensions of shelter, be too hasty in deciding that the minister was wrong. Did you ever see the house that Hawthorne lived in at Lenox? Did you ever see
10   Emerson's house at Concord? They are good houses for Americans to know and remember. They permitted thought.
    A big house is one of the greediest cormorants which can light upon a little income. Backs may go threadbare and stomachs may worry along on indifferent filling, but a house *will* have things, though its occupants go without. It is rarely complete, and constantly tempts the
15   imagination to flights in brick and dreams in lath and plaster. It develops annual thirsts for paint and wallpaper, at least, if not for marble and woodcarving. The plumbing in it must be kept in order on pain of death. Whatever price is put on coal, it has to be heated in winter; and if it is rural or suburban, the grass about it must be cut even though funerals in the family have to be put off for the mowing. If the tenants are not rich enough to hire people to keep their house
20   clean, they must do it themselves, for there is no excuse that will pass among housekeepers for a dirty house. The master of a house too big for him may expect to spend the leisure which might be made intellectually or spiritually profitable, in acquiring and putting into practice fag ends of the arts of the plumber, the bell-hanger, the locksmith, the gas-fitter, and the carpenter. Presently he will know how to do everything that can be done in the house, except enjoy himself. He will
25   learn about taxes, too, and water-rates, and how such abominations as sewers or new pavements are always liable to accrue at his expense. As for the mistress, she will be a slave to carpets and curtains, wallpaper, painters, and women who come in by the day to clean. She will be lucky if she gets a chance to say her prayers, and thrice and four times happy when she can read a book or visit with her friends. To live in a big house may be a luxury, provided that one has a full set of
30   money and an enthusiastic housekeeper in one's family; but to scrimp in a big house is a miserable business. Yet such is human folly, that for a man to refuse to live in a house because it is too big for him, is such an exceptional exhibition of sense that it becomes the favorite paragraph of a day in the newspapers.
    An ideal of earthly comfort, so common that every reader must have seen it, is to get a house
35   so big that it is burdensome to maintain, and fill it up so full of gimcracks that it is a constant occupation to keep it in order. Then, when the expense of living in it is so great that you can't afford to go away and rest from the burden of it, the situation is complete and boarding houses and cemeteries begin to yawn for you. How many Americans, do you suppose, out of the droves that flock annually to Europe, are running away from oppressive houses?

40   When nature undertakes to provide a house, it fits the occupant. Animals which build by instinct build only what they need, but man's building instinct, if it gets a chance to spread itself at all, is boundless, just as all his instincts are. For it is man's peculiarity that nature has filled him with impulses to do things, and left it to his discretion when to stop. She never tells him when he has finished. And perhaps we ought not to be surprised that in so many cases it happens that he

45   does not know, but just goes ahead as long as the materials last.

If another *man* tries to oppress him, he understands that and is ready to fight to death and sacrifice all he has, rather than submit; but the tyranny of *things* is so subtle, so gradual in its approach, and comes so masked with seeming benefits, that it has him hopelessly bound before he suspects his fetters. He says from day to day, "I will add thus to my house;" "I will have one or

50   two more horses;" "I will make a little greenhouse in my garden;" "I will allow myself the luxury of another hired man;" and so he goes on having things and imagining that he is richer for them. Presently he begins to realize that it is the things that own him. He has piled them up on his shoulders, and there they sit like Sinbad's Old Man and drive him; and it becomes a daily question whether he can keep his trembling legs or not.

55   All of which is not meant to prove that property has no real value, or to rebut Charles Lamb's scornful denial that enough is as good as a feast. It is not meant to apply to the rich, who can have things comfortably, if they are philosophical; but to us poor, who have constant need to remind ourselves that where the verbs *to have* and *to be* cannot both be completely inflected, the verb *to be* is the one that best repays concentration.

1A. The tone of the first paragraph of this passage is best described as
    A. hostile.
    B. supportive.
    C. forlorn.
    D. evasive.
    E. patronizing.

1B. Choose the word that best describes the author's feeling toward the minister described in paragraph 1.
    A. condemning
    B. uncertain
    C. frustrated
    D. offended
    E. sympathetic

2A. As used in the first paragraph, *charge* most nearly means
    A. accusation.
    B. debt.
    C. ridicule.
    D. duty.
    E. shock.

2B. Based on the second use of *charge* in line 6, which words from that paragraph best support your answer to question 2A?
    A. amusing, embarrassment
    B. parishioners, given
    C. grown, share
    D. relinquished, sought
    E. covets, wrong

3A. According to the context of the first paragraph, Emerson's and Hawthorne's houses were probably
   A. elaborate and expansive.
   B. practical, plain residences.
   C. constructed more than 200 years ago.
   D. larger than the homes of their neighbors.
   E. simple, one-story homes with dirt floors.

3B. Hawthorne and Emerson are famous literary icons, especially in the time in which the essay was written. They are included as examples in paragraph 1 to demonstrate
   A. the author's appreciation for contemporary artists.
   B. the distractions that small homes provide.
   C. that big homes are conducive to dark story topics.
   D. that modest houses permit high levels of concentration.
   E. that large homes are indicative of wealth and fame.

4A. The *cormorants* in line 12 are probably a metaphor for
   A. matches.
   B. doubts.
   C. boulders.
   D. builders.
   E. thieves.

4B. In the metaphor in line 12, the phrase "a little income" must mean something other than money, which cormorants would not desire. It probably represents
   A. water.
   B. writing.
   C. food.
   D. dreams.
   E. worries.

5A. To whom does the word *man* refer in the following line?

   "Yet such is human folly, that for a man to refuse to live in a house because it is too big for him, is such an exceptional exhibition of sense that it becomes the favorite paragraph of a day in the newspapers."

   A. Emerson
   B. the minister
   C. the carpenter
   D. the housekeeper
   E. the mistress

5B. According to paragraph 2, there is nothing wrong with living in a large house if
   A. the house contains no decorations or furniture.
   B. the occupants are familiar with tax laws, painting, and mowing grass.
   C. the occupants have money and someone to maintain the house.
   D. the house is not in need of immediate or costly repairs.
   E. the occupants have no friends to invite over.

6A. According to the author, people such as the minister are accused of having an "embarrassment of riches" because
  A. few people understand why someone would refuse to live in a large house.
  B. the house offered to the minister comes complete with fine furniture.
  C. everyone wants a larger house than the one he or she currently owns.
  D. ministers generally have few possessions, so wealth embarrasses them.
  E. a modest, wealthy person would never accept a free house.

6B. Which choice is the best interpretation of the following quotation?

"Backs may go threadbare and stomachs may worry along on indifferent filling, but a house *will* have things, though its occupants go without."

  A. The maintenance of a house always takes priority over the comfort of the people living in it.
  B. The price of food and clothing is increasing; it's a bad time to buy real estate.
  C. The best house is one that includes a cook and a full wardrobe.
  D. No matter how much money someone has, a house will ensure that he or she will not be able to afford to eat or buy clothing.
  E. People inevitably spend too much money on their homes.

7A. In the story of Sinbad the Sailor, the "Old Man" is a character who tricks people into carrying him, and then refuses to dismount until the unwitting helper dies from exhaustion. In the passage, the "Old Man" is a symbol of
  A. status.
  B. material possessions.
  C. a slave.
  D. the homeowner.
  E. a critic.

7B. According to paragraph 5 (lines 46-54), a property owner is at risk of becoming enslaved because
  A. virtually no one can turn down lucrative offers.
  B. the owner cannot defeat the oppressors without help.
  C. the owner has never experienced truly difficult work.
  D. political turmoil can upset social hierarchies.
  E. the owner brings it upon him or herself.

8A. The author of the passage would probably describe himself as
  A. a wealthy property owner.
  B. the minister detailed in the passage.
  C. a person who rents property.
  D. the inheritor of a house.
  E. too poor to own a large house.

8B. Which choice best paraphrases the following quotation?

"...but to us poor, who have constant need to remind ourselves that where the verbs *to have* and *to be* cannot both be completely inflected, the verb *to be* is the one that best repays concentration."

   A.   Those who cannot be happy simply existing, or "being," become disillusioned by "wanting" all the time.

   B.   The poor, who need more than they want, are usually happier to think about what kind of people they are.

   C.   Material possessions are nothing compared to those things that define a person.

   D.   The poor, who cannot claim to have or have had material things, are better off considering "what they are" than "what they have."

   E.   Wealthy people, who know who they are and what they want, have little need to worry about owning a large house.

9A. The "tyranny of *things*" entraps people by
   A.   making the greedy appear attractive.
   B.   giving people something to live for.
   C.   causing property owners to buy horses.
   D.   affecting the poor as much as it affects the rich.
   E.   occurring so slowly that no one notices it until it is too late.

9B. Which words from lines 47-53 best support your answer to question 9A?
   A.   benefits, fetters
   B.   subtle, gradual
   C.   bound, greenhouse
   D.   shoulders, drive
   E.   add, luxury

10A. Which of the following statements best supports the theme of this passage?
   A.   Large houses require a lot of work.
   B.   A free house, small or large, is always better than no house.
   C.   People can become slaves to their material possessions.
   D.   Being wealthy and owning a small house is a ridiculous situation.
   E.   Large families should reconsider whether they require large homes.

10B. Choose the statement the author would agree with.
   A.   Both the poor and the rich can enjoy large homes if they stay busy.
   B.   Wealthy homeowners are more likely to end up penniless than poor homeowners are.
   C.   People are inherently lazy and avoid work.
   D.   Human beings are naturally busy; they just don't know when to stop.
   E.   People give up too easily and settle for less.

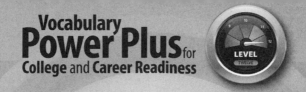

Lesson Three

1. **axiom** (ak´ sē əm) *n.* a universal truth; an established rule
    According to some people, the most important *axiom* of all is, "Do unto others as you would have them do unto you."
    syn: fundamental; theorem   *ant: absurdity*

2. **patronizing** (pā´ trə nīz ing) *adj.* in a condescending manner; with an attitude of superiority
    Despite his *patronizing* treatment of the employees, the foreman was still well liked.
    syn: lofty; arrogant   *ant: humble; friendly*

3. **atelier** (a təl yā´) *n.* an artist's or a designer's workshop
    The painter converted his garage into an *atelier* to work on his creative masterpieces.

4. **scapegoat** (skāp´ gōt) *n.* one who bears the blame for others
    Andy was frequently absent, so other workers made him the *scapegoat* for their own mistakes.
    syn: patsy; sucker

5. **vacillate** (vas´ ə lāt) *v.* to waver; to sway indecisively
    For years Bobby *vacillated* between liking one band and then another.
    syn: fluctuate; swing; waffle   *ant: ductile*

6. **pellucid** (pə lōō´ sid) *adj.* transparent; clear
    Eliminate extraneous words if you want your paper to have a *pellucid* message.
    syn: limpid   *ant: obscure; opaque*

7. **abstemious** (ab stē´ mē əs) *adj.* using or consuming sparingly
    Bill, who wants to lose weight, is *abstemious* in eating foods high in fat.
    syn: frugal; moderate   *ant: gluttonous; greedy*

8. **iniquity** (i nik´ wi tē) *n.* an evil or wicked act
    He heartily repented his *iniquities*, but only after he faced a lifelong prison sentence.
    syn: abomination; injustice; sin

9. **dulcet** (dul´ sit) *adj.* melodious; pleasing to the ear
    The opera singer's *dulcet* voice earned her a prominent place in the upcoming production.
    syn: harmonic; melodic   *ant: cacophonous; dissonant*

10. **peremptory** (pə remp´ tə rē) *adj.* not allowing refusal or delay; imperative
    The guard issued a *peremptory* warning to step away from the fence or be fired upon.
    syn: authoritative; unconditional   *ant: roundabout; passive; equivocal*

11. **arrogate** (ar´ ə gāt) *v.* to claim for oneself without any right or authority
The evil prince *arrogated* the village for his private resort and exiled anyone who
objected.
syn: commandeer; seize   *ant: relinquish; give*

12. **archaic** (är kā´ ik) *adj.* no longer current or applicable; antiquated
Some states still have *archaic* laws that regulate horse-and-buggy traffic.
syn: obsolete; outmoded   *ant: current; modern*

13. **perspicacious** (pûr spi kā´ shəs) *adj.* keen; mentally sharp
The *perspicacious* gambler knew that he would need to make a hasty exit after
winning most of the cowboys' money.
syn: shrewd; clever   *ant: dull; stupid*

14. **talisman** (tal´ is mən) *n.* a magic charm or superstitious object for protection
     or luck
The wizard claimed that no harm would come to anyone holding the *talisman*.

15. **expurgate** (ek´ spûr gāt) *v.* to remove vulgar or objectionable material
Censors sometimes feel that it is necessary to *expurgate* offensive scenes from movies.
syn: censor; bowdlerize; sanitize

Exercise I

Words in Context

From the list below, supply the words needed to complete the paragraph. Some words will not be used.

arrogate	atelier	pellucid	archaic
axiom	dulcet	iniquity	

1. "I prefer to think of this factory as a giant _____, where a team of artists creates not specialized tools, but hand-machined works of art," said Roger, the owner of Calumette Industries. "And as long as our goal remains _____ to every employee, this company will soar." Roger, who took over the failing operation just months ago, sparked life back into the floundering plant by replacing _____ industry practices with new methods guaranteed to increase production; however, despite Roger's many changes to the plant, he was quick to note that he is a firm believer in the _____, "Don't fix things that aren't broken."

    During a tour of the factory, one could see by the smile on Roger's face that the repetitive clanging of electric motors and hydraulic presses was _____ music to the industrialist's ears.

From the list below, supply the words needed to complete the paragraph. Some words will not be used.

scapegoat	atelier	iniquity	vacillate
perspicacious	expurgate	talisman	

2. When an obscene photograph appeared in the school yearbook, the administration immediately sought a[n] _____ to take the blame for what the community called "a[n] _____." Angry students and parents blamed Dora, the yearbook editor, for not being _____ enough to have spotted the photo before the book was sent to the printer. The school collected the books and returned them to the printer to _____ the photograph. Dora, a junior, _____ between signing up for the yearbook staff again next year or not.

From the list below, supply the words needed to complete the paragraph. Some words will not be used.

talisman	archaic	abstemious	scapegoat
patronizing	arrogate	peremptory	

3. Paranoid that someone would _____ control of his latest project, Bob carried the scale model of the building with him all around the office as though it were some kind of _____ that would protect him from any dragons hiding in the cubicles. Some of the employees giggled when Bob walked by, and others gave him _____ looks, which made him feel like a fearful toddler carrying a security blanket. Mrs. Simmons, the manager, began to worry that perhaps Bob was stressed out, so she called a meeting with him. During the meeting, the manager reminded Bob that his _____ use of vacation time was not healthy; he absolutely must get away from the office for a little while. Two weeks later, as Bob basked in the Caribbean sun, he wished that the boss would have prescribed this kind of _____ vacation months earlier.

Exercise II

Sentence Completion

Complete the sentence in a way that shows you understand the meaning of the italicized vocabulary word.

1. Virgil got lost in the city because his *archaic* map did not...

2. To ensure that Adam had a *pellucid* idea of what she was explaining, Sheila...

3. The gymnasium was once open to the public, but owing to the *iniquities* of a few vandals,...

4. At the store, Susan *vacillated* over which...

5. Jerry often muttered the *axiom*, "If you want something done right, do it yourself," when...

6. Chris knew that he would become the *scapegoat* if the police learned that he...

7. Catherine feared that someone would *arrogate* her idea if...

8. The *patronizing* babysitter told the children...

9. To *expurgate* the graffiti sprayed on the walls of the tunnel,...

10. While camping, Liz quickly fell asleep to the *dulcet* sound of...

11. Occasionally, Lisa strayed from her *abstemious* budget in order to...

12. Uncle Pete thought that carrying a *talisman*, such as a rabbit's foot, would...

13. During the bomb scare, the principal issued a *peremptory* order to...

14. In his *atelier*, the carpenter...

15. The fugitive would have escaped if a *perspicacious* citizen had not noticed...

Exercise III

Roots, Prefixes, and Suffixes

Study the entries and answer the questions that follow.

The root *ratio* means "reason."
The root *ment* means "mind."
The root *gno* means "knowledge."
The prefix *de–* means "away."
The prefix *ir–* means "not."
The prefix *a–* means "without."
The prefix *pro–* means "before" or "in advance."

1. Using *literal* translations as guidance, define the following words without using a dictionary.

    A. prognosticate   D. mentality
    B. agnostic   E. rationale
    C. irrational   F. dementia

2. Explain the difference between a *ratio* and a *ration*.

3. What do you think a *mentalist* does?

4. If *dia–* means "through," or "by way of," what does the word *diagnosis* mean literally?

5. List as many words as you can think of that contain the root *ratio*.

Exercise IV

Inference

Complete the sentence by inferring information about the italicized word from its context.

1. If an *archaic* computer system will not run the latest software, the user will need to…

2. The mayor asked citizens to be *abstemious* in their water consumption because…

3. The answer to the calculus problem was not yet *pellucid* to Jack, so he…

Exercise V

Writing

Here is a writing prompt similar to the one you will find on the writing portion of an assessment test.

Plan and write an essay based on the following statement:

> I have never found a companion that was so companionable as solitude. We are for the most part more lonely when we go abroad among men than when we stay in our chambers. A man thinking or working is always alone, let him be where he will.

> –Henry David Thoreau, *Walden*

Assignment: In an essay, explain whether being alone was a depressing or a pleasurable experience for Thoreau. Include an interpretation of the second sentence, about being lonely among other people, and explain why it supports your opinion as to Thoreau's perception of solitude. Support your position by discussing examples from literature, art, science, current events, or your own experience or observation.

Thesis: Write a *one-sentence* response to the above assignment. Make certain this single sentence offers a clear statement of your position.

Example: Thoreau loved solitude because it is much easier to be at ease with oneself than among strangers, especially in a modern world in which selfishness and greed have become acceptable forms of inspiration.

_____

_____

Organizational Plan: List at least three subtopics you will use to support your main idea. This list is your outline.

1. _____

2. _____

3. _____

Draft: Following your outline, write a good first draft of your essay. Remember to support all of your points with examples, facts, references to reading, etc.

Review and Revise: Exchange essays with a classmate. Using the scoring guide for Development on page 272, score your partner's essay (while he or she scores yours). Focus on the development of ideas and the use of language conventions. If necessary, rewrite your essay to incorporate more (or more relevant) support and/or improve your use of language.

Exercise VI

Improving Paragraphs

Read the following passage and then choose the best revision for the underlined portions of the paragraph. The questions will require you to make decisions regarding the revision of the reading selection. Some revisions are not of actual mistakes, but will improve the clarity of the writing.

[1]

(1) The world as we know it would not exist today if it were not for gigantic aircraft capable of carrying <u>hundreds of tons of people</u>,[1] supplies, and equipment. (2) The credit for inspiring such aircraft must go to a versatile Texan by the name of Howard Hughes—the inventor of the first massive "flying boat" that most now remember as the "Spruce Goose."

1. A. NO CHANGE
    B. hundred's of tons of people
    C. hundreds of ton's of people
    D. hundreds' of tons of people

[2]

(3) Howard Hughes was what most would describe as a Renaissance man. (4) He was an actor, a director, a theater owner, a pilot, and a **perspicacious** engineer. (5) Though he never finished high school, Hughes attended classes at California Institute of Technology, thanks to a considerable donation by his father. (6) Hughes's father was wealthy. (7) Hughes's father died when Hughes was only eighteen years old. (8) A judge awarded Hughes legal adulthood just after his nineteenth <u>birthday, that allowed</u>[2] the young man to take control of his father's estate from his uncle. (9) Part of the estate included Hughes Tool Company, and Hughes, taking advantage of the booming aircraft technology industry of the early twentieth century, formed the Hughes Aircraft Company division in 1932. (10) With his company and the designing help of famous shipbuilder Henry Kaiser, <u>they</u>[3] agreed to a contract with the government to build three "flying boats." (11) Hughes never finished building three, but he did successfully complete one.

2. F. NO CHANGE
    G. birthday, which allowed
    H. birthday that allowed
    J. birthday which allowed

3. A. NO CHANGE
    B. Kaiser and Hughes
    C. Hughes
    D. the pair

4. Which sentence can be deleted from paragraph 2 without changing the intent of the paragraph?
    F. sentence 3
    G. sentence 4
    H. sentence 6
    J. sentence 7

[3]

(12) To meet government specifications, Hughes's flying boat had to be capable of transporting cargo and men over long distances. (13) <u>Enemies' were</u>[5] destroying shipping lanes during World War II, and the military needed the flying boat to carry soldiers and supplies high above enemy ships and submarines. (14) The contract awarded Hughes <u>$18 million dollars</u>[6] to build the three aircraft, and Hughes added another seven million of his own fortune to fund the project. (15) With adequate funding and sheer determination, Hughes then proves to the world that human ingenuity could make a 200-ton pile of wood airborne.

5. A. NO CHANGE
   B. Enemy's were
   C. Enemies was
   D. Enemies were

6. F. NO CHANGE
   G. eighteen million dollars
   H. 18 million dollars
   J. eighteen million dollars'

7. Which of the following corrects an error in sentence 15?
   A. Delete the hyphen between *200* and *ton*.
   B. Rewrite the sentence to omit the comma splice.
   C. *Ingenuity* is plural and requires a plural verb.
   D. Change *proves* to *proved*.

[4]

(16) The public nicknamed the flying boat the "Spruce Goose" to mock Hughes for his apparent failure. (17) The flying boat was constructed of mostly birch wood (not spruce) and fabric. (18) It had a single hull, eight of the most powerful engines of the time, and a single vertical tail. (19) Hughes covered the <u>primary, control surfaces in fabric and,</u>[8] the rest of the plane was laminated birch. (20) The plane was a behemoth—the largest aircraft built in the era—a 320-foot wingspan, <u>219 feet in length,</u>[9] and a wing area of 11,430 square feet. (21) Most impressively, the flying boat could take off with a weight of 400,000 pounds, or 200 tons.

8. F. NO CHANGE
   G. the primary, control surfaces in fabric, and,
   H. the primary control surfaces in fabric, and
   J. the primary, control surfaces in fabric and

9. A. NO CHANGE
   B. 219 feet long,
   C. a length of 219 feet,
   D. the length was 219 feet,

[5]

(22) Though the giant plane flew, it flew only once. (23) On November 2, 1947, well after the end of the war and in the midst of **peremptory** Congressional hearings to determine why the planes were not yet completed, Hughes returned to California to run supposed engine tests on his plane. (24) In the waters off Long Beach, Hughes took the controls, shoved the throttles to the stops, and, to the amazement of onlookers, the Spruce Goose took flight. (25) Hughes lifted the plane 70 feet from the ocean and it lumbered along at 80 miles per hour for about a mile before making a perfect landing. (26) Many historians claim that while Congress decided to cancel the contract for the H-4 Hercules, the short flight of the mammoth plane vindicated Howard Hughes. (27) The flying boat may have been late, but it was well ahead of its <u>time to this day.</u>[10] the Spruce Goose is, by wingspan, the largest plane ever built. (28) After the historic flight was made by Hughes, the plane was moved to <u>it's hangar, and</u>[11] was stored and maintained as though active until 1980, four years after the death of Howard Hughes. (29) It now rests in Oregon as a colossal artifact at the Evergreen Aviation Museum. (30) Someday, perhaps, Hughes's invention will inspire a new generation of inventors to do what others say cannot be done.

10. F. NO CHANGE
    G. time, to this day,
    H. time; to this day,
    J. time, to this day:

11. A. NO CHANGE
    B. its' hangar and
    C. its hangar and
    D. its hangar, and

12. Which sentence from paragraph 4 is much more suited to be used in paragraph 5?
    F. sentence 16
    G. sentence 17
    H. sentence 18
    J. sentence 19

13. Which revision would best clarify the term "H-4 Hercules" in sentence 26?
    A. Replace all references to Hughes's plane with "H-4 Hercules."
    B. Mention the official name of the Spruce Goose earlier in the passage.
    C. Explain why the plane is named after a mythical person.
    D. Replace "H-4 Hercules" with "Flying Boat."

14. At which point in paragraph 5 should a new paragraph begin?
    F. between sentence 23 and 24
    G. between sentence 25 and 26
    H. between sentence 26 and 27
    J. between sentence 27 and 28

15. Which of the following suggestions would best improve sentence 28?
    A. Divide it into two separate sentences.
    B. Delete "four years after the death of Howard Hughes."
    C. Change the sentence from the passive voice to the active voice.
    D. Delete "and was stored."

Review Lessons 1-3

Exercise I

Inferences

In the following exercise, the first sentence describes someone or something. Infer information from the first sentence, and then choose the word from the Word Bank that best completes the second sentence.

scapegoat	moratorium	archaic	nonchalant
peremptory	frangible	carte blanche	contemptuous

1. The movie crew built a chair that would easily shatter into pieces when it was used to bludgeon the lead character.

   From this sentence, we can infer that the film crew uses _____ props so that the actors do not sustain injuries.

2. The network server crash occurred just three days after the new employee started working at the office, so many of the senior employees blamed him, even though he really had nothing to do with it.

   From this sentence, we can infer that the new worker was the _____ for the server crash.

3. The failing company summoned an expert in the industry and gave him permission to do whatever was necessary to save the business.

   From this sentence, we can infer that the consultant was granted _____ to make changes to the company.

4. In his mind, the secret agent was in awe of the villain's underground lair, having never seen any facility so advanced, yet he kept his eyes forward and his mouth shut as though he, like the henchmen whose appearance he had assumed, had seen the facility every day for years.

   From this sentence, we can infer that the secret agent's demeanor must remain _____, or he will compromise his cover.

5. The town council voted to revoke the local law banning the sale of livestock on the city green, especially since a shopping mall has stood on the location of the green for the last fifty years.

   From this sentence, we can infer that the council voted to eliminate a[n] _____ law.

Exercise II

Related Words

Some of the vocabulary words from Lessons 1 through 3 have related meanings. Complete the following sentences by choosing the word that best fits the context, based on information you infer from the use of the italicized word. Some word pairs will be antonyms, some will be synonyms, and some will simply be words often used in the same context.

1. Mindy missed her native country, so it brought her joy to speak in her native
    _____ on the rare occasion that an *interlocutor* from her land happened to be
    passing through the customs office.
    A. incantation
    B. vernacular
    C. sophistry
    D. axiom
    E. scapegoat

2. When Jake asked police to be exempted from the _____ on driving on public
    roads during the blizzard, his request received a *peremptory* "Absolutely not!" from
    the police dispatch center.
    A. talisman
    B. axiom
    C. equanimity
    D. moratorium
    E. litany

3. The pipe running up the inside wall of the _____ office is a *vestige* of the
    1890s, when pneumatic tubes were used to send mail from one office to another.
    A. arable
    B. zealous
    C. nonchalant
    D. contemptuous
    E. archaic

4. The artist left his day job and moved to his own *atelier*, where he had _____ to
    work on only the projects he enjoyed.
    A. camaraderie
    B. equanimity
    C. carte blanche
    D. metamorphosis
    E. vestige

5. From the 1950s to the 1980s, fuzzy dice were _____ on the rearview mirrors
    of American cars, although no one is certain of the origin of the *talisman*.
    A. ubiquitous
    B. archaic
    C. peremptory
    D. zealous
    E. cosmopolitan

6. At the end of the workday, the _____ sound of birdsong was a welcome relief to the *interminable* noise of the highway crew's huge asphalt saw, which had run all day right outside Steve's office.
   A. nonchalant
   B. procrustean
   C. dulcet
   D. arable
   E. abstemious

7. Speaking over the audience's repeated _____ of her name, the actress accepted her award and listed a *litany* of people she wanted to thank for having helped her win.
   A. incantation
   B. scapegoat
   C. talisman
   D. sophistry
   E. carte blanche

8. Alone and vastly outnumbered, the police officer maintained total _____ while speaking to the two angry mobs, knowing that they could erupt in a *donnybrook* at any moment with the slightest provocation.
   A. cosmopolitan
   B. metamorphosis
   C. nomenclature
   D. iniquity
   E. equanimity

9. Ramsey had a *nonchalant* reaction to the nation's financial crisis because his _____ lifestyle had kept him out of both debt and bad investments.
   A. dulcet
   B. abstemious
   C. zealous
   D. contemptuous
   E. cosmopolitan

10. The *procrustean* drill sergeant did not bother picking out a[n] _____ for the dirty barracks mirror found during an inspection; he punished the entire platoon for it.
    A. litany
    B. axiom
    C. scapegoat
    D. nomenclature
    E. vestige

Exercise III

Deeper Meanings

Choose a word to replace the italicized word in each sentence. All of the possible choices for each sentence have similar definitions, but the correct answer will have a connotation that best suits the context. For example, the words "delete," "destroy," and "obliterate" all mean "to remove or wipe out," but no one would ever say, "I destroyed the name from the document." The correct choice will be the word that has the best specific meaning and does not render the sentence awkward in tone or content. When choices seem close, look for a clue in the context that makes one choice better than the other.

Note that the correct answer is not always the primary vocabulary word from the lesson.

ancient	seized	typical	careless
zealous	ubiquitous	took	committed
bored	archaic	nonchalant	spread

1. The first handheld electronic calculator cost $300 in 1970, but now, the *frequent* devices can be bought for a dollar, and businesses often give them away for free as advertisements.

    Better word: _____

2. Calculus comes easily for Seth, and his *bored* attitude before big exams amazes the students who must study all night in hopes that they will get passing grades.

    Better word: _____

3. There was no question that Doug had *arrogated* the last ice cream sandwich from the breakroom freezer, even though I had verbally claimed it this morning.

    Better word: _____

4. The *old* law that makes it illegal to leave your horse tied up at a street intersection has not really been relevant since the invention of the automobile more than 100 years ago.

    Better word: _____

5. The *busy* man on the street corner wore a sign that read, "THE END OF THE WORLD IS NEAR," and he yelled doomsday warnings at every driver who stopped at the red light.

    Better word: _____

Exercise IV

Crossword Puzzle

Use the clues to complete the crossword puzzle. The answers consist of vocabulary words from Lessons 1 through 3.

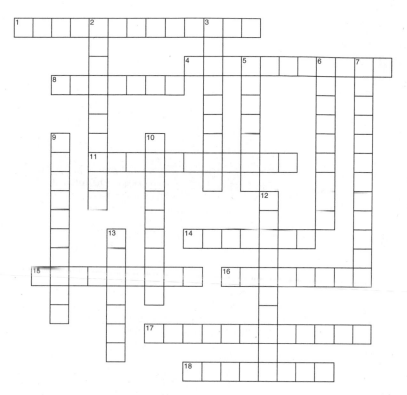

Across

1. You won't be the same after this.
4. being pals
8. eager, over-eager, and this
11. "Double, double, toil and trouble" or "Abracadabra!"
14. extreme darkness
15. foolish arguing
16. This will put a stop to 7 Down.
17. well-rounded
18. like a rabbit's foot or your lucky socks

Down

2. a big time-out
3. takes the blame
5. old, antique, obsolete
6. Take everything out.
7. goes on and on and on
9. very stingy and cheap
10. I like crossword puzzles; I hate crossword puzzles.
12. here, there, everywhere
13. Billy the Kid or Al Capone

Exercise V

Subject Prompts

Here is a writing prompt similar to the one you will find on the writing portion of an assessment test. Follow the instructions below and write a brief, efficient essay.

It has been said that the only thing necessary for the triumph of evil is for good people to do nothing. Indeed, few things are more horrifying than news footage of bystanders witnessing a crime, an assault, or a person in medical distress, and doing nothing to intervene. Like sheep, people simply watch, perhaps wide-eyed as they fumble with cell phones, or else they keep walking with eyes averted, afraid, seemingly, to intervene in the business of others. There is even a name for this repulsive behavior: the bystander effect. In many situations, especially those in which embarrassment might be a consequence of intervening, quiet, cowardly avoidance overpowers the human sense of duty to his or her fellow humans.

Sadly, the bystander effect manifests itself in all facets of life and has contributed to many of the events now regarded as horrors and catastrophes in human history. Tragedies might occur slowly, as residents of a small town watch poisons get dumped into their aquifer for decades, for example, or they might occur at a national level in the form of a specific ethnic group's being blamed and persecuted as the cause of a nation's financial failures. When no one challenges injustices, tragedies occur.

What must be done to help people overcome the bystander effect? Think of activities, exercises, or education that will galvanize people into taking action on behalf of others. You might have an idea for classes, training, camps, or even a convincing story. Detail your solution in a letter to a newspaper and explain the necessity of your program.

Thesis: Write a *one-sentence* response to the above assignment. Make certain this single sentence offers a clear statement of your position.

Example: The first step in getting people to serve others in need is to get them to imagine themselves in situations in which they are in need.

_____

_____

Organizational Plan: List at least three subtopics you will use to support your main idea. This list is your outline.

1. _____

2. _____

3. _____

Draft: Following your outline, write a good first draft of your essay. Remember to support all of your points with examples, facts, references to reading, etc.

Review and Revise: Exchange essays with a classmate. Using the Holistic scoring guide on page 276, score your partner's essay (while he or she scores yours). If necessary, rewrite your essay to correct the problems noted by your partner.

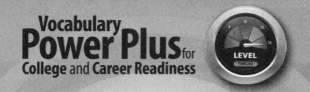

Lesson Four

1. **catharsis** (kə thär´ sis) *n.* a release of emotional tension
The movie lacked a *catharsis* because the villain received no punishment.
syn: purgation

2. **internecine** (in tər ne´ sēn) *adj.* mutually destructive
The *internecine* battle resulted in thousands of casualties, but neither side gained new land.

ant: constructive; beneficial

3. **inundate** (in´ un dāt) *v.* to overwhelm; to fill beyond capacity
Callers *inundated* the radio station with requests for the popular new song.
syn: flood; overwhelm

4. **risible** (ri´ zə bəl) *adj.* relating to laughter; laughable
The *risible* statement made by the gentleman in the front row was completely ridiculous, but amusing.
syn: comical; jocular; jocund   *ant: grave; solemn*

5. **kudos*** (kōō´ dōz) *n.* acclaim or praise
The director of the successful new musical won *kudos* from most critics.
syn: honor; distinction   *ant: disapproval; rejection*
The singular form, Kudo, is very rarely used.

6. **efficacious** (ef i kā´ shəs) *adj.* effective; producing the desired outcome
The shot of adrenaline was *efficacious* in restarting the victim's heart.
syn: productive; useful   *ant: ineffective*

7. **maxim** (mak´ sim) *n.* an established principle; a truth or rule of conduct
The coach frequently spoke the *maxim*, "A chain is only as strong as its weakest link."
syn: axiom; apothegm; proverb

8. **apocryphal** (ə pok´ rə fəl) *adj.* of questionable authenticity, but widely believed
Modern historians dismiss the *apocryphal* story that George Washington cut down a cherry tree.
syn: dubious; equivocal; spurious   *ant: genuine; authentic*

9. **putrid** (pū´ trid) *adj.* rotten and foul smelling
We rolled up the car windows to escape the *putrid* smell of a dead skunk on the road.
syn: fetid; rancid; malodorous   *ant: aromatic; fragrant*

10. **crepuscular** (kri pus´ kyə lər) *adj.* pertaining to twilight
That species of trout has *crepuscular* feeding habits, so you'll catch the most at daybreak or sunset.

11. **revere** (ri vīr´) *v.* to regard with respect, awe, or adoration
    Alexander the Great's soldiers *revered* their leader because he led the troops into every battle.
    syn: venerate; respect; honor   *ant: revile*

12. **sybaritic** (si bə rit´ ik) *adj.* marked by luxury or pleasure
    Ice sculptures, massive chandeliers, and live entertainment were commonplace at Loren's *sybaritic* parties.
    syn: luxurious; ostentatious; grandiose   *ant: modest; simple; plain*

13. **estrange** (i strānj´) *v.* to alienate
    Jill's overbearing mother-in-law *estranged* Jill from her husband.
    syn: disaffect; antagonize   *ant: unite; endear*

14. **intrinsic** (in trin´ sik) *adj.* of or relating to a thing's basic nature; inherent
    Humans have an *intrinsic* desire to be loved.
    syn: basic; elemental; inborn   *ant: extrinsic*

15. **servile** (sûr´ vīl) *adj.* submissive; slavish
    The *servile* dog cowered before its intimidating master.
    syn: subservient; ignoble   *ant: haughty; domineering*

Exercise I

Words in Context

From the list below, supply the words needed to complete the paragraph. Some words will not be used.

sybaritic	crepuscular	apocryphal	servile
maxim	internecine	estrange	

1. When Johnny turned fifteen, he inexplicably began a[n] _____ war with his parents. The Smiths asked Johnny how he was able to afford his new laptop computer, and Johnny gave them a[n] _____ story about how it had fallen from the back of a truck. Enraged, they confiscated the computer and ordered Johnny to sit and listen.

    "When your luck runs out and you end up in prison, it will _____ you from your family and friends, and it will limit your options for the future! Your grades are already suffering, and if you make a criminal record for yourself, you'll end up having a low-paying job in which you must be _____ or be fired, while your successful friends enjoy _____ lifestyles by comparison. Is that what you want?"

From the list below, supply the words needed to complete the paragraph. Some words will not be used.

estrange	efficacious	crepuscular	risible
kudos	inundate	intrinsic	

2. Amy arrived at the empty lot just before sundown, when the _____ animals began to emerge from the forest to feed in the grassy field. The new development would soon ruin the _____ value of Amy's childhood stomping grounds, so she wanted to enjoy it one last time before the construction crews arrived. Amy looked over the rows of beech trees and clusters of mountain laurel and thought of the many _____ lessons she had learned there as a child; for example, that poison ivy should not be added to books of pressed leaves. The visit _____ Amy with childhood memories; she would miss having such a[n] _____ way to forget about her many grown-up responsibilities.

From the list below, supply the words needed to complete the paragraph. Some words will not be used.

catharsis	putrid	efficacious	maxim
kudos	internecine	revere	

3. The young captain earned _____ for leading several successful missions in the past, but his troops did not _____ him when he ordered them to march through the _____ mud of a swamp during the most recent training mission. If anyone complained, the captain simply repeated the _____, "We sweat in peace so that we don't bleed in war."

    What many of the soldiers didn't realize was that the captain had planned this rigorous training mission as a[n] _____ to relieve the tension of living in the confining barracks in the months prior to the troops' deployment.

Exercise II

Sentence Completion

Complete the sentence in a way that shows you understand the meaning of the italicized vocabulary word.

1. The antique watch had little material value, but it had enormous *intrinsic* worth because…

2. The *sybaritic* main cabin of the gigantic yacht has all the pleasures of…

3. The *servile* intern withheld any complaints when the cable television magnate told him to…

4. Flies are not considered *crepuscular* because…

5. A hobby or physical activity in the evening can be a genuine *catharsis* for people who…

6. Most urban legends are *apocryphal* tales simply meant to…

7. Except for one *risible* scene during the opening credits, the movie…

8. The company needed an *efficacious* advertising campaign in order to…

9. The inspirational posters in the guidance counselor's office listed *maxims* about…

10. The relatives all believed they were entitled to a huge inheritance, and *internecine* fighting almost occurred when…

11. When the wind blows just the right way, the *putrid* stench of…

12. Customers *inundated* the department store with orders when…

13. Barb enjoyed *kudos* from her coworkers after she…

14. Jody *estranged* herself from her family when she…

15. Sergeant Butters didn't *revere* the general well enough to volunteer for…

Exercise III

Roots, Prefixes, and Suffixes

Study the entries and answer the questions that follow.

The root *cant* means "sing."
The root *clam* means "shout."
The prefix *in–* means "in," "on," or "onto."
The prefix *re–* means "back."
The prefix *ad–* means "toward."
The prefix *de–* means "down from."
The suffix *–ment* means "result of."

1. Using *literal* translations as guidance, define the following words without using a dictionary.

   A. acclamation   D. incantation
   B. chant   E. canticle
   C. clamorous   F. declamation

2. If *ex–* means "out," then the word _____ means "to shout out suddenly."

3. The famous poem by Dante entitled *The Divine Comedy* is divided into chapters called *cantos*. How do you suppose the chapters got this name?

4. The word *enchantment* is also formed with the root *cant*. If *en–* means "into," what is the literal definition of this word?

5. List as many words as you can think of that contain the prefix *de–*.

Exercise IV

Inference

Complete the sentence by inferring information about the italicized word from its context.

1. Your friends will become *estranged* from you if…

2. If doctors are pleased that Gary's operation proved *efficacious*, then the procedure…

3. During the trial, a judge will usually dismiss *apocryphal* evidence because…

Exercise V

Critical Reading

Below is a pair of reading passages followed by several multiple-choice questions. Carefully read the passages and choose the best answer for each of the questions.

The following passages describe circumstances surrounding the lives of two different young rulers. Alexandrina Victoria, Queen of the United Kingdom of Britain and Empress of India, ruled from 1837 until 1901. Alexander the Great, King of Macedonia, constructed the largest western empire of the ancient world during his reign, which was from 336 to 323 B.C.

Passage 1

In 1792, the French overthrew King Louis XVI and his wife Marie Antoinette, which sparked three decades of bloodshed under the new French Republic and more of conquest because of the imperial designs of Napoleon. After Napoleon was finally silenced at the battle of Waterloo in 1815, the Congress of Vienna restored the monarchy in France. Meanwhile, King George III,
5 the "mad king" of England, neared the end of a sixty-year reign, the latter part of which was marked by bouts of insanity. When Queen Victoria was born in 1819, the continent of Europe was breathing a sigh of relief.

Victoria grew up during the reigns of her uncles, King George IV and King William IV; however, her protective mother, who scorned the **sybaritic** lives of William and George, ensured
10 that Victoria had little exposure to the courts of the two monarchs. Victoria was a kept child, never out of her mother's company, and interacted only with the host of private tutors who provided her with a thorough classical education. Having endured a childhood of isolation and strict control, the eighteen-year-old Victoria found herself Queen when William died in 1837. Knowing that her mother had merely wanted to become regent before Victoria came of age, she quickly shrugged off
15 her mother's domineering influence; however, Victoria had but a fraction of the power of previous English monarchs: by the time of Victoria's reign, the role of a monarch in the creation of policy was little more than that of an advisor who was capable of swaying public opinion if necessary. Reform acts, starting in 1832, granted suffrage to legions of formerly unrepresented working-class voters, further diminishing the power of the aristocracy.
20 The Reform Acts, combined with Victoria's image of honesty and modesty, helped to protect England from the types of upheavals that plagued the rest of Europe at the time. The French revolted in 1830 and then again in 1848, the same year in which revolution wracked Prussia and the Austro-Hungarian Empire. The Communist Manifesto appeared, also in 1848, and the philosophy therein served as the inspiration for revolts around the world for the next century.
25 England enjoyed a period of relative stability, while revolutionary passions ran their course through the rest of the world. In 1840, Queen Victoria married her cousin Prince Albert, and Albert introduced a conservative tone into English politics and society. Albert insisted upon a strict code of conduct in court, and he urged Victoria to voice her opinions among members of the executive cabinet. Under Albert's guidance, Victoria, protecting her dwindling rights as monarch,
30 demonstrated increasingly conservative politics during an era that saw the birth of tradition-challenging ideas such as nationalism, liberalism, democracy, and socialism. She also retained the propriety and restraint inculcated in her youth, demonstrating the values which, emulated by English society, are cataloged today as distinctly Victorian. In the meantime, the British Empire exploded in size, adding ten million square miles of territory and hundreds of millions of subjects.
35 The Empire engaged in no fewer than fifteen wars of varying scale during Victoria's reign.

By the time Queen Victoria died in 1901, the British Empire had added India to its territorial holdings and survived the turmoil and bloodshed concomitant with the revolutions and the creation of two new nations, Germany and Italy, on the European Continent. The anxieties of a teenage queen could easily have sent the British public into a panic, but Victoria's inborn strength
40 and aplomb brought stability and security to her nation, and her subjects **revered** her.

Passage 2

   The father of Alexander the Great, Philip of Macedon, had conquered all of Greece before his assassination in 336 B.C. When Philip died, he left twenty-year-old Alexander with the small task of conquering the Persian Empire. Like a flare that burns with an intense, white-hot flame, Alexander the Great lived fiercely but died young, at the age of thirty-two; however, in his twelve
5 years as king, Alexander built an empire that stretched from Egypt to China.

   One may wonder what type of childhood and adolescent influences must have been at work to create such a powerful ruler. At first glance, Alexander was anything but a charismatic leader—he is described as having been of average appearance and of nervous temperament. His one outstanding feature is said to have been his piercing gaze.
10 Much legend has arisen around Alexander's childhood. He is said to have received a group of envoys from Persia on a day when his father was reviewing his troops, and to have made a more favorable impression on them than his father would have—at the age of six!

   Alexander's first teacher, Leonidas, ingrained his own ascetic personality in young Alexander. He imparted a strong work ethic to the boy, which gave Alexander the **intrinsic** self-discipline he
15 needed to be a good soldier and a young king. When Alexander traveled with his armies, he lived as his soldiers lived, sleeping on the ground and sharing unsavory rations, foregoing extravagant tents, regal vestments, and luxurious meals that had no purpose on the battlefield.

   Alexander's second teacher, Lysimacuis, taught Alexander to appreciate the arts of music, poetry, and drama, but his most famous teacher, the Athenian philosopher Aristotle, passed along
20 his knowledge of science, medicine, philosophy, ethics, and politics, all of which contributed to the background that would soon make the thirteen-year-old Alexander a great leader and champion of his people.

   One story that demonstrates young Alexander's precocious nature is that of Alexander and his horse, Bucephalus. Philoneicus of Thessaly presented a horse to sell to Philip, but none of
25 Philip's farmhands could handle the wild Bucephalus. Alexander noticed that the animal was afraid of its own shadow, so he wagered 13 talents—the price of the horse—that he could tame it. Philip accepted the wager, and Alexander quickly collected his prize after leading the horse toward the sun, so that the animal could not see its shadow, then mounting and riding the horse.

   Not all of the tales associated with Alexander's youth are as charming as that of Bucephalus.
30 Philip took several concubines during his reign, one of whom was Cleopatra, the daughter of a Macedonian aristocrat. During the wedding feast, Cleopatra's uncle, Attalus, suggested that Philip and Cleopatra produce a pure Macedonian heir (Alexander's mother, Olympias, was an Albanian who practiced Dionysian rituals that were not commonly condoned in Macedonia; Alexander was not considered to be a pure Macedonian). Alexander took great offense to the suggestion and a
35 brawl ensued, which **estranged** Alexander from his father until Philip was assassinated in 336.

   Alexander is often described as the ruler who accomplished more in thirteen years than anyone else had accomplished in an entire lifetime. Alexander, like many princes, had a superior education in arts, sciences, and military strategy, but perhaps it was the unconventional education—that which a dysfunctional family presents—that somehow fueled Alexander's
40 ambition. Whatever the deciding factors, Alexander undoubtedly remains among the most powerful military leaders in the history of the world.

1A. The personification used in paragraph 1 of the first passage is used to
   A. describe the mental state of King George III.
   B. demonstrate the purpose of the Congress of Vienna.
   C. express the mood of Europe in 1819.
   D. assess the political hostility of England in the early 1800s.
   E. portray the conflict between Victoria's mother and Victoria's uncles.

1B. Choose the phrase from paragraph 1 that creates the personification in passage 1.
    A.   "sixty year reign"
    B.   "breathing a sigh of relief"
    C.   "finally silenced"
    D.   " 'mad king' of England"
    E.   "three decades of conquest"

2A. As it is used in line 10, *courts* most nearly means
    A.   criminal trials.
    B.   summer homes.
    C.   athletic fields.
    D.   local taverns.
    E.   royal households.

2B. Which description of Victoria's childhood best supports your choice of answer for question 2A?
    A.   the chaos before she was born
    B.   her education
    C.   Victoria's age
    D.   her isolation
    E.   the diminished power of monarchs

3A. As used in line 37 of passage 1, *concomitant* most nearly means
    A.   accompanying.
    B.   sympathetic.
    C.   contradictory.
    D.   uncommon.
    E.   foreign.

3B. What phrase from the final paragraph helps support your answer for 3A?
    A.   "Germany and Italy"
    B.   "inborn strength and aplomb"
    C.   "stability and security"
    D.   "turmoil and bloodshed"
    E.   "revolutions and the creation"

3C. In spite of England's "relative stability" at the time, the period of Queen Victoria's reign, according to the details in passage 1, can be described as
    A.   uneventful.
    B.   a time of powerful rulers.
    C.   a time of frequent conflict.
    D.   Napoleon's dominance.
    E.   a forgotten period of history.

4A. The best title for the first passage would be
  A.   European Revolutions during the Reign of Queen Victoria.
  B.   The Benefits of the Victorian Era in Modern Times.
  C.   England from King George to Communism.
  D.   Queen Victoria: the Birth of English Stability.
  E.   The Expansion of the British Empire.

4B. The tone of passage 1 is best described as
  A.   objective.
  B.   solemn.
  C.   pessimistic.
  D.   critical.
  E.   imaginative.

5A. Which word would be the best antonym for *ascetic* as it appears in line 13 of passage 2?
  A.   spartan
  B.   cynical
  C.   austere
  D.   cheap
  E.   indulgent

5B. Which detail in passage 2, paragraph 4, provides the best evidence for your answer to question 5A?
  A.   Alexander's medical appearance
  B.   Alexander's enduring harsh conditions
  C.   Alexander's anger toward his father
  D.   Alexander's penchant for leadership
  E.   Alexander's ability to tame horses

6A. According to passage 2, which choice was probably *not* a factor in the development of Alexander's personality?
  A.   Philip's dislike of Olympias' religious beliefs
  B.   Leonidas' belief in the denial of the self
  C.   Alexander's skill with horses
  D.   Philip's polygamous practices
  E.   Aristotle's teachings in ethics

6B. In contrast to Victoria's childhood, as it is described in passage 1, young Alexander
  A.   was kept away from any adult other than his father.
  B.   went to war as a child.
  C.   was born to royalty.
  D.   grew into a disciplined leader.
  E.   enjoyed more freedom than Victoria did.

7. As used in line 17 of passage 2, *vestments* most nearly means
   A. robes.
   B. weaponry.
   C. goblets.
   D. scrolls.
   E. attitudes.

8A. The best title for passage 2 would be
   A. An Ambassador at Age Six.
   B. An Imperialistic Mind.
   C. Legends of Alexander's Youth.
   D. The Making of a Warrior King.
   E. Aristotle and Alexander.

8B. Compared to passage 2, the topic of passage 1 is best described as
   A. focused more on the general political climate of the time than on the sovereign.
   B. including many more details of the sovereign's childhood.
   C. relying more heavily on anecdotes of the sovereign's childhood.
   D. being a synopsis of the rulers before and after Victoria's reign.
   E. detailing specific information about the sovereign's early experiences.

9A. Which of the following statements is *not* true about the two passages?
   A. Passage 2 is more skeptical than passage 1.
   B. Passage 1 is more patriotic than passage 2.
   C. Passage 2 is written more formally than passage 1.
   D. Passage 2 is biographical, while passage 1 is historical.
   E. Passage 2 focuses on psychology more than passage 1 does.

9B. Which example of voice from passage 2 best supports your answer choice for question 9A?
   A. "He imparted a strong work ethic"
   B. "Alexander is often described"
   C. "having been of average appearance"
   D. "like a flare that burns with an intense…flame"
   E. "among the most powerful military leaders"

10. Choose the formative element that is central to both Victoria's and Alexander's childhood.
   A. foreign wars
   B. interaction with peers
   C. survival skills
   D. superior education
   E. language skills

Lesson Five

1. **expiate** (ek´ spē āt) *v.* to make amends for
    Johnny mowed the neighbors' lawn free of charge all summer to *expiate* the guilt he felt for breaking their front window with a baseball.
    syn: atone; correct; rectify

2. **anomaly** (ə nom´ ə lē) *n.* a deviation from the norm; an odd or peculiar occurrence
    The sailor immediately notified the captain when he saw an *anomaly* on the sonar screen.
    syn: eccentricity; irregularity; oddity

3. **compendium** (kəm pen´ dē əm) *n.* a list or collection of items
    Jen perused a *compendium* of antique toys to find the value of an old doll.
    syn: compilation; index; anthology

4. **foist** (foist) *v.* to pass off as genuine or valuable
    The secret service arrested the man who *foisted* counterfeit $20 bills off on the unsuspecting country.
    syn: fob

5. **incongruous** (in kong´ grōō əs) *adj.* incompatible; unsuitable for the situation
    Ed's *incongruous* joke about policemen ensured he would get a speeding ticket.
    syn: discordant; improper   *ant: compatible; fitting*

6. **consternation** (kon stər nā´ shən) *n.* alarming dismay or concern
    The announcement of a pop quiz caused *consternation* among the students.
    syn: bewilderment; shock; trepidation   *ant: composure; tranquility*

7. **coterie** (kō´ tə rē) *n.* a small group of people who share interests and meet frequently
    Virginia Woolf was a member of the Bloomsbury Group, a *coterie* of English authors respected for its talent, but ridiculed for its arrogance.
    syn: circle; clique; society

8. **innocuous** (i nok´ yōō əs) *adj.* harmless
    The assassin wore a disguise and a smile to make himself look like an *innocuous* old man.
    syn: inoffensive; innocent   *ant: injurious*

9. **flippancy** (flip´ ənt sē) *n.* disrespect
    His *flippancy* in class often got him sent to the principal's office.
    syn: irreverence; rudeness; impertinence   *ant: respect; reverence*

10. **disconcert** (dis kən sûrt´)   *v.* to frustrate; confuse
    The lengthy calculus problem on the quiz *disconcerted* Nancy.
    syn: agitate; fluster; perplex   *ant: enlighten; comfort;*
                                                                         encourage

11. **preamble** (prē´ am bəl)   *n.* a preliminary statement; an introduction
    After reciting a long-winded *preamble*, the lawyer finally presented some pertinent facts.
    syn: prologue; preface; opening   *ant: epilogue; finale*

12. **vitriolic** (vit rē ol´ ik)   *adj.* harsh in tone; bitterly critical
    The critic's *vitriolic* review of the new film prompted thousands of letters praising the movie.
    syn: caustic; offensive; scathing   *ant: flattering; genial*

13. **comprise** (kəm prīz´)   *v.* to include or consist of; contain
    Canada *comprises* ten provinces and three territories.
    syn: constitute; encompass; incorporate   *ant: exclude; lack*

14. **eidetic** (ī det´ ik)   *adj.* pertaining to extraordinarily detailed and vivid recall
    The author attempted to describe the *eidetic* scenes in his head.
    syn: vivid   *ant: vague*

15. **plethora** (pleth´ ər ə)   *n.* an overabundance; excess
    The library has a *plethora* of information about almost any subject imaginable.
    syn: surplus   *ant: deficiency; shortage; paucity*

Exercise I

Words in Context

From the list below, supply the words needed to complete the paragraph. Some words will not be used.

foist	consternation	coterie	comprise
plethora	innocuous	eidetic	

1. Each month, a[n] _____ of radio-controlled model airplane enthusiasts meets at an open field at the Ames farm, weather permitting. (To the group's _____, rain canceled two meetings this summer already.) The group _____ aviation fans from all over the county, and members with years of aeronautical experience offer a[n] _____ of knowledge and experience to amateurs in the club. The farmer who owns the field sees the meetings as _____, as long as no one crashes a plane into his house or his livestock.

From the list below, supply the words needed to complete the paragraph. Some words will not be used.

foist	vitriolic	innocuous	preamble
anomaly	flippancy	expiate	

2. Heather made a[n] _____ phone call when she realized that the crooked electronics shop had just _____ a cheap replica of a brand-name digital camera on her, but charged her the price of the genuine camera. No one answered the phone at the store, so Heather went, in person, to deal with her concerns. When Heather entered the store, the owner confronted her. In his insulting _____, he scolded Heather for her _____ in spreading such nasty, unfounded rumors about the business; then, quietly, so the other customers didn't hear, the owner offered to _____ his offense by offering Heather a more expensive camera at no additional cost. Heather simply shook her head and demanded her money back.

From the list below, supply the words needed to complete the paragraph. Some words will not be used.

anomaly	coterie	compendium	expiate
eidetic	incongruous	disconcert	

3. Allen has a[n] _____ memory when it comes to remembering faces, so it was quite a[n] _____ when a stranger asked, "Don't you know me?" and Allen was forced to say, "No." The stranger issued a simple, "You'll remember," before leaving Allen's store. The visit was _____ to Allen; he hated having such a[n] _____ gap in the memory he often boasted about. That evening at home, Allen perused every _____ of customer names and addresses he could find, hoping to spark his memory.

Exercise II

Sentence Completion

Complete the sentence in a way that shows you understand the meaning of the italicized vocabulary word.

1. In a *preamble* to the novel, the author writes…

2. The *anomaly* in the clouds turned out to be…

3. Lyle received a *vitriolic* lecture from his teacher for…

4. After a lengthy search, the starving castaways were thrilled to discover that the tiny island offered a *plethora* of…

5. That spider is *innocuous*, so…

6. Ed could not get over his *consternation* when he saw…

7. The average dinner salad usually *comprises*…

8. Mike's fear at the sight of blood was *incongruous* with his…

9. Private Miller quickly departed from his usual *flippancy* when…

10. Heidi could not *expiate* her negative feelings about the divorce, so she…

11. The museum director has a *compendium* that categorizes…

12. Ben saw that discussing evolution was *disconcerting* to his students, so he…

13. To gain membership in the *coterie* of artists, applicants had to…

14. On the street corner, a shady-looking man tried to *foist*…

15. The old man forgot many things, but he still had an *eidetic* memory of the day he…

Exercise III

Roots, Prefixes, and Suffixes

Study the entries and answer the questions that follow.

The root *ject* means "throw."
The root *tract* means "drag" or "draw."
The prefix *con–* means "together."
The prefix *de–* means "down."
The prefix *in–* means "not."
The prefix *pro–* means "forward."

1. Using *literal* translations as guidance, define the following words without using a dictionary.

    A. conjecture
    B. dejected
    C. intractable
    D. injection
    E. detract
    F. protracted

2. What does a *projector* literally do?

3. When the prefix *ex–*, which means "out," is added to the root *ject*, a letter drops out. What word do we get from this prefix and root?

4. Something that *draws* people *together* legally is a _____.

5. List as many words as you can think of that contain the root *ject*.

6. List as many words as you can think of that contain the prefix *con–*.

Exercise IV

Inference

Complete the sentence by inferring information about the italicized word from its context.

1. If the editor's *vitriolic* critique of the novel brings the writer to tears, then the editor must think that...

2. A cheese merchant might have a *compendium* that...

3. If a doctor finds an *anomaly* on someone's X-ray, then the patient will probably want to...

Exercise V

Writing

Here is a writing prompt similar to the one you will find on the writing portion of an assessment test.

Plan and write an essay based on the following statement:

> "Rules and models destroy genius and art."
>
> —William Hazlitt (1778–1830), "On Taste"

Assignment: Artists and creative personalities are often contrasted with mathematicians and practical thinkers, even though the two types exist in, and overlap, almost every person. Hazlitt's quote seems to suggest that rules and models destroy art; but without them, can art, as we know it, exist? In an essay, explain whether or not you agree with Hazlitt, and explain how you think art should be judged or determined. Support your opinion using evidence from your reading, studies, or experience and observations.

Thesis: Write a *one-sentence* response to the above assignment. Make certain this single sentence offers a clear statement of your position.

Example: Rules and models do nothing but restrict new ways of thinking and stifle the endeavors of the next Einsteins and Michelangelos of the world.

_____

_____

Organizational Plan: List at least three subtopics you will use to support your main idea. This list is your outline.

1. _____

2. _____

3. _____

Draft: Following your outline, write a good first draft of your essay. Remember to support all of your points with examples, facts, references to reading, etc.

Review and Revise: Exchange essays with a classmate. Using the scoring guide for Sentence Formation and Variety on page 274, score your partner's essay (while he or she scores yours). Focus on sentence structure and the use of language conventions. If necessary, rewrite your essay to improve the sentence structure and/or your use of language.

Exercise VI

English Practice

Identifying Sentence Errors

Identify the grammatical error in each of the following sentences. If the sentence contains no error, select answer choice E.

1. Everyone in the office laughs at Betty <u>because she felt she was</u> the smartest person
   (A) (B)
   <u>who</u> <u>had ever worked</u> for the company. <u>No error</u>
   (C)   (D)   (E)

2. The <u>man in the water shouted,</u> <u>"Help!"</u> when he <u>started to get tired from</u> all the
        (A)   (B)   (C)
   <u>swimming he done.</u> <u>No error</u>
        (D)   (E)

3. If you dig <u>farther and deeper</u> into Bill's reason for embezzling the money from
            (A)
   <u>his father's company,</u> you will see <u>that the crime began</u> when the older man
        (B)   (C)
   <u>removed him from the will.</u> <u>No error</u>
        (D)   (E)

4. The <u>children all of who had all been playing noisily in their backyard fled</u> to the
        (A)
   <u>safety of the back porch</u> at the <u>first sound of thunder,</u> which is exactly what
        (B)   (C)
   <u>their parents had told them to do.</u> <u>No error</u>
        (D)   (E)

5. <u>No one</u> in the entire class <u>could understand exactly</u> what the teacher
   (A)   (B)
   <u>meant when she</u> talked about oxygen and <u>it's properties.</u> <u>No error</u>
        (C)   (D)   (E)

Improving Sentences

The underlined portion of each sentence below contains some flaw. Select the answer choice that best corrects the flaw.

6. I saw that <u>everyone at the dance was dressed formally. This meant that I needed</u> to change out of my jeans.
   A. everyone at the dance was dressed formally, and this meant that I needed
   B. everybody at the dance was dressed formally. This meant that I needed
   C. everyone at the dance was dressed formally. That meant that I needed
   D. everyone at the dance was dressed formally, which meant that I needed
   E. everyone at the dance was dressed formally; their attire means I had

7. <u>The butterflies, which emerged from their cocoons this year, will</u> not be the same ones that migrate to Mexico for the winter.
   A. The butterflies, that emerged from their cocoons this year, will
   B. The butterflies, which emerged from their cocoons this year will,
   C. The butterflies, which emerged from their cocoons this year will
   D. The butterflies that emerged from their cocoons this year will
   E. Whichever butterflies that have emerged from their cocoons this year will

8. <u>Everybody involved in the student plays last Saturday and Sunday are to receive</u> an extra day to study before finals.
   A. Everyone involved in the student plays last Saturday and Sunday are to receive
   B. Everybody involved in the student plays last Saturday and Sunday is to receive
   C. Everybody involved in the student plays last Saturday and Sunday will have received
   D. Everybody in the student plays last Saturday and Sunday are to receive
   E. Everybody involved in last Saturday's and Sunday's student plays are to receive

9. <u>Playing in the park, the stormy weather ruined the childrens' game of dodge ball.</u>
   A. The stormy weather ruined the childrens' game of dodge ball playing in the park.
   B. The stormy weather ruined the childrens' game of dodge ball.
   C. Playing in the park, the stormy weather ruined the children's game of dodge ball.
   D. The stormy weather ruined the childrens' game of dodge ball who were playing in the park.
   E. The stormy weather ruined the children's dodge ball game in the park.

10. <u>Anyone who comes to the football game wearing a player's T-shirt receive</u> 50% off the price of admission.
    A. Anyone, who comes to the football game wearing a player's T-shirt, will receive
    B. Everybody who come to the football game wearing a player's T-shirt will receive
    C. Anyone who comes to the football game wearing a player's T-shirt receives
    D. Anyone who comes to the game wearing a T-shirt will receive
    E. Anyone who comes to the football game, and also wears a player's T-shirt receives

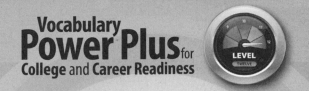

Lesson Six

1. **accoutrement** (ə kōō′ trə mənt) *n.* an accessory item of dress or equipment
Various *accoutrements* dangled from the workbelt of the telephone repairman.
syn: device; gear

2. **hubris** (hyōō′ bris) *n.* overbearing pride; arrogance
Hubris is the character flaw found in many tragic heroes.
syn: conceit; smugness; pompousness *ant: humility; modesty*

3. **prognosticate** (prăg năs′ tə kāt) *v.* to predict
Meteorologists are attempting to *prognosticate* the path of the hurricane.
syn: forecast; foreshadow

4. **contrive** (kən trĭv′) *v.* to plan cleverly; to devise
After four days in captivity, Steve *contrived* an escape plan that could not fail.
syn: concoct; design; engineer

5. **sectarian** (sek târ′ ē ən) *adj.* narrowly confined to a particular group
Members of the *sectarian* cult gave no thought to the beliefs of outsiders.
syn: insular; dogmatic *ant: tolerant*

6. **scullion** (skul′ yən) *n.* a servant for menial tasks
Scullions scrubbed the castle floors for hours prior to the king's feast.
syn: peon; toiler *ant: patrician; aristocrat*

7. **antediluvian** (an ti də lōō′ vē ən) *adj.* extremely old; antiquated
Especially tall structures were rare in the ancient world because *antediluvian*
architecture could not withstand the enormous forces.
syn: ancient; archaic *ant: modern; new*

8. **imbroglio** (im brōl′ yō) *n.* a difficult and embarrassing situation
His infatuation with a married co-worker led to an *imbroglio* at the office picnic.
syn: predicament *ant: peace; serenity*

9. **quotidian** (kwō ti′ dē ən) *adj.* everyday; commonplace
Earthquakes were *quotidian* events for the people living near the volcano.
syn: ordinary; routine *ant: rare; uncommon*

10. **platitude** (plat′ i tōōd) *n.* an obvious remark; a cliché
The two candidates offered plenty of *platitudes,* but no practical solutions.
syn: maxim; truism; banality

11. **peregrination** (per i grə nā´ shən) *n.* travel by walking
    Vince planned a summer of *peregrination* throughout Europe.
    syn: trekking; exploration

12. **venerate** (ven´ ə rāt) *v.* to respect or revere
    Young scholars often *venerate* the ideas of the great philosophers.
    syn: glorify; treasure   *ant: abhor; despise*

13. **sanctimonious** (sangk tə mō´ nē əs) *adj.* showing false piety or righteousness
    The *sanctimonious* landlord made public contributions to charities, but threatened
    his tenants with eviction if they didn't pay the rent on time.
    syn: hypocritical; specious   *ant: humble; modest*

14. **stringent** (strin´ jənt) *adj.* restrictive; imposing demanding standards
    The dynamite factory imposed *stringent* safety rules to prevent any catastrophe.
    syn: severe; rigid; inflexible   *ant: lenient; flexible*

15. **haughty** (hô´ tē) *adj.* condescendingly proud; arrogant
    The *haughty* boy thought that his family's wealth made him better than other
    students.
    syn: conceited; snobbish; supercilious   *ant: humble; modest*

Exercise I

Words in Context

From the list below, supply the words needed to complete the paragraph. Some words will not be used.

imbroglio	quotidian	sanctimonious	scullion
peregrination	hubris	prognosticate	

1. There was a[n] _____ at the garage. A customer arrived and demanded to see his car, after having been told that the repairs were nearly finished, but found that the work had not even begun.
    "Two weeks ago, you said that the job would take three or four days, but that _____ was wrong," the customer sarcastically said to Jane, the receptionist. "Give me the keys; I'll take my car to a different garage." Jane complied, still smiling as usual; she never worried about losing an occasional customer, though she did feel bad about mistakenly telling the customer that his car was finished. Angry customers were a[n] _____ occurrence in the auto repair business; most people have a tendency to become emotional when they receive bills for hundreds or even thousands of dollars, especially for repairs to cars that are still relatively new. Jane knew that every garage in town was overloaded. Upon hearing the customer's story, the other garage would offer some _____ criticism of Jane's garage, accept the job, and then do exactly what Jane's garage did, since the car required a tedious repair that yielded little profit. The whole frustrating process simply causes many drivers to abandon their cars and resort to _____ as their primary form of transportation.

From the list below, supply the words needed to complete the paragraph. Some words will not be used.

platitude	haughty	contrive	stringent
sectarian	quotidian	scullion	

2. After reviewing the pamphlets for the private school, Veronica's parents thought that the school might be too _____ because of its religious affiliation, but they favored the _____ educational requirements to which the students were held.
    Veronica assumed that the private school would be full of _____, rich children who probably treated middle-class people like _____. She was about to _____ a way to get out of going to the school, but at the last minute, she decided to give it a try.

From the list below, supply the words needed to complete the paragraph. Some words will not be used.

accoutrement	hubris	platitude	prognosticate
venerate	antediluvian	contrive	

3. Most people rendered a typical _____ to Tracey before the triathlon, such as "Good luck," or "Pace yourself," but Tracey's mother, who _____ famous women and _____ conquerors such as Cleopatra, simply said, "Win the race or don't bother starting it." Tracey smiled as she removed her watch, earrings, and other _____ before confidently walking to the triathlon's registration booth. Tracey also hoped that her own _____ hadn't clouded her expectations of how well she would do in the race; she was in excellent shape, but so were the other two hundred competitors.

Exercise II

Sentence Completion

Complete the sentence in a way that shows you understand the meaning of the italicized vocabulary word.

1. Ashley bought the new dress, but she still needed *accoutrements* such as...

2. Despite the claims of being able to *prognosticate* the future, most...

3. The thief found himself in an *imbroglio* when he...

4. People of the remote mountain village retained *antediluvian* traditions that...

5. Rachel warned her son that his *hubris*, left unchecked, would...

6. *Peregrination* was the most common form of transportation before...

7. Our *sectarian* neighbors seldom speak to us because they...

8. Carol, the secretary, began to feel like the boss's *scullion* when he told her to...

9. Rabbits and woodchucks were eating the vegetables in the garden, so Bob *contrived* a way to...

10. Dana was certain that she could meet the *stringent* training requirements of...

11. The corrupt police commissioner often made the *sanctimonious* claim that he...

12. Kevin left the country club because he didn't like the way in which *haughty* members...

13. Cindy *venerates* the huge walnut tree on the property line, but Bill, her neighbor, would like to...

14. Nathan was tired of watching *quotidian* television sitcoms, so he...

15. Watching a movie with our father is difficult because he feels obligated to voice some *platitude* every time...

Exercise III

Roots, Prefixes, and Suffixes

Study the entries and answer the questions that follow.

The prefix *pre–* means "before."
The root *bene* means "good" or "well."
The root *optim* means "best."
The root *dict* means "speech."
The root *ven* means "come."
The prefix *contra–* means "against."
The prefix *con–* means "together."

1. Using *literal* translations as guidance, define the following words without using a dictionary.

A.	contradiction	D.	optimal
B.	optimistic	E.	contravene
C.	convene	F.	benediction

2. The root *male* has the opposite meaning of the root *bene*. What, then, is a *malediction*?

3. What do you suppose a *venue* is?

4. If you *talk* about something *before* it happens, then you might be making a[n]
   _____ .

5. List as many words as you can think of that contain the root *dict*.

6. List as many words as you can think of that contain the root *bene*.

Exercise IV

Inference

Complete the sentence by inferring information about the italicized word from its context.

1. Devoted fans might *venerate* their idol long after…

2. During a *quotidian* visit to the grocery store, you probably wouldn't expect to…

3. A university might have *stringent* academic requirements for admission to ensure that…

Exercise V

Critical Reading

Below is a reading passage followed by several multiple-choice questions. Carefully read the passage and choose the best answer for each of the questions.

The following passage describes the characteristics of the Maya, Inca, and Aztec cultures of Central and South America.

To the average North American, the mere mention of Maya, Aztec, or Inca civilization evokes thoughts of great, flat-topped pyramids of mysterious origin, secret cities perched on remote mountaintops, and booby-trapped temples brimming with treasure-hoards of gold. Indeed, impressions have not changed much since the age of the Spanish explorers, who, despite
5 intentions of conquest, were also mystified by the cryptic civilizations of Mesoamerica and South America. Explorers may not have found the mythical golden city of El Dorado, but they did find three amazing cultures, each with unique characteristics.

Maya civilization, often considered to be the most exalted and mysterious of the three, inhabited the Yucatan Peninsula of Eastern Mexico as long ago as 2,600 B.C. Emerging from a
10 collection of city-states with no central government, the Maya reached a cultural peak between A.D. 250 and 900. The Maya, who developed an astrological calendar that allowed them to grow crops in poor soil, were originally thought to be a peaceful people, but archaeologists have since determined that intertribal warfare brought about their decline. Maya, like the Aztecs and Inca, also practiced human sacrifice. Ancient pyramids inscribed with weathered glyphs and characters
15 from the most advanced ancient alphabet in the western hemisphere now sit abandoned, obscured by centuries of jungle growth. Maya descendants still inhabit the Yucatan, but the technology, religion, and practices of the ancient civilization must now be slowly exhumed and catalogued by archaeologists—a difficult task considering the Maya had no central ruling capital. The Maya existed in a network of city-states, with each ruling its immediate territory. Neither did
20 the Maya have a single emperor, though its kings were **venerated** as godlike, as in the Inca and Aztec cultures.

The Aztecs, noted perhaps most often for their penchant for battle and human sacrifice, composed the second-largest pre-Columbian civilization in central America. Originally a nomadic society inhabiting the central basin of **antediluvian** Mexico, the various tribes who identified
25 themselves as Aztec settled in the marshy region near Lake Texcoco and, in 1325, founded the city of Tenochtitlan at the present site of Mexico City. Despite vicious religious practices, the Aztec demonstrated ingenuity by inventing an innovative farming technique to grow crops among the 30 canals of Tenochtitlan. Farmers **contrived** chinampas, or artificial, fertile islands floating in canals, to grow crops of beans, peppers, avocados, tomatoes, and, most important,
30 corn. Ironically, the seemingly bloodthirsty culture, when not participating in an estimated 20,000 human sacrifices a year, took great interest in the beauty of nature; Aztecs, who lacked plows or beasts of burden, took the time to grow beautiful flowers strictly for decoration. Before falling to the Spanish in 1521, the Aztecs left several permanent contributions to history and to the explorers of the New World: chocolate, derived from indigenous cacao beans; tomatoes, potatoes,
35 and numerous other vegetables that have long become staples to the rest of the world; and, as testament to the artisans among the Aztecs, an accurate, 24-ton limestone calendar that took more than fifty years to construct.

Inca, whose feats of engineering baffle modern architects, dominated the west coast of South America from 1300 to 1535. Like the Aztecs, the Inca practiced human sacrifice and
40 lacked a written language; however, the Inca made up for language shortcomings with advanced architecture and a complex government. In addition to having the most advanced medical and surgical techniques of the ancient Americas, the Inca constructed more than 12,000 miles of roadway and aqueducts to supply taxpaying and labor-contributing tribes throughout the empire.

The precise, intricate stonemasonry of Inca pyramids, fortresses, and walls commands the respect
45 of even modern masons. Inca architecture still dots the Andean mountains and highlands as the
timeless endeavors of a lost people.

In spite of the achievements and predominance of the two civilizations intact after
Columbus arrived in the New World, they found themselves at the mercy of the Spaniards during
the sixteenth century. Hernando Cortez, who sought control of the Aztec Empire, or Mexican
50 Empire, began his quest in 1519 by forming alliances with tribes who were displeased with the
leadership of Montezuma II in Tenochtitlan. Cortez went to the city and took Montezuma hostage,
taking advantage of the fact that Aztecs thought that the Spaniards were descendants of their god,
Quetzalcoatl, and had come to fulfill a prophecy. Aztec prophets had **prognosticated** that bearded
men would arrive from the east, or the land of the sun god—the Aztec conception of heaven.
55 Montezuma was killed during a short uprising in 1521 while instructing the Aztecs to make peace
with the Spaniards. The Spaniards were forced to retreat from the city, but they soon regrouped
and besieged the Aztec capital. After the eventual surrender, Cortez burned the city and destroyed
the greatest monuments of Aztec culture.

The Inca Empire shared a fate similar to that of the Aztec, but at the hands of a conquistador
60 more sinister than Cortez. Francisco Pizarro, motivated by legends of treasure, captured the Inca
ruler Atahualpa during their first meeting. Atahualpa offered a ransom for himself that consisted
of a roomful of gold. Atahualpa revealed the location of the treasure to Pizarro, and Pizarro
promptly executed the ruler and seized control of Cuzco, the Inca capital. Pizarro was eventually
killed by his own people, but the Inca Empire was forever lost.
65 Aztecs, Inca, and Maya who escaped the iron swords and gunpowder of the Europeans
instead suffered the old world diseases that accompanied the explorers. Entire tribes vanished
as smallpox, scarlet fever, and influenza decimated the native population of the Americas. Those
who survived were forced to abandon their customs and live beneath Spanish rule for the next
three centuries.
70 Millions of tourists now visit Mexico and Peru to see the remnants of the Maya, Aztec, and
Inca civilizations. Though weathered or overgrown, the relics stand as permanent markers of the
ingenuity and art of the pre-Columbian civilizations. Archaeologists and treasure hunters scour
newly discovered burial platforms and caves in search of knowledge that might contribute to the
modern understanding of the lost cultures, and also, undoubtedly, to find relics made of that one
75 material valued by both the ancient and modern worlds: gold.

1A. The purpose of this passage is to
    A.   explain how Spanish explorers decimated other cultures.
    B.   demonstrate the differences among three early cultures.
    C.   show early cultural advances.
    D.   show the relationships among three cultures.
    E.   explain how three civilizations began.

1B. The organization of the passage is best described as
    A.   chronological.
    B.   cause and effect.
    C.   persuasive.
    D.   problem and solution.
    E.   topical.

2A. The term *Mesoamerica* in line 5 most nearly means
    A.   South America.
    B.   coastal America.
    C.   prehistoric America.
    D.   ancient America.
    E.   Middle America.

2B. Which clues from lines 1-15 best support your answer to question 2A?
   A.   secret cities, crops
   B.   archaeologists, Peninsula
   C.   conquest, alphabet
   D.   Mexico, North America
   E.   intertribal, cryptic

3A. It is ironic that the Aztecs grew flowers because
   A.   flowers do not grow well where the Aztecs lived.
   B.   flower cultivation was indicative of a society with leisure time.
   C.   the Aztecs were violent and warlike.
   D.   the Aztecs had no calendar to determine the best time to grow flowers.
   E.   Pre-Columbian cultures did not use plants for decoration.

3B. As it is used in line 22, *penchant* most nearly means
   A.   aversion.
   B.   religion.
   C.   teaching.
   D.   tendency.
   E.   future.

4A. In paragraph 3, the term "pre-Columbian" describes
   A.   all civilization that preceded the nation of Columbia.
   B.   the time leading to the foundation of Washington, D.C.
   C.   everything before the year in which the Inca Empire fell.
   D.   the new name that Cortez gave to Tenochtitlan.
   E.   the time before Columbus arrived in the Americas.

4B. Choose the phrase from the passage that best supports your answer to question 4A.
   A.   "…20,000 human sacrifices a year…"
   B.   "…after Columbus arrived in the New World…"
   C.   "Cortez went to the city and took Montezuma hostage…"
   D.   "…Yucatan Peninsula of Eastern Mexico…"
   E.   "…dominated the west coast of South America…"

5A. The word *staples,* as it is used in line 35, most nearly means
   A.   fasteners.
   B.   basics.
   C.   luxuries.
   D.   features.
   E.   surplus.

5B. A *staple* can probably be described as
   A.   unobtainable.
   B.   fruit.
   C.   common.
   D.   meat.
   E.   rare.

6A. Which of the following statements is implied by the following quotation (lines 42-43)?

"…the Inca constructed more than 12,000 miles of roadway and aqueducts to supply taxpaying…tribes throughout the empire."

    A.   The Inca had some type of central government.
    B.   Inca roadways were elevated high above the ground.
    C.   High taxes probably accelerated the fall of the Inca Empire.
    D.   The Inca wasted resources on building roadways.
    E.   The Inca decorated their aqueducts with gold.

6B. How does your answer to question 6A draw a contrast between the Inca and the Maya, according to the passage?
    A.   The Maya's roads were crudely made and inefficient.
    B.   The Maya did not pay taxes.
    C.   The Maya had no central ruling power.
    D.   The Inca calendar was not created to sustain agriculture.
    F.   Gold was not available to the Maya.

7A. Unlike the Aztecs and the Inca, the Maya had
    A.   knowledge of planting crops.
    B.   a written language.
    C.   human sacrifice.
    D.   chinampas.
    E.   a calendar.

7B. Choose the cultural element shared by all three of the civilizations described in the passage.
    A.   stone calendars
    B.   written language
    C.   artificial islands
    D.   roadways
    E.   human sacrifice

8A. The passage contains no details about the Spanish conquering the Maya because
    A.   the Maya welcomed the Spaniards.
    B.   all Maya people mysteriously disappeared in A.D. 1450.
    C.   the Portuguese, not the Spanish, conquered the Maya.
    D.   the Maya civilization declined before the Europeans arrived.
    E.   Europe had no interest in the Yucatan peninsula.

8B. According to the passage, which choice best explains the disappearance of the Maya?
    A.   disease
    B.   war
    C.   enslavement
    D.   emigration
    E.   genocide

9A. Which choice would be the best title for this passage?
   A. Differentiating Ancient Cultures
   B. Human Sacrifice in Mesoamerican Civilizations
   C. Aztec, Inca, and Maya in South America
   D. Three Lost Civilizations
   E. The History of Ancient Mexico and Parts of South America

9B. Why would the passage be better suited for a travel brochure instead of a social studies textbook?
   A. The passage contains academic references and citations.
   B. The content of the passage is too violent for school texts.
   C. The author offers no opinion about the Spanish explorers.
   D. The three cultures in the passage were not native to the United States.
   E. The passage contains only generalizations of the specific cultures.

10A.The author of this passage would probably agree that
   A. explorers should not have interfered with the Mesoamerican or South American cultures.
   B. ancient civilizations were justified in practicing human sacrifice.
   C. the Aztecs were far more advanced than the Inca were.
   D. gold is more important than information about the civilizations.
   E. the Spaniards were devious in the way they conquered the Aztecs and the Inca.

10B.Which detail from the passage best supports your answer to question 10A?
   A. descriptions of the Inca religion
   B. floating gardens and agriculture
   C. the central influence of gold in the motives of explorers
   D. the conquistadors' strategies for success
   E. specific dates for the cultural peak of each civilization

Review Lessons 4-6

Exercise I

Inferences

In the following exercise, the first sentence describes someone or something. Infer information from the first sentence, and then choose the word from the Word Bank that best completes the second sentence.

platitudes	intrinsic	eidetic	internecine
imbroglio	hubris	disconcerted	sectarian

1. The tiny wind-up train made of copper and tin cost only pennies to make, but that single, imported toy sparked the Industrial Age in the small nation in which such technology had never been seen before.

   From this sentence, we can infer that the toy train had little monetary value, but immense _____ value to the people it inspired.

2. The reporter's surprise question left the candidate stammering as he tried desperately to articulate an answer while standing on the stage in front of a large crowd.

   From this sentence, we can infer that the reporter's question _____ the candidate.

3. The heavyweight champion was so sure that he was the greatest boxer in the world that he failed to train well for his match to defend his title and was knocked out in the second round.

   From this sentence, we can infer that the boxer's _____ brought about the loss of his title.

4. Jarvis won't send greeting cards because he dislikes the generic, impersonal sentiments they typically contain, so he writes letters instead.

   From this sentence, we can infer that Jarvis does not think highly of the _____ found in greeting cards.

5. For decades, the gangs fought, occasionally gaining or losing a block of territory, and with it, the block's illicit drug sales, but ultimately ensuring that their families and friends would live in fear and misery.

   From this sentence, we can infer that no one would win the _____ gang wars.

Exercise II

Related Words

Some of the vocabulary words from Lessons 4 through 6 have related meanings. Complete the following sentences by choosing the word that best fits the context, based on information you infer from the use of the italicized word. Some word pairs will be antonyms, some will be synonyms, and some will simply be words often used in the same context.

1. The cryptozoologist endured much _____ while investigating an *apocryphal* story about sasquatch because none of the storytellers knew who had told the story first.
   A. consternation
   B. catharsis
   C. kudos
   D. hubris
   E. accoutrement

2. The aging hip hop artist expected to hear the usual *platitudes* from fans about how much they liked his latest album, but instead he was shocked to read _____ reviews of his songs from harsh critics.
   A. apocryphal
   B. vitriolic
   C. crepuscular
   D. intrinsic
   E. putrid

3. The witches _____ that Macbeth would one day be king, which *disconcerted* him because it seemed like an unlikely prediction, unless some horrible things were to occur.
   A. venerated
   B. comprised
   C. prognosticated
   D. estranged
   E. foisted

4. The whole town _____ the late doctor, and they *venerated* his legacy by crafting a statue in his likeness at the park.
   A. estranged
   B. inundated
   C. revered
   D. comprised
   E. expiated

5. The sight of a rat running through the restaurant's dining room on live television was an *imbroglio* that _____ customers and the eatery for years after the event.
   A. comprised
   B. estranged
   C. contrived
   D. revered
   E. venerated

6. Unable to harm the federally protected albino squirrels nesting in his house and destroying the attic, Armando used his carpentry skills to *contrive* a[n] _____ trap that he could use to capture the rodents without injuring them and then transport them far away.
   A. vitriolic
   B. stringent
   C. innocuous
   D. sybaritic
   E. risible

7. Walt's *eidetic* memories, revealed during his lectures, gave his world travels a[n] _____ value that exceeded the value and novelty of photographs or souvenirs.
   A. incongruous
   B. vitriolic
   C. haughty
   D. quotidian
   E. intrinsic

8. Nolan's _____ ensured his self-confidence was never lacking when it was time to perform on stage, but his *flippancy* toward fans slowly alienated him from the music scene.
   A. kudos
   B. hubris
   C. platitude
   D. imbroglio
   E. plethora

9. Though the _____ school admitted only people of a specific faith, its library contained a *plethora* of text about all the world's religions and cultures.
   A. anomaly
   B. eidetic
   C. incongruous
   D. sectarian
   E. servile

10. After months of trials, the research scientist found what appeared to be a[n] _____ cure to the disease, but he still had to prove that the success was more than a mere *anomaly*.
    A. efficacious
    B. putrid
    C. servile
    D. vitriolic
    E. haughty

Exercise III

Deeper Meanings

Choose a word to replace the italicized word in each sentence. All of the possible choices for each sentence have similar definitions, but the correct answer will have a connotation that best suits the context. For example, the words "delete," "destroy," and "obliterate" all mean "to remove or wipe out," but no one would ever say, "I destroyed the name from the document." The correct choice will be the word that has the best specific meaning and does not render the sentence awkward in tone or content. When choices seem close, look for a clue in the context that makes one choice better than the other.

Note that the correct answer is not always the primary vocabulary word from the lesson.

remarks	innocuous	enraged	judgmental
sanctimonious	annoyed	dysfunctional	weak
internecine	platitudes		

1. Audrey's *detrimental* struggle with her sister over a boyfriend left both of them alone and miserable.

    Better word: _____

2. Roz panicked after being bitten by the snake until the guide assured her that the creature was a[n] *friendly* species.

    Better word: _____

3. Though the celebrity is genuinely thankful for his many fans, he rarely engages in conversation with them because most of them offer the same, predictable *sayings* about how great he was in the latest film.

    Better word: _____

4. The *arrogant* lady complained about the noisy teenagers outside playing basketball, forgetting that her dog's barking wakes up the whole neighborhood in the middle of the night at least three times a week.

    Better word: _____

5. Tiffany's endless pencil tapping *enraged* everyone else sitting in study hall.

    Better word: _____

Exercise IV

Crossword Puzzle

Use the clues to complete the crossword puzzle. The answers consist of vocabulary words from Lessons 4 through 6.

Across

2. what comes before the beginning
6. an amazing collection of antique books
9. worry, worry, worry
10. HaHa, LOL
13. not true, just made up
15. what the champion gets for winning
16. servant
17. sunset
18. like a limousine with gold wheels and a hot tub

Down

1. a stroll down the street
3. to know what the winning lottery numbers will be
4. to worship or respect
5. gets the job done
7. a turtle with two heads, for example
8. gold chain, tie, bracelet, bling
11. not causing any harm
12. better than everyone else
14. more, more, more

Exercise V

Subject Prompts

Here is a writing prompt similar to the one you will find on the writing portion of an assessment test. Follow the instructions below and write a brief, efficient essay.

Living beyond one's means has become a way of life in America, one in which the status quo would seem to suggest everyone needs to have a new car (and car payment), high speed Internet access, cable television, and the latest smart phone. Those who cannot pay cash for these luxuries charge them on credit cards with astronomical interest rates, rendering repayment of the debt nearly impossible.

People who have substantial consumer debt have made themselves slaves for a few trivial comforts, trophies, or novelties. Some simply try to walk away from the debt they racked up, declaring bankruptcy and leaving their bills unpaid after having already enjoyed the pleasures they never paid for. Others pay debt using borrowed money, digging the hole yet deeper.

Certainly, debt is nothing anyone wants, but it is often necessary; few people, for example, have enough cash to purchase a house (though it's a great idea). What is your opinion of debt? What is acceptable debt, if there is such a thing, and what makes it acceptable? When is it okay to borrow money? When is borrowing money a poor idea?

As the new writer for your local newspaper's advice column, address the question of when it is wise to incur debt. Create at least one example situation to support your argument. Be sure that you take a position on when, or if, there is a good time to borrow money.

Thesis: Write a *one-sentence* response to the above assignment. Make certain this single sentence offers a clear statement of your position.

Example: Borrowing money is acceptable only if it is needed to survive, and no more should be borrowed than is absolutely necessary.

_____

_____

Organizational Plan: List at least three subtopics you will use to support your main idea. This list is your outline.

1. _____

2. _____

3. _____

Draft: Following your outline, write a good first draft of your essay. Remember to support all of your points with examples, facts, references to reading, etc.

Review and Revise: Exchange essays with a classmate. Using the scoring guide for Word Choice on page 275, score your partner's essay (while he or she scores yours). Focus on word choice and the use of language conventions. If necessary, rewrite your essay to improve word choice and/or your use of language.

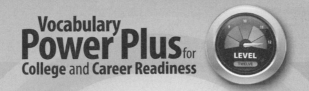
Lesson Seven

1. **convoluted**   (kon´ və lōōt əd)   *adj.*   complicated; intricate
Few people in class understood the teacher's *convoluted* explanation of the problem.
syn: involved; jumbled   *ant: simple; obvious*

2. **nexus**   (nek´ səs)   *n.*   a link, tie, or bond
The desire for acceptance by others is a *nexus* for all humankind.
syn: connection; correlation   *ant: disruption; gap*

3. **gibberish**   (jib´ ər ish)   *n.*   nonsense; unintelligible speech
A foreign language might sound like *gibberish* until you learn key words and phrases.
syn: babble; chatter; prattle

4. **staid**   (stād)   *adj.*   showing dignity and often strait-laced propriety
The *staid* general spoke softly, seldom dismounted his horse, and never smiled.
syn: composed; serious; solemn   *ant: agitated; excited; nervous*

5. **incumbent**   (in kum´ bənt)   *adj.*   obligatory; necessary
It is *incumbent* on the night watchman to stay awake during his shift.
syn: required; essential   *ant: voluntary; unnecessary*

6. **cogent**   (kō´ jənt)   *adj.*   convincing; reasonable
Bert's *cogent* justification for a new desk convinced management to buy one for him.
syn: compelling; pertinent; influential   *ant: ineffective; weak*

7. **entreat**   (en trēt´)   *v.*   to earnestly request or petition
At the supermarket, the child first *entreated* his mother for the candy bar, and then cried for it.
syn: importune; implore   *ant: demand*

8. **churlish**   (chûr´ lish)   *adj.*   boorish or vulgar
The wild cowboys' *churlish* behavior offended the genteel townspeople.
syn: uncouth; rude; surly   *ant: courteous; polished; civil*

9. **coeval**   (kō ē´ vəl)   *adj.*   of the same time period
Scientists assert that the two ancient, *coeval* civilizations, though thousands of miles apart, were aware of each other.
syn: contemporaneous

10. **inimical**   (i nim´ i kəl)   *adj.*   unfriendly; hostile; injurious
The stranger's *inimical* voice made me wonder if I had done something wrong.
syn: mean; malicious; harmful   *ant: encouraging; flattering*

11. **dilatory** (di´ lə tōr ē) *adj.* tending to delay or procrastinate
The teacher warned the *dilatory* students that any paper turned in after the deadline
would be an instant failure.
syn: dallying; laggard; unhurried   *ant: diligent; prompt*

12. **anecdote** (an´ ik dōt) *n.* a short account of an incident
New parents often share *anecdotes* about their children.
syn: narrative

13. **promulgate** (prom´ əl gāt) *v.* to announce; to make known
During the drought, the city *promulgated* strict rules about water usage.
syn: declare; exhibit

14. **livid** (liv´ id) *adj.* extremely angry
When I was brought home by the police, my father was *livid*; he yelled at me for
hours.
syn: enraged; furious; fuming   *ant: contented; pleased*

15. **lurid** (lōōr´ id) *adj.* shocking; explicit
The *lurid* crime appeared in every newspaper in the city.
syn: sensational; extreme   *ant: dull; boring; mediocre*

Exercise I

Words in Context

From the list below, supply the words needed to complete the paragraph. Some words will not be used.

gibberish	**livid**	**staid**	**promulgate**
cogent	**incumbent**	**nexus**	

1. The boss was _____ after he learned about the accounting error that cost the company thousands of dollars, but he vowed to remain calm and _____ while he sought a[n] _____ explanation for the mistake. This was the second major error in six months, and it was _____ on the company to find the source of the problem. When confronted, the nervous accountant quickly listed possible excuses for what might have gone wrong.

    "Spare me your _____ and tell me exactly where the error originated," ordered the boss.

From the list below, supply the words needed to complete the paragraph. Some words will not be used.

lurid	**cogent**	**anecdote**	**entreat**
inimical	**nexus**	**coeval**	

2. When the children asked their father about an old, abandoned cabin in the forest behind their house, he responded with a[n] _____ about the day he discovered it, when he, too, was eleven years old.

    "Enos, a[n] _____ hermit, once lived in that shack," said the father, "and he used to shoot at anyone who dared to trespass on his property. The old man, rumored to be an escaped convict hiding from the law, was the last member of a family _____ with the bootlegging industry that flourished in these woods during the Prohibition Era."

    The _____ story so fascinated the children that they had to venture into the forest to look at the rotting timbers of the overgrown cabin once again. The father's memory was now a[n] _____ that connected the children's generation to a lost era, and the children planned to access that link more often in the future.

From the list below, supply the words needed to complete the paragraph. Some words will not be used.

dilatory	**convoluted**	**entreat**	**gibberish**
churlish	**promulgate**	**nexus**	

3. Roger _____ his teacher for more time, but she told him to put his pencil down and hand in his test like everyone else. Once again, Roger's _____ approach to test-taking had resulted in another incomplete exam, but he blamed it on the _____ word problems on which he had spent too much time. He stood and _____ his obvious failure to the rest of the class by making the whistling sound of a bomb falling from the sky and then exploding on the ground. The teacher then asked Roger to take his _____ behavior outside.

Exercise II

Sentence Completion

Complete the sentence in a way that shows you understand the meaning of the italicized vocabulary word.

1. The *lurid* crime of Irene's next-door neighbor…

2. When the teacher saw the *churlish* message on Gary's T-shirt, she told him to…

3. Maggie failed to give Sam a *cogent* reason for…

4. The government *promulgated* the false concept that…

5. Aaron could speak only *gibberish* after having his wisdom teeth removed because…

6. A song that never seems to fade in popularity is sometimes called a generational *nexus* because…

7. Craig was *livid* after learning that…

8. Shawn knew that his *dilatory* work habits would…

9. The athlete remained *staid*, despite…

10. Dinosaurs were not *coeval* with humankind, so early humans did not need to…

11. Dave *entreated* his messy roommate to…

12. Getting an occasional checkup is *incumbent* on anyone who…

13. The detective's voice had an *inimical* tone when he…

14. At the class reunion, alumni shared *anecdotes* about…

15. The teacher asked the student to revise the *convoluted* essay so that…

Exercise III

Roots, Prefixes, and Suffixes

Study the entries and answer the questions that follow.

The root *spect* means "look."
The roots *vid* and *vis* mean "see."
The root *aud* means "hear."
The prefix *circum–* means "around."
The prefix *in–* can mean "not," "upon," or "against."

1. Using *literal* translations as guidance, define the following words without using a dictionary.

     A. auditory   D. spectator
     B. circumspect   E. envy
     C. inaudible   F. spectrum

2. A place specifically designed for *hearing* music, speeches, or recitals is called a[n] _____ .

3. What do you suppose a *specter* is?

4. List as many words as you can think of that contain the root *spect*.

5. List as many words as you can think of that contain the root *vis*.

Exercise IV

Inference

Complete the sentence by inferring information about the italicized word from its context.

1. Someone who gives you an *inimical* stare might…

2. It was *incumbent* on the team…

3. If you miss an important exam, you might *entreat* the teacher to…

Exercise V

Writing

Here is a writing prompt similar to the one you will find on the writing portion of an assessment test.

Plan and write an essay on the following statement:

> In the ordinary course of nature, the great beneficent changes come slowly and silently. The noisy changes, for the most part, mean violence and disruption. The roar of storms and tornadoes, the explosions of volcanoes, the crash of thunder, are the result of a sudden break in the equipoise of the elements; from a condition of comparative repose and silence they become fearfully swift and audible. The still small voice is the voice of life and growth and perpetuity. In the history of a nation, it is the same.
>
> –John Burroughs (1837–1921)

Assignment: In an essay, explain whether Burroughs is accurate in his comparison of nature with civilization. Is the *voice* of civilization ever truly *small*? Cite an example or examples from American history that best illustrate Burroughs's comparison. Support your position by discussing examples from literature, art, history, or experience or observation.

Thesis: Write a *one-sentence* response to the above assignment. Make certain this single sentence offers a clear statement of your position.

Example: Burroughs is indeed correct that mankind follows the same pattern as that of the natural world, and this parallelism is quite visible in the United States Civil War.

_____

_____

Organizational Plan: List at least three subtopics you will use to support your main idea. This list is your outline.

1. _____

2. _____

3. _____

Draft: Following your outline, write a good first draft of your essay. Remember to support all of your points with examples, facts, references to reading, etc.

Review and Revise: Exchange essays with a classmate. Using the scoring guide for Word Choice on page 275, score your partner's essay (while he or she scores yours). Focus on word choice and the use of language conventions. If necessary, rewrite your essay to improve word choice and/or your use of language.

Exercise VI

Improving Paragraphs

Read the following passage and then answer the multiple-choice questions that follow. The questions will require you to make decisions regarding the revision of the reading selection.

1   (1) Have you ever driven down the road, seemingly at ease, perhaps exceeding the speed limit to arrive at your destination a bit more quickly. (2) Then you see a long line of cars waiting in line to pay the toll and realize that you now have to join them and become one of the poor idiots wasting time and costly gasoline. (3) People have engaged in this meaningless exercise ever since toll roads and toll bridges were invented. (4) Stop, go a few feet, brake, stop again, and then repeat the process more times than you can count as cars jostle for better positions like basketball players near the hoop. (5) **Dilatory** drivers nervously dig in ashtrays and between car seats, fumbling for the correct change, dropping coins on the ground or attempting to back up, or their cars scrape the side of the tollbooth, leaving paint chips and chipped concrete as permanent marks of futility. (6) Sometimes you're in line for ten minutes or more before you reach the toll-taker and surrender your quarter, dollar, or life savings for the privilege of being on a supposedly fast route home.

2   (7) Modern technology has finally given drivers the means of escaping the horrors of paying tolls by hand. (8) New microchip transmitters affixed to windshields can be read by machines above the tollbooths, and the charges are billed automatically to drivers' credit cards. (9) This easy process requires drivers to register their cars, set up accounts, and pay the bill, that's all there is to it, it's as simple as that. (10) The driver can pass through the toll lane without stopping, while the fools in the pay-by-cash lane wait their turns.

3   (11) The rewards of using the simple, plastic toll boxes are enormous: drivers save time and gas; some states offer discounts to those who use the devices; pollution decreases; fewer accidents occur; and there's no worrying about having enough cash for the toll.

4   (12) Few things in life compare to the thrill of watching other drivers suffer the wrenching pain of losing time waiting in long lines—even such joys as graduation, finding money on the ground, getting a bike for Christmas, and falling in love. (13) It is this great pleasure in observing someone elses misfortune that separates us from the animals—not our ability to reason or use tools. (14) Humans love to gloat! (15) My own toll transmitter will arrive in the mail next week, and I'll then be able to enjoy the pleasure of smoothly gliding through booth after booth without having to stop.

5   (16) So, if you're in the long line waiting to move an inch at a time for an hour because you're not intelligent enough to join the modern world, wave to me as I glide on by, because I'll be looking over at you with a smile on my face and a transmitter on my windshield.

6   (17) Some paranoid people think this new use of electronic gadgetry is just another **inimical** invention of the government for tracking citizens, so that it knows where we are, where we go, what we buy, and what we do. (18) That form of reasoning is illogical and false. (19) If the government wants to follow people's whereabouts, there are already plenty of ways to do so, like security cameras, Internet data gathering, bank reports, passport information, credit card statements, social security numbers, taxes, cell phone monitoring, etc. (20) One more intrusion into our personal lives will not make any difference at all. (21) To those people who refuse to get these electronic passes, I say, "If you don't have anything to hide, why worry?"

1. Which choice best corrects an error in paragraph 1?
    A. Find a substitute for the word *idiots*.
    B. Delete sentence 4.
    C. Exchange sentence 2 and sentence 5.
    D. End the first sentence with a question mark.
    E. Rewrite the first paragraph from the first-person point of view.

2. To correct an error in paragraph 2, an editor would need to
    A. create two sentences from sentence 7.
    B. place a semicolon between sentence 7 and sentence 8.
    C. fix the comma splices in sentence 9.
    D. change "drivers' credit cards" to "driver's credit cards" in sentence 8.
    E. delete the hyphens in "pay-by-cash" in sentence 10.

3. Which choice corrects a grammatical error in sentence 13?
    A. Change the dash after *animals* to a semicolon.
    B. Replace *elses* with *else's*.
    C. Create an antecedent for *else*.
    D. Remove the comma splice.
    E. Make "use tools" parallel with "to reason."

4. Which of the following revisions would improve the chronology of the passage?
    A. Exchange paragraphs 1 and 2.
    B. Exchange paragraphs 2 and 3.
    C. Exchange paragraphs 3 and 4.
    D. Exchange paragraphs 5 and 6.
    E. Exchange paragraphs 1 and 6.

5. If one paragraph must be removed from the passage, the best choice would be
    A. paragraph 1 because an introduction is not necessary.
    B. paragraph 2 because an introduction to the microchip transmitters is not necessary.
    C. paragraph 3 because it does not support the topic of the passage.
    D. paragraph 4 because it digresses into personal philosophy.
    E. paragraph 6 because it discusses an opposing viewpoint.

Lesson Eight

1. **puerile** (pyu´ ər əl) *adj.* childish; juvenile
   Uncle Joe refused to tolerate his teenage nephew's *puerile* behavior.
   syn: immature; infantile   *ant: mature*

2. **inveigh** (in vā´) *v.* to disapprove angrily; to protest
   Irene *inveighed* against her company's hiring of a former competitor for a
   prominent position.
   syn: berate; condemn; remonstrate   *ant: commend; laud; praise*

3. **ameliorate** (ə mēl´ yə rāt) *v.* to make better; to improve
   The manager asked for suggestions that might *ameliorate* working conditions at
   the factory.
   syn: enhance; upgrade   *ant: weaken; damage; corrupt*

4. **renunciation** (ri nun sē ā´ shən) *n.* rejection; refusal to acknowledge
   Members of the club responded to Bill's *renunciation* of their doctrine by asking
   him to leave.
   syn: denial; refusal   *ant: admittance; concession*

5. **vitiate** (vish´ ū āt) *v.* to corrupt morally; to contaminate
   Mark claims that prisons simply *vitiate* the spirits of the inmates.
   syn: defile; devalue; spoil   *ant: purify; clarify; cleanse*

6. **profligate** (prof´ li gət) *adj.* wasteful and immoral
   The young heir lived a *profligate* life of alcohol, excess, and greed.
   syn: licentious; decadent   *ant: virtuous; principled*

7. **otiose** (ō´ shē ōs, tē) *adj.* useless; futile
   The director decided to remove the *otiose* scenes that increased the length of the
   film but failed to add to the suspense.
   syn: unimportant; worthless   *ant: productive; necessary*

8. **lionize** (lī´ ə nīz) *v.* to assign great social importance to; to treat as a celebrity
   The public *lionized* the boy for saving the child from the burning building.
   syn: acclaim; exalt; honor   *ant: ignore; overlook*

9. **recalcitrant** (ri kal´ si trənt) *adj.* stubbornly resistant; showing opposition
   The *recalcitrant* child kicked and screamed when the barber tried to give him his
   first haircut.
   syn: defiant; insubordinate; unwilling   *ant: agreeable; obedient*

10. **pander** (pan´ dər) *v.* to exploit weaknesses of others; to cater to the vices of others
The trendy clothing store *pandered* to materialistic clients by selling shoddy clothing at outrageously high prices.
syn: cajole; indulge

11. **aleatory** (ā´ lē ə tôr ē) *adj.* dependent on luck or chance
Because of the uncertain weather forecast, the success of our company picnic is purely *aleatory*.

12. **asperity** (a sper´ i tē) *n.* roughness or harshness; severity
The teacher felt bad after his *asperity* caused a student to cry.
syn: acerbity; irascibility   *ant: mildness; kindness*

13. **unimpeachable** (un im pē´ chə bəl) *adj.* unquestionable; beyond doubt
The Internet is not an *unimpeachable* source of information for academic research.
syn: trustworthy; infallible   *ant: questionable; flawed*

14. **allay** (ə lā´) *v.* to relieve; to alleviate
Mom tried to *allay* my fear of flying by reading favorable airline statistics.
syn: calm; ease; pacify   *ant: excite; intensify; agitate*

15. **exegesis** (ek sə jē´ sis) *n.* an explanation of a text; a critical interpretation
The students read an *exegesis* of *Macbeth* to understand the play better.
syn: analysis; exposition; commentary

Exercise I

Words in Context

From the list below, supply the words needed to complete the paragraph. Some words will not be used.

unimpeachable	exegesis	otiose	renunciation
puerile	pander	recalcitrant	

1. The defense attorney's _____ efforts to win the trial simply delayed the inevitable; the _____ evidence had quickly convinced the jury that the defendant was guilty. When the verdict was read, the defendant, a former executive, shocked courtroom observers with _____ remarks. Bailiffs then dragged the _____ prisoner from the courtroom, while he kicked and clawed at any court official within reach.

    "The defendant's blatant disregard for the law implies a complete _____ of it," said the judge, "and demands a strict reprisal, which will be determined at the sentencing hearing tomorrow."

From the list below, supply the words needed to complete the paragraph. Some words will not be used.

aleatory	ameliorate	profligate	exegesis
inveigh	otiose	asperity	

2. Tina liked her new first-floor apartment, but she couldn't stand the _____ upstairs tenants, who partied incessantly though the night, keeping everyone awake. After enduring several days of nonstop music and stomping, Tina visited the noisy neighbor and spoke with a[n] _____ she usually reserved for dealing with the most difficult of people.

    "You shouldn't require a[n] _____ of the lease to know that it's not proper to disturb every tenant in the building with your noise!" screamed Tina, in order to be heard over the blaring stereo. The offending neighbor simply closed the door, leaving Tina standing in the hall alone. During the week that followed, Tina encouraged her other neighbors to call the landlord and _____ against the habits of the noisy tenants so as to _____ the living conditions within the apartment building.

From the list below, supply the words needed to complete the paragraph. Some words will not be used.

pander	lionize	unimpeachable	aleatory
vitiate	allay	asperity	

3. The world of pop culture _____ the talk-radio host for his racy programs, but thousands of angry listeners claimed that his low humor and poorly supported arguments simply _____ his younger listeners. The host, they claimed, _____ to the young by supplying their vivid imaginations with scenarios that defy traditional morality. Raising children properly is _____ enough, they argued, without adding counterproductive distractions. Network executives held a meeting, and in the following week, the network attempted to _____ the angry listeners' concerns by rescheduling the show to a late-night slot.

Exercise II

Sentence Completion

Complete the sentence in a way that shows you understand the meaning of the italicized vocabulary word.

1. The man *pandered* to concert fans by selling T-shirts for twenty dollars each, even though he...

2. It took three hours to convince the *recalcitrant*...

3. The drill sergeant claimed that her *asperity* was necessary because it...

4. Dan's *otiose* attempt to ski resulted in...

5. To *allay* the pain of your headache, you might...

6. The *profligate* senator was voted out shortly after...

7. Ryan read an *exegesis* of the cryptic poem because...

8. The baseball player made an *aleatory* promise to the sick youngster that he would...

9. Ted thought that firing more people would *ameliorate* the company's finances, but instead...

10. The inmate failed to convince the parole board of his complete *renunciation* of...

11. Some citizens feared that the new casino would *vitiate*...

12. Teresa *inveighed* against the proposed landfill because...

13. The criminal mistakenly thought that the public would *lionize* him if he...

14. The professor expected *puerile* comments from four-year-olds, but not...

15. Harvey had an *unimpeachable* belief in ghosts after...

Roots, Prefixes, and Suffixes

Study the entries and answer the questions that follow.

The roots *nat* and *nasc* mean "to be born."
The root *viv* means "to live."
The root *mort* means "to die."
The prefix *con–* means "together."
The prefix *pre–* means "before."
The suffix *–fy* means "to make."

1. Using *literal* translations as guidance, define the following words without using a dictionary.

    A. mortify D. nascent
    B. convivial E. vivify
    C. prenatal F. vivid

2. A person born in a country is _____ to that country.

3. The root *sect* means "to cut apart"; *vivisection*, therefore, literally means _____.

4. What does a *mortician* do for a living?

5. List as many words as you can think of that contain the root *viv*.

Inference

Complete the sentence by inferring information about the italicized word from its context.

1. Someone might *inveigh* against your plan if…

2. Your motives must be *unimpeachable* if you plan to attempt something that…

3. A *recalcitrant* child might refuse to…

Exercise V

Critical Reading

Below is a pair of reading passages followed by several multiple-choice questions. Carefully read the passages and choose the best answer for each of the questions.

The authors of the following passages offer two different perspectives on the significance of the Internet.

Passage 1

From protecting American lives to enriching the lives of people all over the world, the Internet stands as one of the greatest collaborative inventions of all time. In 1969, the Pentagon sponsored a network of computers at four major universities, creating a system that allowed the United States military to communicate and maintain control over missiles during a simulated
5 nuclear war. Researchers named the network ARPANET after the Advanced Research Projects Agency, a military technological think-tank. By the early seventies, thirty-seven computers communicated with each other via ARPANET. Ironically, what began as an effort to **allay** the chaos of a nuclear holocaust soon morphed into a chaotic, but infinitely useful, world of its own.

Beginning in 1972 with the invention of electronic mail, ARPANET also functioned as a high-
10 speed post office. At the First International Conference on Computers and Communication held in Washington, D.C., demonstrations of the network in action stimulated interest and research, and soon many more networks appeared. In 1974, researchers began using a common language, Transmission Control Protocol and Internet Protocol (TCP/IP), which allowed the networks to communicate with each other. Stanford University researchers introduced a commercial version of
15 ARPANET that same year, and they officially dubbed the ever-expanding network, the "Internet." In the years since, schools, libraries, hospitals, and corporations hurried to connect to the Net; thus, the Internet revolutionized society's way of learning and sharing information.

Today, the Information Superhighway (as the Net was slugged to generate interest in Al Gore's 1991 High Performance Computing Act) entices everyone to cruise its main drags and back
20 roads; computer companies and Internet service providers boast incredible features at affordable prices, making it easier than ever to merge into the fast lane. Combined with incredible video technology, the Internet offers casual users a scenic route for their information road trip, on which they can enjoy the picturesque views of vacation spots, pictures from their grandchildren, or the photographic evidence that the perfect chocolate cake recipe really does exist.

25 Educators and their students use the Internet's many reputable news and reference sites to access valuable information. Scientists still use the Internet, only now they can communicate images, data, and ideas with other scientists all over the world. Medical professionals exchange life-saving information with each other, and post that information for patient access. A confused student can find a complete **exegesis** of an obscure novel for free. An accessible wealth of
30 information **ameliorates** the spread of the latest research. Gone are the days when the Internet belonged solely to military scientists and university researchers. The road less traveled has become the main thoroughfare, and to be without access has become quite pedestrian.

Passage 2

Created in the 1960s to protect America in the aftermath of a nuclear attack, the Internet now threatens to **vitiate** the nation, slowly, insidiously, and completely. Rather than nuclear explosions, Americans face Internet-induced implosion that will cause morals and values to crumble and decay in the dust of apathy. Independent intelligent thought will go up in
5 a nauseating, miasmic mushroom cloud of muddled misinformation, and relationships and community will cease altogether.

Since the Internet, born of a partnership between government and academia, became available to ordinary citizens, people no longer use libraries, encyclopedias, or their own brains to solve problems. When boredom strikes and an original idea does not, people surf the sea of mediocrity
10 known as the World Wide Web. They accept as truth everything they see there. They dismiss their powers of logic and common sense in favor of following blindly the simulacra-strewn path of Internet misinformation. Thus, overuse and abuse of the Internet promotes banality of thought, slovenliness of research habits, and sheer idiocy of behavior.

Young people are especially susceptible to the propagation of half-truths and myths found
15 on the Internet. The Internet hampers their ability to focus by constantly interrupting with pop-up advertisements and instant messages begging for response. Students cannot concentrate, and they become frustrated; after all, fact checking and attribution take time. Today's young people are growing up accustomed to instant gratification; that is precisely why the Internet appeals to them. Meanwhile, plagiarism is becoming commonplace as students attempt to download instant
20 good grades, even if the source belongs to someone else.

Furthermore, the Internet promotes hate, and hate unchecked decimates faster than the Black Death. Prejudice prevails thanks to a plethora of propaganda-based websites espousing ethnic and cultural superiority. Even the most ignorant cretin can post on any number of Internet locations with malicious intent and simultaneous impunity. Hatemongers remain anonymous
25 by using screen names—web pseudonyms that cannot be traced; thus, these insolent Internet users participate in online anarchy, avoiding censorship, regulation, and accountability. Internet-induced and -abetted hate crimes and acts of terrorism are sure to follow.

Many people **lionize** the Internet as a valuable tool used by upstanding citizens strictly in the pursuit of professional and personal excellence. Apparently, "personal excellence" must have
30 been redefined over the past decade: The Internet is a **profligate**, virtual altar at which millions of sex addicts faithfully worship. Over 260 million pages of pornography clog the web. Common sense holds, and statistics prove, that Internet pornography contributes to marital problems and the increasing divorce rate; yet even so-called respectable members of society use the Internet to indulge their perversions. Curiously, the mere thought of a gentle family practitioner or a respected
35 member of the clergy engaging in such lewd pursuits should generate concern; however, moral decay flourishes in an atmosphere of apathy, a byproduct of the Internet.

Spending a lot of time online (regardless of the activity pursued) also leads to isolationism and the deterioration of social relationships. Who needs to visit friends when an e-mail will suffice? Who needs to attend religious services when groups can worship online? Virtual
40 communities fill the emptiness with pseudo-socialization that requires no commitment, laying waste to real families and real neighborhoods. Lazy consumers no longer need to leave the house to shop. Slacking singles can go on virtual dates that require no preparation. Uninformed patients can visit web doctors for dubious professional opinions, sight unseen. Soon, a generation of children with bold, gregarious chat room personalities will refuse to leave their own homes
45 because they might be required—it's frightening—to speak to an actual stranger in person.

The Internet monster shall soon have thrust its tentacles into every aspect of American life, weakening the nation from the inside out. From horoscopes to horror films to horticulture, everything will exist digitally, and Internet-induced agoraphobia will reduce this nation to a collective of pale, atrophied, hermits who buy groceries, go to college, get married, and have
50 children online.

1A. According to passage 1, researchers developed the Internet to
  A. enrich lives through enhanced communication.
  B. send e-mail from universities to military bases.
  C. assist medical research.
  D. provide a cheap means of intercollegiate communication.
  E. maintain control of weapons after a nuclear attack.

1B. According to passage 1, which choice best explains the difference between the Internet and the ARPANET?
    A.   The ARPANET was a state secret before 1991.
    B.   The Internet is a nonmilitary network for civilian use.
    C.   The ARPANET had its own computer language.
    D.   The Internet is limited to school communication.
    E.   "Internet" is simply the current name for the ARPANET.

2A. In paragraph 3 of passage 1, the author uses a metaphor to
    A.   foreshadow the expansion of the Internet.
    B.   compare the Internet to a highway.
    C.   add humor to the passage.
    D.   explain how language changes to reflect technology.
    E.   personify the Internet.

2B. Which words from passage 1, paragraph 3, best support your answer to question 2A?
    A.   Computing Act, Net, prices
    B.   vacation spots, video technology, picturesque
    C.   back roads, fast lane, scenic route
    D.   information, casual users, grandchildren
    E.   companies, chocolate cake, evidence

3.   As used in line 18 of passage 1, the term *slugged* most nearly means
    A.   struck.
    B.   hit with a bat.
    C.   named.
    D.   fought.
    E.   derided.

4A. Which of the following best describes the tone of passage 1?
    A.   light and informative
    B.   comical and humorous
    C.   critical and judgmental
    D.   technical and authoritative
    E.   biased and dogmatic

4B. Which characteristic of passage 1 would preclude its being described as formal writing?
    A.   the use of historical facts
    B.   organized in chronological order
    C.   the use of figurative language
    D.   written in third-person point of view
    E.   the absence of negative information

5. In line 13 of passage 2, the word *sheer* most nearly means
    A. transparent.
    B. difficult to understand.
    C. a small amount of.
    D. without restrictions.
    E. very steep.

6A. In passage 2, line 23, the word *cretin* most nearly means
    A. an innocent person.
    B. an insensitive person.
    C. a hindered person.
    D. a silly person.
    E. a physically disabled person.

6B. Which phrase from lines 22-26 identifies the author's reason for using the word *cretin?*
    A. "screen names"
    B. "propaganda-based"
    C. "cultural superiority"
    D. "malicious intent"
    E. "Internet users"

7A. In paragraphs 1 and 4 of the second passage, the author uses a series of words that begin with the same sounds. The author uses this alliteration in order to
    A. make the paragraph read like a poem
    B. impart an encoded message to readers.
    C. personify independent, intelligent thought.
    D. demonstrate the language of anonymous chat rooms.
    E. emphasize the condemning tone of the paragraph.

7B. Which one of the following Internet-induced problems is *not* addressed in passage 2?
    A. diminishing mental focus
    B. social isolation
    C. loss of intelligence
    D. breakup of families
    E. overdependence on socializing

8A. The tone of passage 2 is
    A. encouraging and supportive.
    B. mildly critical.
    C. judgmental and contentious.
    D. educational and informative.
    E. light and humorous.

8B. The topic of passage 1 is the history of the Internet. The topic of passage 2 is best described as
   A.   the moral implications of the Internet.
   B.   the history of e-mail.
   C.   the discovery of ARPANET.
   D.   the world without the Internet.
   E.   the economic effects of the Internet.

9A. The authors of both passages would agree that
   A.   the Internet should be abolished.
   B.   military researchers developed the Internet.
   C.   the Internet should be celebrated.
   D.   the Internet has a bright future.
   E.   the Internet is a threat to the American public.

9B. Choose the line that best describes the similarity in the argument between the passages.
   A.   The passages both refer to religion.
   B.   Both passages use famous historical figures as examples.
   C.   Neither passage offers a counterargument to its main point.
   D.   Both passages rely heavily on highway and travel metaphors.
   E.   Neither passage addresses the negative consequences of the Internet.

10A.Which statement most accurately describes both passages?
   A.   Passage 1 is argumentative, and passage 2 is objective.
   B.   Passage 1 and passage 2 were written by the same author.
   C.   Passage 1 is likely to appear in a newspaper.
   D.   Both passages are informal.
   E.   Both passages are scholarly.

10B. Choose the title that is most suitable for both passages.
   A.   The Information Superhighway
   B.   The Internet and a Changing World
   C.   The Internet and the Decline of Humanity
   D.   Time to Unplug
   E.   A Bright, New World

Lesson Nine

1. **penultimate** (pi nul´ tə mət) *adj.* next to last
    The *penultimate* step before graduation will be passing my final examinations.

2. **bumpkin** (bump´ kin) *n.* an unsophisticated, awkward person
    Pickpockets often prey on *bumpkins* who forget to protect their wallets while
    visiting the city.
    syn: yokel; hayseed; rube   *ant: intellectual*

3. **pervasive** (pər vā´ siv) *adj.* permeating; spreading throughout
    In two days, everyone in the small town had heard the *pervasive* rumor.
    syn: sweeping; persistent   *ant: contained; restricted; limited*

4. **provocative** (prə vok´ ə tiv) *adj.* tending to excite or stimulate
    The daughter considered her mother's short skirt too *provocative*.
    syn: provoking; exciting   *ant: dull; boring*

5. **recrimination** (ri krim ə nā´ shən) *n.* a counteraccusation
    The burglar had the nerve to express *recriminations* against the homeowner for
    hitting him with a shovel.
    syn: countercharge

6. **soporific** (sop ə rif´ ik) *adj.* tending to induce sleep
    I stopped reading the *soporific* novel and found a more exciting one.
    syn: somniferous; monotonous   *ant: dramatic; exciting;*
    stimulating

7. **hortatory** (hor´ tə tōr ē) *adj.* encouraging; inciting
    The troops cheered during the general's *hortatory* speech.
    syn: exhorting   *ant: discouraging; dampening*

8. **toady** (tō´ dē) *n.* a person who flatters for personal gain
    The *toady* followed the young queen around, agreeing with every idiotic statement
    she uttered.
    syn: sycophant; flatterer

9. **corroborate** (kə rob´ ə rāt) *v.* to strengthen by adding evidence
    The doctor's note *corroborated* Bill's excuse for missing a week of work.
    syn: confirm; substantiate; validate   *ant: contradict*

10. **frenetic** (frə net´ ik) *adj.* wildly excited
The neighbors heard the *frenetic* barks of the dog that fell into the well.
syn: frenzied; frantic   *ant: calm; composed*

11. **blithe** (blīth) *adj.* carefree and lighthearted
The sight of his childhood home caused Jerry to reminisce about his *blithe* days of
picking blueberries and fishing in the creek behind the house.
syn: cheerful; radiant   *ant: burdened; worried; troubled*

12. **culpable** (kul´ pə bəl) *adj.* deserving blame or condemnation; guilty
The prosecutor said that the crime boss was *culpable* for the murders even though
he himself did not kill the victims.
syn: blameworthy; liable   *ant: innocent; blameless*

13. **orotund** (ôr´ ə tund) *adj.* full and rich in sound (in speech)
The narrator of the movie advertisement spoke in a deep, *orotund* voice.
syn: resonant; resounding   *ant: quiet; reserved*

14. **benign** (bi nīn´) *adj.* beneficial; favorable
She let down her guard when she saw his *benign* expression.
syn: benevolent; harmless   *ant: harmful; malevolent*

15. **indecorous** (in dek´ ər əs) *adj.* lacking good taste; improper
The heckler made *indecorous* comments during the candidate's speech.
syn: inappropriate; vulgar   *ant: decent*

Exercise I

Words in Context

From the list below, supply the words needed to complete the paragraph. Some words will not be used.

benign	soporific	indecorous	bumpkin
pervasive	corroborate	frenetic	

1. David loved to spend time with his grandparents, but he loathed the _____ drive through three hundred miles of midwestern cornfields. Halfway through the trip, Dave pulled over at a dusty little gas station for coffee and fuel. Two _____ clad in bib overalls sat in lawn chairs near the front door, staring at Dave—they didn't often see city folk at their tiny outpost. He gave a[n] _____ nod to them before placing the pump nozzle into his fuel tank; he didn't want to be _____ during his first visit to the country in years. As the ancient pump made audible "dings" to mark each gallon of gas, Dave stepped away from the car and breathed in the _____ smell of corn husks.

From the list below, supply the words needed to complete the paragraph. Some words will not be used.

frenetic	orotund	provocative	pervasive
toady	hortatory	culpable	

2. The successful novelist knew that her latest book, a[n] _____ tale of star-crossed lovers and murder-for-hire, was not her best, but her agent, a fawning _____ who simply wanted more money and fame, said it was her best writing to date. Anne knew better than to take her agent's _____ comments seriously; he was simply _____ about receiving his guaranteed dividend as stated in the contract. Anne was the one who was _____ in imparting sudden, undeserved wealth to her agent, though she had prematurely signed a six-year contract before she realized that she didn't need an agent to sell her books in the first place.

From the list below, supply the words needed to complete the paragraph. Some words will not be used.

recrimination	blithe	toady	orotund
corroborate	bumpkin	penultimate	

3. A[n] _____ group of children abandoned their game of marbles to flock around the burly man delivering a[n] _____ sales pitch from the top of a wagon in the town square. He was selling genuine musical instruments, he said, and he _____ his claims by unveiling samples of trumpets, clarinets, flutes, and even some snare drums. In response to those in the crowd who asserted that he was simply a scam artist who would take everyone's money and leave town without providing the instruments, the quick-witted man expressed overly forceful _____, suggesting that his accusers simply feared that the town's children might have an opportunity that their parents never had. In three days, the salesman had collected enough orders—and cash—to complete the _____ step in his plan: to get as far away from the little town as he possibly could before the people realized that they had been conned. Having assumed a new name in a new town, the so-called music man would start all over again.

Exercise II

Sentence Completion

Complete the sentence in a way that shows you understand the meaning of the italicized vocabulary word.

1. Fans came from all around to hear the *orotund* voice of…

2. The sound of the ocean had a *soporific* effect that caused…

3. Victor said that *recriminations* against…

4. The child's mother's *frenetic* shouts became…

5. When the doctor explained that the growth was *benign*, the patient…

6. Charles looked forward to the *blithe* days he'd have during…

7. It was once considered *provocative* for people to…

8. No single person is *culpable* for…

9. The villagers grabbed their pitchforks and torches after the mayor's *hortatory* rallying cries to…

10. During our trek through the desert, the *pervasive* dust and sand…

11. Talking on a cellular phone is *indecorous* behavior when you are…

12. Without realizing the danger, the poorly informed *bumpkin* walked right into…

13. For many people, the *penultimate* step before going to sleep at night is to…

14. The wealthy broker grew tired of *toadies* who…

15. Unless you can *corroborate* your need for additional funding, the government will…

Exercise III

Roots, Prefixes, and Suffixes

Study the entries and answer the questions that follow.

The root *spir* means "to breathe."
The root *hal* means "to breathe."
The root *neur* means "nerve."
The prefix *con–* means "together."
The prefix *ex–* means "out."
The prefix *a–* means "towards."
The suffix *–osis* means "sickness," "condition," or "process."

1. Using *literal* translations as guidance, define the following words without using a dictionary.

    A. exhalation   D. halitosis
    B. conspire   E. aspire
    C. expire   F. neurosis

2. If you are said to have _____, then you are full of energy, or the "breath of life."

3. A device that helps asthma sufferers breathe is called a[n] _____.

4. If *per* means "through," then *perspire* literally means _____.

5. List as many words as you can think of that contain the prefix *ex–*.

Exercise IV

Inference

Complete the sentence by inferring information about the italicized word from its context.

1. If no one can *corroborate* your story that you were home on the night of the burglary, the court might…

2. On the school bus, the children's *frenetic* behavior caused…

3. The inspectors at the factory will need to find the person *culpable* for the tragic explosion so they can…

Exercise V

Writing

Here is a writing prompt similar to the one you will find on the writing portion of an assessment test.

Plan and write an essay based on the following statement:

> "But, Rome, 'tis thine alone, with awful sway,
> To rule mankind, and make the world obey,
> Disposing peace and war by thy own majestic way;
> To tame the proud, the fetter'd slave to free:
> These are imperial arts, and worthy thee."

–Virgil (70–19 B.C.), *Aeneid:* Chapter VI

Assignment: In the above quotation, Aeneas, the hero of Virgil's epic poem *Aeneid*, addresses the duties of newly founded Rome: to impose order, peace, and war as necessary; to free those people enslaved during the conquest to create Rome; and to "tame the proud." In an essay, explain the meaning of the phrase, "To tame the proud." To whom is Virgil alluding, and how would you feel if the president of the United States used the same language today? Support your opinion using evidence from reading, studies, current events, and your observation or experience.

Thesis: Write a *one-sentence* response to the above assignment. Make certain this single sentence offers a clear statement of your position.

Example: Aeneas, like all great rulers, suggests that "the proud," or enemies of Rome, must be controlled if the new nation is to survive.

_____

_____

Organizational Plan: List at least three subtopics you will use to support your main idea. This list is your outline.

1. _____

2. _____

3. _____

Draft: Following your outline, write a good first draft of your essay. Remember to support all of your points with examples, facts, references to reading, etc.

Review and Revise: Exchange essays with a classmate. Using the Holistic scoring guide on page 276, score your partner's essay (while he or she scores yours). If necessary, rewrite your essay to correct the problems noted by your partner.

Exercise VI

English Practice

Identifying Sentence Errors

Identify the grammatical error in each of the following sentences. If the sentence contains no error, select answer choice E.

1.   However hard it rains, the frogs in my pond continue to enjoy themselves; when the
        (A)   (B)   (C)
     · weather changes, though, they begin to prepare for hibernation.   No error
        (D)   (E)

2.   Betty, who had the best average of anyone in math class, could not believe her ears
        (A)
     when the teacher said, "Betty, you must not have studied for this test; you missed half
                  (B)   (C)
     the answers."   No error
        (D)   (E)

3.   The lost campers wandered through the mountains, camped each night wherever
                                            (A)
     they could, ate wild berries, managed to avoid bears and mountain lions and never
            (B)   (C)   (D)
     gave up hope.   No error
                            (E)

4.   The little children chased the rabbits into burrows and didn't worry about
                                        (A)
     anything, while the kid's parents worried about mosquitoes' biting.   No error
        (B)   (C)   (D)   (E)

5.   Tiffany's new car, that requires premium fuel, can really fly down the highway.
        (A)   (B)   (C)   (D)
     No error
        (E)

Improving Sentences

The underlined portion of each sentence below contains some flaw. Select the answer choice that best corrects the flaw.

6.   During the hot, dry summer, commercial farmers growing fruits and grains in low
     elevations recognized they needed more water to survive, they installed new
     irrigation systems.
     A.   that farmers needed more water to survive so they installed new irrigation systems.
     B.   that the plants would not survive without more water; for that reason,
          the farmers installed new irrigation systems.
     C.   the plant's key to survival was water, possible only with new irrigation systems.
     D.   they would need more water, they, therefore, installed new irrigation systems.
     E.   they needed more water for the plants, and the plants would not survive so
          they, the farmers, installed new irrigation systems.

7. The family of doctors traces <u>their medical heritage back to the sixteen hundreds.</u>
    A. its medical heritage to the seventeenth century.
    B. their medical heritage back to the 1600s.
    C. their heritage back to the seventeenth century.
    D. medical heritage to the sixteenth century.
    E. its medical heritage back to the sixteen hundred's.

8. <u>Playing until one o'clock in the morning, the police were called</u> to shut down the concert.
    A. Playing until one o'clock in the morning, someone called the police
    B. Playing until 1:00 a.m., the police were called
    C. At one o'clock in the morning, the police were called
    D. By playing until one o'clock in the morning, the police were called
    E. The police were called; someone was playing until one o'clock in the morning,

9. <u>Because the math problems were difficult for me to do, I had forgotten all the equations.</u>
    A. I had forgotten all the equations, because the math problems were difficult for me to complete.
    B. Because the math problems were difficult for me to do, I forgot all the equations.
    C. The math problems were difficult for me because I had forgotten to do all the equations.
    D. The math problems were difficult to do, but all the equations had been forgotten by me.
    E. The math problems were difficult to do because I had forgotten all the equations.

10. <u>After Mr. Edwards died, workers at his company realize how much he did for the neighborhood, and they have been circulating</u> a petition to have a street named after him.
    A. After Mr. Edwards died, workers at his company realized how much he had done for the neighborhood, and they have been circulating
    B. After Mr. Edwards has died, workers at his company have realized how much he did for the neighborhood, and, since then, they had been circulating
    C. After Mr. Edwards passed away, workers at his company realized what he did for the neighborhood and they have circulated
    D. When Mr. Edwards died, workers at his company, realizing how much he does for the neighborhood, had been circulating
    E. Mr. Edwards died, and workers at his company realize how much he has done for the neighborhood, and they have been circulating

Review Lessons 7-9

Exercise I

Inferences

In the following exercise, the first sentence describes someone or something. Infer information from the first sentence, and then choose the word from the Word Bank that best completes the second sentence.

pervasive	culpable	benign	asperity
exegesis	pander	dilatory	entreat

1. Knowing that backup would arrive at any moment, the undercover detective attempted to stall the wanted murderer by starting a conversation with him.

   From this sentence, we can infer that the detective's conversation was a[n] _____ tactic to prevent the suspect from leaving.

2. Grandpa, who left home at the age of twelve, sailed through typhoons, and fought in three wars, said that he feels bad for anyone whose life is too easy.

   From this sentence, we can infer that grandpa believes enduring some _____ in life is not always a bad thing.

3. Everyone loved the new hit song—that is, until the song had been played several times a day on every radio and television station and in all the dance clubs.

   From this sentence, we can infer that a song can wear out quickly once it becomes _____.

4. Citizens criticized the state for allowing a casino to be built in the poorest county, claiming it would prey upon people who could not even afford food, let alone gambling.

   From this sentence, we can infer that some people believe the casino will _____ to people already in poor financial situations.

5. Everyone knew that Dr. Sybil had done everything she could for the patient, but she forever felt that she could have done more to save the man.

   From this sentence, we can infer that Dr. Sybil feels _____ for the patient's death.

Exercise II

Related Words

Some of the vocabulary words from Lessons 7 through 9 have related meanings. Complete the following sentences by choosing the word that best fits the context, based on information you infer from the use of the italicized word. Some word pairs will be antonyms, some will be synonyms, and some will simply be words often used in the same context.

1. The original novel is so _____ that most students first read a popular *exegesis* of the text that explains its structure and symbolism.
    A. churlish
    B. livid
    C. lurid
    D. convoluted
    E. benign

2. Three runs behind in the fifth inning, the coach *ameliorated* the team's low confidence with a[n] _____ speech in the dugout.
    A. culpable
    B. penultimate
    C. inimical
    D. pervasive
    E. hortatory

3. The wanderer made a[n] _____ living as he roamed from state to state, relying on good luck to find jobs to pay for his *blithe* pursuits and simple pleasures.
    A. staid
    B. puerile
    C. convoluted
    D. livid
    E. aleatory

4. It is *incumbent* upon the investigator to _____ his accusations with evidence of the crime, or else the judge will dismiss the charges against the suspect.
    A. entreat
    B. ameliorate
    C. corroborate
    D. pander
    E. lionize

5. A major sponsor of the radio station withdrew its sponsorship and published a *renunciation* of the popular talkshow host after his _____ language offended millions of listeners.
    A. indecorous
    B. otiose
    C. frenetic
    D. soporific
    E. recalcitrant

6. The owners of the overpriced souvenir stores _____ their phony antiques to vacationing *bumpkins* who believe the junk to be genuine artifacts.
   A. promulgate
   B. lionize
   C. corroborate
   D. pander
   E. inveigh

7. Though she was _____ over the damage the neighbor's dogs did to her front yard, Nikki forced herself to be *staid* while discussing it because the neighbors were otherwise very nice people.
   A. convoluted
   B. indecorous
   C. livid
   D. pervasive
   E. provocative

8. The judge said that neither side was _____ in the lawsuit, so each party would be held *culpable* for half the replacement cost of the broken windshield.
   A. churlish
   B. unimpeachable
   C. pervasive
   D. blithe
   E. livid

9. The raunchy music video celebrated a *profligate* lifestyle achieved through crime and violence, and its _____ imagery repulsed almost anyone who watched it.
   A. staid
   B. frenetic
   C. inimical
   D. convoluted
   E. lurid

10. The demanding teacher claimed that using mild *asperity* on students had a _____ effect on their progress because it motivated them to pass the class on the first attempt.
   A. benign
   B. convoluted
   C. soporific
   D. pervasive
   E. culpable

Exercise III

Deeper Meanings

Choose a word to replace the italicized word in each sentence. All of the possible choices for each sentence have similar definitions, but the correct answer will have a connotation that best suits the context. For example, the words "delete," "destroy," and "obliterate" all mean "to remove or wipe out," but no one would ever say, "I destroyed the name from the document." The correct choice will be the word that has the best specific meaning and does not render the sentence awkward in tone or content. When choices seem close, look for a clue in the context that makes one choice better than the other.

Note that the correct answer is not always the primary vocabulary word from the lesson.

irritated	overpopulated	trade	indecorous
worshipped	pander	pervasive	lionized
heinous	disturbed		

1. Sean was *livid* for a few moments when he saw that the deli was out of the good salami, but he simply sighed and ordered something else.

    Better word: _____

2. When young Antonov *praised* Josef Stalin, a dictator responsible for millions of deaths, his grandmother, who had survived Stalin's terrifying policies, gave him an immediate history lesson.

    Better word: _____

3. Bars and gambling houses sprouted all around the frontier mining town, ready to *sell* to the many young men with plenty of free time and more money than sense.

    Better word: _____

4. Talking on a cell phone during a funeral service is a[n] *hostile* act.

    Better word: _____

5. English speakers are *spread* throughout the country, so your trip should be easy even though you don't speak the native language.

    Better word: _____

Exercise IV

Crossword Puzzle

Use the clues to complete the crossword puzzle. The answers consist of vocabulary words from Lessons 7 through 9.

Across

2. like a maze or a difficult math problem
6. giving it up
9. no danger or damage
15. Make it all better.
16. please, please, please
17. Make it feel better.
18. zzzzzzzzzzzzzzzzz

Down

1. baby talk
3. a servant to a froggy, perhaps
4. spending time together
5. makes a lot of sense
7. Show me some proof.
8. right before the end
10. a story
11. responsible
12. need some luck
13. What does it all mean?
14. throwing a water balloon during class, for example

Exercise V

Subject Prompts

Here is a writing prompt similar to the one you will find on the writing portion of an assessment test. Follow the instructions below and write a brief, efficient essay.

Entertainment today, including both film and literature, often excites our misdirected judgment. When we read books or watch films set in historical contexts of the mid-1800s or earlier, we tend to weigh the behavior of characters against our expectations for people of the present. The featured heroes, or even the sympathetic characters, tend to be those who stand out among their contemporaries by espousing beliefs or attitudes of the present. This causes the other characters, representing the status quo, to seem primitive, or even barbaric, by comparison.

This often unconscious "judgment" that we render upon fiction is best described as *presentism*, an act of applying the values and beliefs of the present to the people—real or fictional—of past generations, cultures, and civilizations. There is a perpetual debate, for example, over the virtue of the founders of America, some of whom blazed frontiers, engaged in fierce battles, and established a successful republic, but were simultaneously practitioners of slavery or participants in campaigns against Native Americans.

By present-day mores and beliefs, of course, slavery and genocide are regarded as abject evils, but does this make the successful figures of the past, and the fruits of their labor—the nation—evil? Should our predecessors be regarded as evil because they espoused corporal punishment, or profited from child labor, at a time when such activities were acceptable?

Take a position and explain whether or not the heroes of the past, or the people regarded as notable figures in history, should be celebrated for their achievements or forgotten due to their participation in societal norms that offend modern sensibilities. Imagine that your argument will become the preface to a collection of biographies of people known for their historical achievements in science, exploration, literature, or any other field.

Thesis: Write a *one-sentence* response to the above assignment. Make certain this single sentence offers a clear statement of your position.

Example: Because society's expectations, choices, and more were different in earlier times, people who lived then should not be judged by today's mores.

_____

_____

Organizational Plan: List at least three subtopics you will use to support your main idea. This list is your outline.

1. _____

2. _____

3. _____

Draft: Following your outline, write a good first draft of your essay. Remember to support all your points with examples, facts, references to reading, etc.

Review and Revise: Exchange essays with a classmate. Using the scoring guide for Organization on page 271, score your partner's essay (while he or she scores yours). Focus on the organizational plan and the use of language conventions. If necessary, rewrite your essay to improve the organizational plan and/or your use of language.

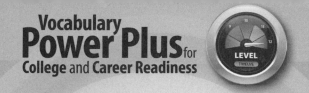

Lesson Ten

1. **veneer** (və nēr´) *n.* a thin, attractive layer that conceals something common or coarse
   He disguised his greed with a *veneer* of smiles and charitable words.
   syn: disguise; gloss; facade

2. **luminous** (lōō´ mə nəs) *adj.* emitting light
   That wristwatch has *luminous* numbers so you can see them at night.
   syn: glowing; radiant   *ant: dim; dark*

3. **tacit** (tas´ it) *adj.* indicated but not expressed; implied silently
   Dad didn't want me to go to the concert, but he gave his *tacit* approval by saying nothing when I asked permission to go.
   syn: hinted; suggested; unspoken   *ant: explicit; frank*

4. **untenable** (un ten´ ə bəl) *adj.* impossible to defend or justify
   The judge's dismissal of the defendant's *untenable* claim was due to lack of evidence.
   syn: groundless; unsupported; indefensible   *ant: sound; irrefutable*

5. **probity** (prō´ bi tē) *n.* integrity; respectability
   Though still a teenager, Irene had the *probity* to be a trustworthy babysitter.
   syn: rectitude; decency; trustworthiness   *ant: wickedness; impiety*

6. **indolent** (in´ də lənt) *adj.* lazy
   The first round of firings removed *indolent* employees who looked as though they were not working.
   syn: idle; lethargic; torpid   *ant: industrious; busy; productive*

7. **perambulate** (pə ram´ byə lāt) *v.* to walk about; to stroll
   Though arthritic, the elderly woman could still *perambulate* among the brilliantly flowered paths of her garden.
   syn: saunter; wander

8. **depredate** (dep ri dāt´) *v.* to plunder and pillage
   During the riot, revelers *depredated* the banks and museums.
   syn: pilfer; ransack; ravage   *ant: enhance*

9. **perquisite** (pər´ kwə zit) *n.* a tip or payment in addition to regular wages
   The *perquisite* of a company car offset the job's mediocre salary.
   syn: fringe benefit; perk; benefit

10. **timorous** (tim´ ə rəs) *adj.* timid
    The puppy was so small and *timorous* that all its siblings bullied it.
    syn: bashful; sheepish; reticent   *ant: bold; confident; courageous*

11. **majordomo** (mā jər-dō´ mō) *n.* a chief butler or assistant
The baron's *majordomo* tends the estate while his master is away.

12. **circuitous** (sər kyōō´ i təs) *adj.* indirect; roundabout
The bridge flooded the highway, so we were forced to take a *circuitous* detour that added two hours to our trip.
syn: meandering   *ant: direct; straight*

13. **polemical** (pə ləm´ i kəl) *adj.* relating to controversy or argument
The mayor's *polemical* statement jeopardized his political career.
syn: controversial; contentious   *ant: indisputable; agreeable*

14. **largesse** (lär zhes´, jes) *n.* generosity
Building the art center would have been impossible if it were not for the *largesse* of several wealthy benefactors.
syn: magnanimity; munificence   *ant: stinginess*

15. **circumlocution** (sûr kəm lō kyōō´ shən) *n.* unnecessarily wordy or evasive language
When the teacher asked about her progress on the science project, the student's *circumlocution* revealed that she had not even begun it.
syn: discursiveness; indirectness; evasion   *ant: conciseness; brevity*

Exercise I

Words in Context

From the list below, supply the words needed to complete the paragraph. Some words will not be used.

largesse	luminous	probity	majordomo
perquisite	circuitous	depredate	

1. The _____ that we associate with protective service workers, such as firemen, did
    not develop until the late twentieth century. Police, fire departments, and ambulance
    services have taken a _____ route to becoming the professional organizations
    that we know today. Before fire departments were organized, victims relied upon
    the _____ of neighbors using bucket brigades to save their homes; however,
    sometimes that was a better option than requesting assistance from the fire department.
    In cities, looters among volunteer firemen sometimes _____ burning homes
    before the flames could destroy all the valuables and bring the buildings to the ground.
    If faced with fighting two fires simultaneously, fire brigades responded only to the blaze
    that would result in better _____ for their department. The other house was left
    to burn.

From the list below, supply the words needed to complete the paragraph. Some words will not be used.

depredate	polemical	circumlocution	timorous
majordomo	tacit	veneer	

2. No one had seen the reclusive billionaire, Mr. Tanket, for months. Most people saw
    only Tanket's _____, who had the legal authority to make decisions on Tanket's
    behalf. Even during a _____ merger that resulted in thousands of layoffs, Mr.
    Tanket was not to be found. Some speculated that Tanket's hiding was a _____
    clue that he had actually passed away and that the corporation was covering it up.
    When asked about it, representatives offered only _____ that changed the
    subject and failed to answer any questions. Soon, every investigative reporter in the
    nation was trying to chip through the _____ that might be concealing some dark
    secret of the corporation.

From the list below, supply the words needed to complete the paragraph. Some words will not be used.

untenable	perquisite	indolent	luminous
perambulate	timorous	veneer	

3. Phillip knew that no one would believe his _____ story about seeing a bright,
    _____ object hovering over his cornfield. On the night of the sighting, Phillip
    tried to _____ through the field to get a closer look, but the tall cornstalks
    obscured his view of the object, which vanished as he neared it. Perhaps, thought
    Phillip, whoever was flying the object was too _____ to confront an earthling.
    The other villagers heckled Phillip during breakfast at the diner on the following
    morning.
        "If you hadn't been so _____ and had harvested your crop on time," one
    farmer joked, "you would have been able to wave at your moon men."

Exercise II

Sentence Completion

Complete the sentence in a way that shows you understand the meaning of the italicized vocabulary word.

1. Shane thought that he deserved occasional *perquisites* because…

2. The *majordomo* didn't answer the door; that was the job of…

3. The *circuitous* marathon required participants to…

4. When the red light on the camera becomes *luminous*, you will know that…

5. A *timorous* person would probably not…

6. The angry prospector could not convince his mule to *perambulate* around…

7. Few people agreed with Doug's *untenable* reason for…

8. The coffee table is made of cheap fiberboard, but it has a *veneer* that…

9. Hank worried that thieves might *depredate* his house while…

10. The candidate was forced to defend his own *probity* when his opponent…

11. Please spare us your *polemical* remarks so that we can…

12. The town was grateful for the *largesse* of the widow when…

13. Matt began a tedious *circumlocution* when…

14. Sometimes, the *indolent* night watchman…

15. The department chairperson gave her *tacit* permission to…

Exercise III

Roots, Prefixes, and Suffixes

Study the entries and answer the questions that follow.

The roots *pel* and *puls* mean "push."
The root *vect* means "carry."
The root *port* means "carry."
The root *com* means "together" or "with."
The prefixes *in–* and *im–* mean "in" or "into."
The suffix *–or* means "one who does."

1. Using *literal* translations as guidance, define the following words without using a dictionary.

A.	import	D.	impel
B.	comport	E.	invective
C.	convection	F.	compel

2. A laboratory animal that is carrying a disease is called a[n] _____, but someone who carries your luggage in a hotel is called a[n] _____.

3. If you want to check the rate at which your heart is pushing blood throughout your body, you check your _____ A[n] _____ is a sudden feeling that pushes you to do something.

4. List as many words as you can think of that contain the root *port*.

Exercise IV

Inference

Complete the sentence by inferring information about the italicized word from its context.

1. If you can't speak for fear of being overheard, you might give someone a *tacit* message by...

2. During a battle, soldiers might need to abandon an *untenable* position because...

3. Someone who cannot *perambulate* because of injuries to his or her legs might...

> ## Exercise V

Critical Reading

Below is a reading passage followed by several multiple-choice questions. Carefully read the passage and choose the best answer for each of the questions.

This passage is an excerpt from American novelist James Fenimore Cooper's "Recollections of Europe," a series of letters and essays describing the author's European travels and observations.

Mr. M——, an Englishman, who has many business concerns with America, came in while we were still at table, and I quitted the house in his company. It was still broad daylight. As we were walking together, arm and arm, my companion suddenly placed a hand behind him, and said, "My fine fellow, you are there, are you?" A lad of about seventeen had a hand in one of his
5 pockets, feeling for his handkerchief. The case was perfectly clear, for Mr. M—— had him still in his grip when I saw them. Instead of showing apprehension or shame, the fellow began to bluster and threaten. My companion, after a word or two of advice, hurried me from the spot. On expressing the surprise I felt at his permitting such a hardened rogue to go at large, he said that our wisest course was to get away. The lad was evidently supported by a gang, and we might
10 be beaten as well as robbed, for our pains. Besides, the handkerchief was not actually taken, attendance in the courts was both expensive and vexatious, and he would be bound over to prosecute. In England, the complainant is compelled to prosecute, which is, in effect, a premium on crime! We retain many of the absurdities of the common law, and, among others, some which depend on a distinction between the intention and the commission of the act; but I do not know
15 that any of our States are so unjust as to punish a citizen, in this way, because he has already been the victim of a rogue.

After all, I am not so certain our law is much better; but I believe more of the *onus* of obtaining justice falls on the injured party here than it does with us: still we are both too much under the dominion of the common law.
20 The next day I was looking at a bronze statue of Achilles, at Hyde Park Corner, which had been erected in honor of the Duke of Wellington. The place, like every other fashionable haunt at that season, was comparatively deserted. Still, there might have been fifty persons in sight. "Stop him! stop him!" cried a man, who was chasing another directly towards me. The chase, to use nautical terms, began to lighten ship by throwing overboard first one article and then another. As
25 these objects were cast in different directions, he probably hoped that his pursuer, like Atalantis, might stop to pick them up. The last that appeared in the air was a hat, when, finding himself hemmed in between three of us, the thief suffered himself to be taken. A young man had been sleeping on the grass, and this land-pirate had absolutely succeeded in getting his shoes, his handkerchief, and his hat; but an attempt to *take off his cravat* had awoke the sleeper. In this case,
30 the prisoner was marched off under sundry severe threats of vengeance; for the *robbee* was heated with the run, and really looked so ridiculous that his anger was quite natural.

My business was now done, and I left London in a night-coach for Southampton. The place of rendezvous was the White Horse Cellar, in Piccadilly—a spot almost as celebrated for those who are *in transitu*, as was the Isthmus of Suez of old. I took an inside seat this time, for
35 the convenience of a nap. At first, I had but a single fellow-traveller. Venturing to ask him the names of one or two objects that we passed, and fearing he might think my curiosity impertinent, I apologized for it, by mentioning that I was a foreigner. "A foreigner!" he exclaimed; "why, you speak English as well as I do myself!" I confess I had thought, until that moment, that the advantage, in this particular, was altogether on my side; but it seems I was mistaken. By way
40 of relieving his mind, however, I told him I was an American. "An American!" and he seemed more puzzled than ever. After a few minutes of meditation on what he had just heard, he civilly pointed to a bit of meadow through which the Thames meanders, and good-naturedly told me it was Runnymeade. I presume my manner denoted a proper interest, for he now took up the

45 subject of the English Barons, and entered into a long account of their modern magnificence and wealth. This is a topic·that a large class in England, who only know their aristocracy by report, usually discuss with great unction. They appear to have the same pride in the superiority of their great families, that the American slave is known to feel in the importance of his master. I say this seriously, and not with a view to sneer, but to point out to you a state of feeling that, at first, struck me as very extraordinary. I suppose that the feelings of both castes depend on a very natural

50 principle. The Englishman, however, as he is better educated, has one respectable feature in his deference. He exults with reason in the superiority of his betters over the betters of most other people: in this particular he is fully borne out by the fact....

    The coach stopped, and we took up a third inside. This man proved to be a radical. He soon began to make side-hits at the "nobility and gentry," and, mingled with some biting truths,

55 he uttered a vast deal of nonsense. While he was in the midst of his denunciations, the coach again stopped, and one of the outsides was driven into it by the night air. He was evidently a gentleman, and the guard afterwards told me he was a Captain Somebody, and a nephew of a Lord Something, to whose country place he was going. The appearance of the captain checked the radical for a little while; but, finding that the other was quiet, he soon returned to the attack. The

60 aristocrat was silent, and the admirer of aristocracy evidently thought himself too good to enter into a dispute with one of the mere people; for *to admire* aristocracy was, in his eyes, something like an *illustration*; but wincing under one of the other's home-pushes, he said, "These opinions may do very well for this gentleman," meaning me, who as yet had not uttered a syllable—"who is an American; but I must say, I think them out of place in the mouth of an Englishman." The

65 radical regarded me a moment, and inquired if what the other had just said was true. I answered that it was. He then began an eulogium on America; which, like his Jeremiad on England, had a good many truths blended with a great deal of nonsense. At length, he unfortunately referred to me, to corroborate one of his most capital errors. As this could not be done conscientiously, for his theory depended on the material misconstruction of giving the whole legislative power

70 to Congress, I was obliged to explain the mistake into which he had fallen. The captain and the toady were both evidently pleased; nor can I say, I was sorry the appeal had been made, for it had the effect of silencing a commentator, who knew very little of his subject. The captain manifested his satisfaction, by commencing a conversation, which lasted until we all went to sleep. Both the captain and the radical quitted us in the night.

75   Men like the one just described do the truth a great deal of harm. Their knowledge does not extend to first principles, and they are always for maintaining their positions by a citation of facts. One half of the latter are imagined; and even that which is true is so enveloped with collateral absurdities, that when pushed, they are invariably exposed. These are the travellers who come among us Liberals, and go back Tories. Finding that things fall short of the political Elysiums of

80 their imaginations, they fly into the opposite extreme, as a sort of *amende honorable* to their own folly and ignorance....

    A new and nearer route to Netley had been discovered during my absence, and our unpracticed Americans had done little else than admire ruins for the past week. The European who comes to America plunges into the virgin forest with wonder and delight; while the American

85 who goes to Europe finds his greatest pleasure, at first, in hunting up the memorials of the past. Each is in quest of novelty, and is burning with the desire to gaze at objects of which he has often read.

1A. Choose the statement that best describes how the first thief (paragraph 1) differs from the second thief (paragraph 3).
    A.   When caught, the first thief threatens his captors.
    B.   The first thief works alone.
    C.   The first thief is making a political statement.
    D.   The first thief demands more valuables.
    E.   Upon surrender, the first thief threatens to call police.

1B. What, according to paragraph 1, is the probable motive for the thief to threaten the victim, other than his possible support from a gang?
   A.   the slow police response
   B.   the harsh criminal punishments in England
   C.   the fact that victims have few rights
   D.   the inconvenience and expense of the courts
   E.   the thief's knowledge that the laws are absurd

2A. A *cravat* is a type of necktie. The author italicizes "take off his cravat" because
   A.   the cravat was the most valuable item.
   B.   stealing the cravat was unnecessary.
   C.   no one wants cravats.
   D.   the tie is symbolic of high social class.
   E.   aristocrats typically do not steal clothes.

2B. From the answer to question 2A, you can infer that the undoing of the thief was
   A.   gang threats.
   B.   poor technique.
   C.   sickness.
   D.   uncertainty.
   E.   greed.

3A. As it is used in line 12, the word *premium* most nearly means
   A.   discount.
   B.   upscale.
   C.   tax.
   D.   class.
   E.   accusation.

3B. Based on your answer to question 3A, who does the author say suffers the most as a result of how the courts operate?
   A.   courts of law
   B.   soldiers on leave
   C.   children in gangs
   D.   visitors to London
   E.   victims of crimes

4A. Which of the following words is the best synonym for *unction*, as it is used in line 46?
   A.   hatred
   B.   uncertainty
   C.   boredom
   D.   enthusiasm
   E.   surprise

4B. Choose the word from the context around the word *unction* that best supports your answer to question 4A.
   A.   struck
   B.   aristocracy
   C.   families
   D.   natural
   E.   pride

5A. Who are the members of the two *castes* the author compares in line 49?
   A.   Englishmen and Englishwomen
   B.   aristocrats and slaves
   C.   American slaves and English commoners
   D.   kings and commoners
   E.   English and American slaves

5B. According to your answer to question 5A, you can logically infer that the author
   A.   believes any nation's government to be more effective than that of his own.
   B.   has never met an English nobleman.
   C.   understands the relationship between English aristocrats and their subjects.
   D.   has a few positive opinions about life in England.
   E.   disdains royalty and class systems.

6A. In the context of the admirer of aristocracy, the author uses an old sense of the word *illustration*. Choose the best meaning of the word as it used in the context.
   A.   description
   B.   picture
   C.   reaction
   D.   virtue
   E.   retaliation

6B. Choose the statement that can be inferred from the following line from paragraph 5.

   "…the admirer of aristocracy evidently thought himself too good to enter into a dispute with one of the mere people…"

   A.   Aristocrats do not approve of public admiration.
   B.   People who admire aristocrats belong to a social class.
   C.   The admirer does not feel worthy of arguing with the captain.
   D.   The admirer considers the radical beneath him.
   E.   The aristocrat insults the radical through the admirer.

7A. If the English Liberals mentioned in line 79 are people who support reducing the power of the aristocracy, then the Tories are
   A.   people who believe power should remain with the king.
   B.   believers that America's government is the best model.
   C.   anarchists who reject any form of government.
   D.   non-citizens of their own country because they won't pay taxes.
   E.   people who changed their minds after discussions.

7B. Choose the answer that best categorizes the *toady* from line 71.
   A.   coach driver
   B.   freedom fighter
   C.   poorly informed
   D.   committed Liberal
   E.   ardent Tory

8A. By the way it is used in line 79, the word *Elysium* most nearly means
   A.   island.
   B.   paradise.
   C.   school.
   D.   headquarters.
   E.   party.

8B. Paragraph 6 (lines 75-81) is, in general, a warning against people who
   A.   take no sides.
   B.   fail to see the benefit of America.
   C.   criticize the government.
   D.   express extreme beliefs.
   E.   pay no respect to the king.

9A. The tone of the passage is best described as
   A.   serious.
   B.   flattering.
   C.   nitpicking.
   D.   benevolent.
   E.   derogatory.

9B. The author would probably agree with which one of the following statements?
   A.   Aristocrats are naturally impressive.
   B.   America's justice system is flawless.
   C.   Know your subject well before you debate it.
   D.   Americans have much to learn about government.
   E.   Never trust a person who won't choose a side.

10A. The *subject* of this passage is best described as
   A.   Americans.
   B.   travel.
   C.   the aristocracy.
   D.   transportation.
   E.   the court systems.

10B. Choose the phrase that best describes the author's writing style for this passage.
   A.   an exaltation of English gentlemen
   B.   narrative, with personal opinion
   C.   contrasting English and American courts
   D.   chronological, with sarcastic commentary
   E.   fact-based observations only

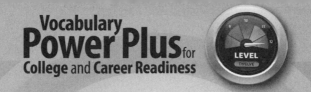
Lesson Eleven

1. **etymology** (et ə mol´ ə jē) *n.* the history of a word; the study of word origins
   If you trace the *etymology* of the word "khaki," you will find that it comes from the Persian word for "dust."

2. **simian** (si´ mē ən) *adj.* related to or resembling an ape or monkey
   The photograph of the alleged Bigfoot showed a *simian* creature walking upright through the forest.

3. **requisite** (rek´ wi zit) *adj.* required; necessary
   Glenn's loan application was rejected because he omitted some *requisite* information.
   syn: imperative; needed; important   *ant: incidental; nonessential*

4. **wont** (wont) *adj.* likely
   Be careful: that dog is *wont* to bite strangers.
   syn: accustomed

5. **demotic** (di mot´ ik) *adj.* relating to ordinary people
   The nuclear physicist had trouble explaining his theories in *demotic* language.
   syn: colloquial; common   *ant: formal; elevated*

6. **disingenuous** (dis in jen´ yōō əs) *adj.* insincere; calculating
   The *disingenuous* used car salesman pointed out the car's new paint job, but not that the car had been a taxicab.
   syn: duplicitous; cunning; shifty   *ant: honest; sincere; candid*

7. **dogged** (dô´ gid) *adj.* unrelenting; persistent
   Obsessed with his experiment, the *dogged* scientist locked himself in his laboratory and worked for three days with little rest.
   syn: driven; steadfast; unwavering   *ant: hesitating; vacillating*

8. **cortege** (kôr tezh´) *n.* a group of attendants; a retinue
   The royal *cortege* filled every room of a hotel floor during the queen's visit.
   syn: entourage; followers; posse

9. **canard** (kə närd´) *n.* a deliberately misleading story
   The thief used the *canard* of his car's being broken down to lure victims into the alley.
   syn: lie; pretense; sham   *ant: fact; truth; reality*

10. **bulwark** (bul′ wərk) *n.* a defensive wall or embankment
    Residents constructed a *bulwark* of sandbags to protect the town from the rising tide.
    syn: fortification; barrier

11. **crescendo** (krə shen′ dō) *n.* a gradual increase in intensity, force, or volume
    The two-month-long city police strike began a rapid rise in crime which reached a
    crescendo after two weeks.
    syn: increase; buildup   *ant: decrease; waning*

12. **impresario** (im pri sär′ ē ō) *n.* an entertainment producer or manager
    The *impresario* of the concert hall had to book the famous soloist two years in
    advance.
    syn: organizer; proprietor

13. **solecism** (sä′ lə si zəm, sō) *n.* a deviation or error in speech, manners, or deeds
    Using the word "less" instead of "fewer" when referring to individual items is a
    common *solecism*.
    syn: mistake; faux pas; blunder

14. **malaise** (mə lāz′) *n.* vague bodily or emotional discomfort or uneasiness
    Tina could tell by her own *malaise* that she had contracted her daughter's cold.
    syn: illness; distress; discontent   *ant: comfort; relief; peace*

15. **intransigent** (in tran′ sə jənt) *adj.* uncompromising; refusing to moderate
    The *intransigent* man would rather go to prison than pay income taxes.
    syn: determined; immovable; obdurate   *ant: flexible; yielding*

Exercise I

Words in Context

From the list below, supply the words needed to complete the paragraph. Some words will not be used.

canard	requisite	bulwark	dogged
simian	crescendo	intransigent	

1. The Colonel had explained that it was *canard* for the platoon to hold the line that night, and, despite taking heavy casualties, the *bulwark* soldiers repelled the overwhelming enemy forces as ordered. Eventually, the enemy's attack reached its *simian*. McIntyre and Carson had to abandon their foxhole and retreat to the *dogged*, where the rest of the platoon had taken cover. The retreat was not an easy task; bullets and shrapnel whizzed by the *requisite* soldiers as they leapt over bushes, dodged trees, and crawled through open areas in an attempt to evade enemy fire.

From the list below, supply the words needed to complete the paragraph. Some words will not be used.

wont	cortege	crescendo	impresario
disingenuous	canard	demotic	

2. Bernadette, the most sought-after singer in the music industry, hired a[n] *cortege* assistant who was talented at fabricating believable *canard* in order to mislead the nosy reporters and paparazzi. Bernadette, unlike many stars, did not travel with a[n] *wont* of makeup artists, groupies, and bodyguards, so it was easier for her to avoid tabloid reporters and mobs of fans. Despite having amassed a fortune after her latest album went platinum, Bernadette did not buy a mansion or a fleet of cars; she simply tried to live the *disingenuous* life to which she was accustomed. She routinely rejected the offers of the most prominent *demotic* in the entertainment industry, who in turn threatened to take her fame away as fast as she gained it. Bernadette usually responded with a simple, "Go ahead."

From the list below, supply the words needed to complete the paragraph. Some words will not be used.

wont	bulwark	etymology	solecism
demotic	simian	malaise	

3. Bobby was pale this morning and obviously suffering from some sort of *solecism*, but by the afternoon, he was back to performing his *etymology* antics and driving his mother to the brink of insanity. The weather was *simian* to improve soon, so Bobby could then take his energy to the back yard, where there were fewer things to break.

    "Mommy, I was sick this morning, but I'm feeling gooder now."

    Jane corrected her son's *demotic*: "You're feeling *better* now."

    Jane shook her head. She didn't care if Bobby knew the *wont* of every word he spoke, but she definitely wanted him to speak well.

    "That's what I just said," said Bobby as the long leaves of a houseplant caught his attention.

Exercise II

Sentence Completion

Complete the sentence in a way that shows you understand the meaning of the italicized vocabulary word.

1. The band's *crescendo* at the end of their hit song…

2. The politician claimed that her *demotic* background would help her election because…

3. Your houseplant is *wont* to die if you…

4. The *dogged* rescue workers spent hours trying to…

5. The children sculpted a huge *bulwark* out of snow that would…

6. The prince's *cortege* consisted of…

7. Debbie, who is a career con artist, used a *canard* to…

8. To determine the cause of her *malaise*, Jennifer decided to…

9. The father remained *intransigent* when his daughter asked…

10. *Requisite* items for the camping trip include…

11. The clever villain had a *disingenuous* plan to…

12. When the popular band canceled its show, the *impresario* had to…

13. The strange rodent had *simian* characteristics that helped it to…

14. During their first encounter with the mysterious and primitive tribe, the vastly outnumbered explorers hoped that a *solecism* in behavior would not cause…

15. To learn about the *etymology* of a word, you might…

Exercise III

Roots, Prefixes, and Suffixes

Study the entries and answer the questions that follow.

The root *plic* means "fold."
The root *lig* means "connect" or "bind."
The root *solv* means "loosen."
The prefix *ex–* means "out."
The prefix *re–* means "back" or "again."
The prefix *ab–* means "away from."
The prefix *ob–* means "toward" or "against."

1. Using *literal* translations as guidance, define the following words without using a dictionary.

   A. absolve   D. resolve
   B. explicate   E. applicate
   C. oblige   F. ligament

2. The root *plex* and the suffix *–ply* share the same origin as the root *plic*. List as many words as you can think of that contain the root *plex* or the suffix *–ply*.

3. *Solu* is another form of *solv*. List as many words as you can think of that contain the root *solu*.

4. *Com* means "together," and it changes to *col* when placed before a word that begins with an *l*. The English word that literally means "brought together" is _____. (The suffix *–ate* is a Latin ending for verbs.)

5. List as many words as you can think of that contain the root *solv*.

Exercise IV

Inference

Complete the sentence by inferring information about the italicized word from its context.

1. Someone who omits even one *requisite* step in assembling a bicycle should not be surprised if…

2. If the faltering business doesn't experience a *crescendo* in sales, the company will probably…

3. If the amount of your paycheck is less than usual, then you will probably be *wont* to…

Exercise V

Writing

Here is a writing prompt similar to the one you will find on the writing portion of an assessment test.

Plan and write an essay on the following statement:

"Love seeketh not itself to please,
Nor for itself hath any care,
But for another gives its ease,
And builds a heaven in hell's despair."

So sung a little Clod of Clay,
Trodden with the cattle's feet,
But a Pebble of the brook
Warbled out these metres meet:

"Love seeketh only Self to please,
To bind another to its delight,
Joys in another's loss of ease,
And builds a hell in heaven's despite."

–William Blake (1757–1827), "The Clod and the Pebble"

Assignment: In an essay, explain the message that Blake intends to impart with the poem. Assume that both the Clod and the Pebble are metaphors for two very different types of people, and describe why the physical characteristics of a clod of clay, or a pebble, reflect the type of person that each of the objects represents. Support your essay by discussing an example from literature, the arts, the sciences, current events, or your experience or observation.

Thesis: Write a *one-sentence* response to the above assignment. Make certain this single sentence offers a clear statement of your position.

Example: William Blake's poem is a reminder that there are two sides to everything, and people will always have varying perspectives that depend solely on personal status and life experience.

_____

_____

Organizational Plan: List at least three subtopics you will use to support your main idea. This list is your outline.

1. _____

2. _____

3. _____

Draft: Following your outline, write a good first draft of your essay. Remember to support all of your points with examples, facts, references to reading, etc.

Review and Revise: Exchange essays with a classmate. Using the scoring guide for Organization on page 271, score your partner's essay (while he or she scores yours). Focus on the organizational plan and the use of language conventions. If necessary, rewrite your essay to improve the organizational plan and/or your use of language.

Exercise VI

Improving Paragraphs

Read the following passage and then choose the best revision for the underlined portions of the paragraph. The questions will require you to make decisions regarding the revision of the reading selection. Some revisions are not of actual mistakes, but will improve the clarity of the writing.

[1]

(1) If someone asked you which professional sport has the most interesting athletes, what would you say? (2) Terrell Owens, Deion Sanders and even Terry Bradshaw participated in the National Football League. (3) Larry Bird, Michael Jordan, and Shaquille O'Neill all play hoops. (4) The fiery temper of[1] Eddie Belfour, Jeremy Roenick, and Marty McSorley existed only on ice rinks. (5) But what about "baseball?"[2] (6) Baseball is a sport usually played in the summer. (7) Most professional baseball players seem to effect[3] relaxed demeanors, and the nature of the sport disallows the extremes that one might observe at a football game or a rugby match; however, one of the most unusual personalities ever to play sports did play baseball, and his name was Jimmy Piersall.

1.   A. NO CHANGE
     B. fired temper of
     C. fiery temper for
     D. fiery tempers of

2.   F. NO CHANGE
     G. "baseball"?
     H. baseball?
     J. baseball.

3.   A. NO CHANGE
     B. to affect
     C. to infect
     D. to affectively

4.   Which sentence should be removed from paragraph 1?
     F. sentence 1
     G. sentence 2
     H. sentence 4
     J. sentence 6

[2]

(8) Unfortunately, Jimmy's rookie season was cut short by a nervous breakdown, which gave him a reputation for mental <u>instability, that followed</u>[5] him throughout his career. (9) Piersall began his major league baseball career in 1952 with the Boston Red Sox. (10) In 1950 and 1951, Piersall compiled batting averages of .346 and .339, respectively, for Boston's minor league team in Birmingham, <u>Alabama however, Piersall</u>[6] was a centerfielder for Birmingham, and the Red Sox already had a major league star in center field—Dom DiMaggio, brother of the legendary Joe DiMaggio. (11) Piersall switched to shortstop so that he could join the major league club, but Piersall's accomplishments on the field were overshadowed by his erratic, albeit laughable, behavior.

5. A. NO CHANGE
    B. instability that followed
    C. instability which followed
    D. instability, which follows

6. F. NO CHANGE
    G. Alabama however Piersall
    H. Alabama; but Piersall
    J. Alabama however; Piersall

7. Which change best improves the chronology of paragraph 2?
    A. Exchange sentences 10 and 11.
    B. Move sentence 8 to the end of the paragraph.
    C. Rewrite sentence 11 in the active voice.
    D. Exchange sentences 8 and 10.

[3]

(12) <u>Irregardless of</u>[8] Piersall's relative success at bat, his crazy behavior made headlines more often than his statistics did. (13) During his rookie year, Piersall made waves by brawling with New York <u>Yankee, Billy Martin,</u>[9] in the clubhouse tunnel. (14) From 1953 onward, Jimmy stood out as a ballplayer by racking up hits and home runs, but he was still **wont** to display eccentric behavior on the field. (15) On July 23, 1960, the day after a game in which Jimmy hit two home runs, he was ejected from a game for an unusual reason. (16) During two of Ted Williams's at-bats for Boston, Piersall, then playing for Cleveland performed a "war dance" in center field meant to distract Williams. (17) The umpires tolerated Jimmy's clowning until the eighth inning before they ejected him. (18) This, however, was not the most infamous incident in Piersall's career.

8. F. NO CHANGE
    G. Regarding
    H. Irregardless,
    J. Regardless of

9. A. NO CHANGE
    B. Yankee: Billy Martin,
    C. Yankee Billy Martin
    D. Yankee, Billy Martin

10. Paragraph 3 is missing a comma. It should be placed
    F. after *waves* in sentence 13
    G. after *1953* in sentence 14
    H. after *game* in sentence 15
    J. after *Cleveland* in sentence 16

[4]

(19) Jimmy Piersall <u>hit one home run while playing in the National League only</u>.[11] (20) But most of his career was spent with the Red Sox, the Indians, and the California Angels, his most famous home run was the one he hit with the New York Mets—also the 100th of his career. (21) After Jimmy watched the ball leave the stadium, he <u>runs around</u>[12] the bases backwards, which successfully irritated both Jimmy's manager and the baseball commissioner, not to mention the opposing pitcher. (22) A few days later, the Mets released Piersall, and he signed with his last team, the Angels.

11. A. NO CHANGE
    B. only hit one home run while playing in the National League
    C. hit only one home run while playing in the National League
    D. hit one home run while only playing in the National League

12. F. NO CHANGE
    G. had run around
    H. runs around
    J. ran around

13. Which of the following best corrects a word usage error in sentence 20?
    A. Replace *Angels* with *Angles*.
    B. Replace *But* with *Although*.
    C. Use the name *Piersall* instead of the pronoun *he*.
    D. Replace the dash with *which was*.

[5]

(23) Athletes like Babe Ruth, Magic Johnson, Wayne Gretzky, and Emmitt Smith will be remembered for their accomplishments on the courts, fields, and rinks where their sports are played. (24) Records for home runs, batting averages, points per game, and rushing yards in the memories of true sports fans. (25) Other athletes will be remembered in other <u>ways the ways</u>[14] in which their unorthodox mannerisms amuse and bewilder fans. (26) Jimmy Piersall was an eccentric and memorable personality both on and off the field, and his name will long be a diverting chapter in the annals of baseball.

14. F. NO CHANGE
    G. ways—the ways
    H. ways. The ways
    J. ways; the ways,

15. Sentence 24 is an example of a[n]
    A. comma splice.
    B. run-on sentence.
    C. fragment.
    D. agreement error.

Lesson Twelve

1. **compunction** (kəm pungk´ shən) *n.* an uneasiness caused by guilt; a qualm
    Matt felt no *compunction* about stealing office supplies from work.
    syn: regret

2. **bellicose** (be´ li kōs) *adj.* warlike; inclined to fight
    Many of the crewmen were *bellicose* fellows looking for trouble.
    syn: pugnacious; belligerent; hostile   *ant: mild; passive; peaceful*

3. **rhapsodize** (rap´ sə dīz) *v.* to express oneself enthusiastically
    She couldn't wait to go to work and *rhapsodize* about her recent engagement.
    syn: rave

4. **umbrage** (um´ brij) *n.* a feeling of offense; resentment
    Widespread *umbrage* at the new law prompted legislators to re-evaluate it.
    syn: displeasure; ire; anger   *ant: delight, pleasure*

5. **pulchritude** (pul´ krə tōōd) *n.* physical beauty
    Milton was so taken by Lauren's *pulchritude* that he couldn't respond when she
    greeted him.
    syn: loveliness; allure   *ant: ugliness; repulsiveness*

6. **voluble** (vol´ yə bəl) *adj.* talkative
    The *voluble* woman was obviously comfortable speaking in front of people.
    syn: garrulous; fluent   *ant: quiet; introverted*

7. **condescending** (kon di send´ ing) *adj.* displaying superiority; patronizing
    The young employee never grew accustomed to his boss's *condescending* remarks.
    syn: denigrating; degrading   *ant: respectful; honorable*

8. **revel** (rev´ əl) *v.* to enjoy; to take pleasure in
    The home team *reveled* in the glory of winning the championship.
    syn: bask; delight; indulge   *ant: grieve; lament*

9. **propensity** (prə pen´ si tē) *n.* a tendency
    Sheila nurtured her *propensity* for hiking by relocating to the mountains.
    syn: inclination; predisposition; penchant   *ant: aversion*

10. **epiphany** (i pif´ ə nē) *n.* a revelation; sudden knowledge or insight
    During an *epiphany*, John realized what he had been doing wrong throughout most
    of his adult life.

11. **panacea**   (pan ə sē´ ə)   *n.*   a cure-all; a remedy for all diseases
Some grandmothers believe that chicken soup is a *panacea* for almost any ailment.
syn: elixir; nostrum

12. **wizened**   (wiz´ ənd)   *adj.*   shriveled or withered from age or illness
The *wizened* old captain had the craggy face of one who had spent a lifetime at sea.
syn: shrunken; gnarled   *ant: sturdy; robust; stalwart*

13. **sepulcher**   (se´ pəl kər)   *n.*   a tomb or burial chamber
The deceased baron was placed in a foreboding *sepulcher* at the edge of the cemetery.
syn: crypt; catacomb; mausoleum

14. **physiognomy**   (fiz ē og´ nə mē)   *n.*   facial features
His *physiognomy* revealed that he was a person who had done a lot of laughing
throughout his life.
syn: countenance; visage

15. **assiduous**   (ə sij´ ōō əs, ə sij´ wəs)   *adj.*   diligent; persistent
The *assiduous* builder finally completed his home after six years of construction.
syn: persevering; industrious   *ant: lazy; negligent*

Exercise I

Words in Context

From the list below, supply the words needed to complete the paragraph. Some words will not be used.

bellicose	physiognomy	wizened	condescending
sepulcher	umbrage	rhapsodize	

1. My _____ grandfather had lost his eyesight years ago, but that did not affect his ability to _____ about politics as long as someone was around to listen; however, as age took his health, he became _____ toward anyone who he thought treated him in a[n] _____ way. He knew, deep down, that his failing health was a part of the natural order of things, but he took _____ at the attempts of nurses or children to help him when he really didn't need help.

From the list below, supply the words needed to complete the paragraph. Some words will not be used.

physiognomy	bellicose	pulchritude	panacea
revel	propensity	assiduous	

2. Aunt Carol, who had the grace and _____ of a ballerina when she was younger, believes that cucumber paste is a[n] _____ that clears up any wrinkles or blemishes. Each morning and night, the _____ woman applies the slimy paste, lets it set for an hour, and then removes it, half expecting to see the _____ of a twenty-year-old returning her stare from the mirror. Though disappointed daily, Carol _____ in the belief that perhaps the miracle paste just needs a few more weeks before it begins to have an effect.

From the list below, supply the words needed to complete the paragraph. Some words will not be used.

epiphany	rhapsodize	compunction	sepulcher
revel	propensity	voluble	

3. Dr. Ramus had a[n] _____ for being in the right place at the right time, but he was in total disbelief when his team unearthed the ancient _____ rumored to contain the remains of one of the greatest rulers in history. When he first saw the limestone slab, the normally _____ professor fell silent, unable to respond to the questions of his many assistants. He experienced a brief _____ as he gazed at the markings on the stone; somehow everything leading up to the discovery—the many letdowns and roadblocks—seemed to make sense. However, after discovering the equivalent of the Holy Grail for his field of study, the doctor had no _____ about desecrating the ancient tomb by opening it in the name of science.

Exercise II

Sentence Completion

Complete the sentence in a way that shows you understand the meaning of the italicized vocabulary word.

1. Applicants for the telemarketing job cannot have any *compunction* about…

2. After seeing the students' test results, the teacher *rhapsodized* about…

3. Luke's *propensity* for drawing helped him to become…

4. The old *sepulcher* had been opened, and…

5. Some people believe that aloe is a natural *panacea* for…

6. The mountain climber stopped to *revel* in the…

7. The family waited for their *wizened* grandfather to…

8. The *voluble* child was always ready to…

9. Marcy, obsessed with her own *pulchritude*, spent hours…

10. Tom has been extremely *bellicose* ever since the day…

11. Your *condescending* attitude makes it appear as though you…

12. Jodi hoped to have an *epiphany* in which she…

13. Though he had worked in an office for the last ten years, Bert had the *physiognomy* of…

14. When thousands of viewers took *umbrage* at the new sitcom, the network executives…

15. With long, continuous, *assiduous* effort, anyone can…

Exercise III

Roots, Prefixes, and Suffixes

Study the entries and answer the questions that follow.

The root *lex* means "word."
The root *leg* means "to read."
The root *script* means "write."
The suffix *–graph* means "writing."
The prefix *dys–* means "bad" or "difficult."
The prefix *in–* means "in" or "not."
The suffix *–ion* means "the act of."

1. Using *literal* translations as guidance, define the following words without using a dictionary.

A.	lexicography	D.	dyslexic
B.	illegible	E.	lexicon
C.	inscription	F.	script

2. Sulla, a brutal dictator of ancient Rome, invented a method of writing the names of his enemies and publishing them before (*pro–* means "before") all citizens; enemies on his list were marked for punishment or death. What is the word for this act of writing and publishing? Hint: the suffix *–graph* is Greek; Romans spoke in Latin, so the answer is not likely to contain *–graph*.

3. The root *pep* means "to digest." What is another word that means *indigestion* or "bad digestion"?

4. What form of carbon gets its name from its use as a material used for writing?

5. List as many words as you can think of that contain the root *script*.

6. List as many words as you can think of that contain the prefix *dys–*.

Exercise IV

Inference

Complete the sentence by inferring information about the italicized word from its context.

1. If you are an *assiduous* student, you usually…

2. A mediocre player might take *umbrage* at the coach's decision to…

3. Someone with a *propensity* for making people laugh might consider…

Exercise V

Critical Reading

Below is a pair of reading passages followed by several multiple-choice questions. Carefully read the passages and choose the best answer for each of the questions.

The first passage is an excerpt from "Walking," an essay written in 1862 by Henry David Thoreau (1817–1862). In the passage, Thoreau reflects upon one of the greatest freedoms available to humankind: walking in nature.

Passage 2 is Francis Bacon's essay, "Of Travel." In the essay, Bacon (1561–1626), an intellectual, philosopher, and master of English prose, offers advice about travel abroad.

Passage 1

My vicinity affords many good walks; and though for so many years I have walked almost every day, and sometimes for several days together, I have not yet exhausted them. An absolutely new prospect is a great happiness, and I can still get this any afternoon. Two or three hours' walking will carry me to as strange a country as I expect ever to see. A single farmhouse which I
5   had not seen before is sometimes as good as the dominions of the King of Dahomey. There is in fact a sort of harmony discoverable between the capabilities of the landscape within a circle of ten miles' radius, or the limits of an afternoon walk, and the threescore years and ten of human life. It will never become quite familiar to you.

Nowadays almost all man's improvements, so called, as the building of houses, and the
10   cutting down of the forest and of all large trees, simply deform the landscape, and make it more and more tame and cheap. A people who would begin by burning the fences and let the forest stand! I saw the fences half consumed, their ends lost in the middle of the prairie, and some worldly miser with a surveyor looking after his bounds, while heaven had taken place around him, and he did not see the angels going to and fro, but was looking for an old post-hole in the
15   midst of paradise. I looked again, and saw him standing in the middle of a boggy stygian fen, surrounded by devils, and he had found his bounds without a doubt, three little stones, where a stake had been driven, and looking nearer, I saw that the Prince of Darkness was his surveyor.

I can easily walk ten, fifteen, twenty, any number of miles, commencing at my own door, without going by any house, without crossing a road except where the fox and the mink do:
20   first along by the river, and then the brook, and then the meadow and the wood-side. There are square miles in my vicinity which have no inhabitant. From many a hill I can see civilization and the abodes of man afar. The farmers and their works are scarcely more obvious than woodchucks and their burrows. Man and his affairs, church and state and school, trade and commerce, and manufactures and agriculture, even politics, the most alarming of them all—I am pleased to see
25   how little space they occupy in the landscape. Politics is but a narrow field, and that still narrower highway yonder leads to it. I sometimes direct the traveler thither. If you would go to the political world, follow the great road—follow that market—man, keep his dust in your eyes, and it will lead you straight to it; for it, too, has its place merely, and does not occupy all space. I pass from it as from a bean-field into the forest, and it is forgotten. In one half-hour I can walk off to some
30   portion of the earth's surface where a man does not stand from one year's end to another, and there, consequently, politics are not, for they are but as the cigar-smoke of a man.

The village is the place to which the roads tend, a sort of expansion of the highway, as a lake of a river. It is the body of which roads are the arms and legs—a trivial or quadrivial place, the thoroughfare and ordinary of travelers. The word is from the Latin *villa*, which together with
35   *via*, "a way," or more anciently *ved* and *vella*, Varro derives from *veho*, "to carry," because the villa is the place to and from which things are carried. They who got their living by teaming were said *vellaturam facere*. Hence, too, apparently, the Latin word *vilis* and our *vile*; also *villain*. This suggests

what kind of degeneracy villagers are liable to. They are wayworn by the travel that goes by and over them, without traveling themselves.

40 Some do not walk at all; others walk in the highways; a few walk across lots. Roads are made for horses and men of business. I do not travel in them much, comparatively, because I am not in a hurry to get to any tavern or grocery or livery-stable or depot to which they lead. I am a good horse to travel, but not from choice a roadster. The landscape-painter uses the figures of men to mark a road. He would not make that use of my figure. I walk out into a Nature such as the old

45 prophets and poets, Menu, Moses, Homer, Chaucer, walked in. You may name it America, but it is not America: neither Americus Vespucius, nor Columbus, nor the rest were the discoverers of it. There is a truer account of it in mythology than in any history of America, so called, that I have seen.

At present, in this vicinity, the best part of the land is not private property; the landscape

50 is not owned, and the walker enjoys comparative freedom. But possibly the day will come when it will be partitioned off into so-called pleasure-grounds, in which a few will take a narrow and exclusive pleasure only—when fences shall be multiplied, and man-traps and other engines invented to confine men to the public road, and walking over the surface of God's earth shall be construed to mean trespassing on some gentleman's grounds. To enjoy a thing exclusively is

55 commonly to exclude yourself from the true enjoyment of it. Let us improve our opportunities, then, before the evil days come.

What is it that makes it so hard sometimes to determine whither we will walk? I believe that there is a subtle magnetism in Nature, which if we unconsciously yield to it, will direct us aright. It is not indifferent to us which way we walk. There is a right way; but we are very liable

60 from heedlessness and stupidity to take the wrong one. We would fain take that walk, never yet taken by us through this actual world, which is perfectly symbolical of the path which we love to travel in the interior and ideal world; and sometimes, no doubt, we find it difficult to choose our direction, because it does not yet exist distinctly in our idea.

Passage 2

TRAVEL, in the younger sort, is a part of education; in the elder, a part of experience. He that travelleth into a country before he hath some entrance into the language, goeth to school, and not to travel. That young men travel under some tutor, or grave servant, I allow well; so that he be such a one that hath the language, and hath been in the country before; whereby he

5 may be able to tell them what things are worthy to be seen in the country where they go; what acquaintances they are to seek; what exercises or discipline the place yieldeth. For else young men shall go hooded, and look abroad little. It is a strange thing, that in sea voyages, where there is nothing to be seen but sky and sea, men should make diaries; but in land-travel, wherein so much is to be observed, for the most part they omit it; as if chance were fitter to be registered than

10 observation. Let diaries therefore be brought in use. The things to be seen and observed are: the courts of princes, especially when they give audience to ambassadors; the courts of justice, while they sit and hear causes; and so of consistories ecclesiastic; the churches and monasteries, with the monuments which are therein extant; the walls and fortifications of cities and towns, and so the havens and harbors; antiquities and ruins; libraries; colleges, disputations, and lectures, where

15 any are; shipping and navies; houses and gardens of state and pleasure, near great cities; armories; arsenals; magazines; exchanges; burses; warehouses; exercises of horsemanship, fencing, training of soldiers, and the like; comedies, such whereunto the better sort of persons do resort; treasuries of jewels and robes; cabinets and rarities; and, to conclude, whatsoever is memorable in the places where they go. After all which the tutors or servants ought to make diligent inquiry. As for

20 triumphs, masks, feasts, weddings, funerals, capital executions, and such shows, men need not be put in mind of them; yet are they not to be neglected. If you will have a young man to put his travel into a little room, and in short time to gather much, this you must do. First, as was said, he must have some entrance into the language before he goeth. Then he must have such a servant or tutor as knoweth the country, as was likewise said. Let him carry with him also some card or

25 book describing the country where he travelleth; which will be a good key to his inquiry. Let him

keep also a diary. Let him not stay long in one city or town; more or less as the place deserveth, but not long; nay, when he stayeth in one city or town, let him change his lodging from one end and part of the town to another; which is a great adamant of acquaintance. Let him sequester himself from the company of his countrymen, and diet in such places where there is good
30 company of the nation where he traveleth. Let him, upon his removes from one place to another, procure recommendation to some person of quality residing in the place whither he removeth; that he may use his favor in those things he desireth to see or know. Thus he may abridge his travel with much profit. As for the acquaintance which is to be sought in travel; that which is most of all profitable is acquaintance with the secretaries and employed men of ambassadors: for
35 so in traveling in one country he shall suck the experience of many. Let him also see and visit eminent persons in all kinds, which are of great name abroad; that he may be able to tell how the life agreeth with the fame. For quarrels, they are with care and discretion to be avoided. They are commonly for mistresses, healths, place, and words. And let a man beware how he keepeth company with choleric and quarrelsome persons; for they will engage him into their own quarrels.
40 When a traveler returneth home, let him not leave the countries where he hath traveled altogether behind him; but maintain a correspondence by letters with those of his acquaintance which are of most worth. And let his travel appear rather in his discourse than his apparel or gesture; and in his discourse let him be rather advised in his answers, than forward to tell stories; and let it appear that he doth not change his country manners for those of foreign parts; but only prick in
45 some flowers of that he hath learned abroad into the customs of his own country.

1A. The metaphor in paragraph 2 of passage 1 suggests that
   A. the devil burned down the fence to harass the landowner.
   B. the man who owns the fence is selling his soul to the devil.
   C. the surveyor is angry about losing his fence to a fire.
   D. building fences and developing land is evil.
   E. the smoke from the burning fence is making the sky dark.

1B. In paragraph 2, passage 1, the miser is described as
   A. conducting a satanic ritual among witches.
   B. oblivious to the beauty of the nature surrounding him.
   C. weary of the toils of tending his land on the prairie.
   D. a surveyor of property.
   E. reluctant to confine himself to fenced boundaries.

2A. According to lines 32-42 of the first passage, the author thinks very little of
   A. the beauty of nature.
   B. undeveloped countryside.
   C. the benefits of village life.
   D. walking through woods instead of on roads.
   E. simple curiosities.

2B. The source of ills among villagers, according to the author, is
   A. too much travel, which makes them weary.
   B. the reason the word *village* comes from a root that means *villain*.
   C. diseases brought into their villages from travelers.
   D. a lack of fences, which causes frequent property disputes.
   E. their confinement to one place while witnessing others in transit.

3A. Choose the statement that best exemplifies the following quote from passage 1.

"To enjoy a thing exclusively is commonly to exclude yourself from the true enjoyment of it."

A. Many people feel guilty when given the opportunity to enjoy themselves.
B. Someone who builds a nice fence will soon fail to notice it.
C. The wealthy squander their fortunes on wildlife conservation causes.
D. Parks require so much work to maintain that no one gets to enjoy them.
E. Cities build wonderful parks, but disallow people to walk on the grass.

3B. Choose the situation that best parallels your answer to question 3A.
A. charging admission to see a movie
B. finding an undiscovered island paradise
C. owning a great masterpiece but not allowing anyone to see it
D. eating the same meal every day of the year
E. discovering a gold mine and selling off shares of it

4A. In passage 1, the author's attitude toward the achievements of mankind can be described as one of
A. dismissiveness.
B. rudeness.
C. contempt.
D. happiness.
E. praise.

4B. The author of passage 1 would agree with which of the following statements?
A. Man is champion over nature.
B. Having a plan is very important to travel.
C. A place takes on the characteristics and expectations of its name.
D. Politics is one of the few forces as potent as that of nature.
E. Man cannot improve upon nature.

5A. The purpose of passage 2 is
A. to retort.
B. to defend European culture.
C. to brag about wealth.
D. to dissuade from travel.
E. to counsel.

5B. The most suitable title for passage 2 would be
A. Freedom of Travel.
B. Finding the Self Through Travel.
C. How to Travel Wisely.
D. Escaping Civilization.
E. The Importance of the Journey.

6A. According to passage 2, which is *not* a requirement for a young person traveling abroad?
    A. fluency in the language of one's destination
    B. a book about the destination
    C. a servant or guide
    D. a means of defending oneself
    E. having a diary

6B. To Francis Bacon, travel should be
    A. a very controlled experience.
    B. a reason to abandon, temporarily, one's own culture.
    C. a source of good stories of adventure.
    D. spontaneous and unplanned.
    E. only within a nation that speaks the traveler's language.

7A. As used in line 28 of passage 2, *adamant* means
    A. a way to save money.
    B. an inflexible quality.
    C. a choleric person.
    D. a source of attraction.
    E. a lack of understanding.

7B. According to Bacon's advice, the act of *acquaintance* is
    A. best limited to one's own countrymen.
    B. best used for business or trading.
    C. most valuable if done randomly.
    D. to be avoided.
    E. desirable in general.

8A. Which of the following quotes from passage 2 is in direct conflict with the ideology of passage 1?
    A. "TRAVEL, in the younger sort, is a part of education…" (line 1)
    B. "It is a strange thing, that in sea voyages, where there is nothing to be seen but sky and sea, men should make diaries…" (lines 7-8)
    C. "Let diaries therefore be brought in use." (line 10)
    D. "As for triumphs, masks, feasts, weddings…men need not be put in mind of them…" (lines 19-21)
    E. "For quarrels, they are with care and discretion to be avoided." (line 37)

8B. Based on your answer to question 8A, Francis Bacon, the author of passage 2, would most resemble which figure from Thoreau's essay?
    A. Thoreau himself
    B. Americus Vespucius
    C. the miser who cannot see "heaven"
    D. the surveyor "devil"
    E. one of the villagers

9A. Which choice best describes the authors' preferences in travel destinations?
    A.   The author of passage 2 prefers traveling to centers of culture abroad, while the author of passage 1 prefers to avoid the public.
    B.   The author of passage 1 prefers nature to civilization, while the author of passage 2 appreciates manmade buildings and objects.
    C.   The author of passage 1 has a deep desire to travel abroad.
    D.   The author of passage 2 would probably sleep comfortably in a tent.
    E.   The author of passage 2 has a greater sense of social propriety than the author of passage 1.

9B. The authors of the passages would agree that
    A.   it is important to designate a travel destination.
    B.   people should maintain journals wherever they go.
    C.   cities and monuments are the best destinations for travelers.
    D.   some form of travel in one's life is important.
    E.   no one needs a guide to enjoy a trip.

10. Passage 1 would be best classified as which one of the following genres?
    A.   history
    B.   philosophy
    C.   humor
    D.   science
    E.   poetry

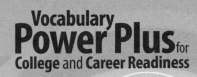

Review Lessons 10-12

Exercise I

Inferences

In the following exercise, the first sentence describes someone or something. Infer information from the first sentence, and then choose the word from the Word Bank that best completes the second sentence.

panacea	intransigent	largesse	requisite
perquisite	compunction	probity	malaise

1. Working as an assistant greenskeeper at the country club golf course involved tough labor during the hot summer, but Jeff didn't mind because he got to play golf for free.

    From this sentence, we can infer that free golf was a[n] _____ to Jeff's job at the golf course.

2. Because Pete always managed to avoid paying for his share of the tab when he and his friends went out to eat, his friends stopped inviting him along when they went out.

    From this sentence, we can infer that Pete took advantage of his friends' _____ too often.

3. The spoiled child refused to leave the toy store without the expensive playset and had to be dragged out by his mother, with help from the store's security guard.

    From this sentence, we can infer that the _____ child threw a tantrum over the toy.

4. Mr. White swore that he was sorry and ashamed for having caused the accident, but the fact that he continued to his party after the wreck, rather than checking on the condition of the victim, made it difficult to believe his statement.

    From this sentence, we can infer that Mr. White failed to show any _____ for having caused the accident.

5. Tara is a hypochondriac, so every time she experiences even the mildest symptoms of a cold or an allergy, she assumes that she has contracted some incurable, fatal, tropical disease.

    From this sentence, we can infer that Tara can't experience general _____ without thinking that she is dying.

Exercise II

Related Words

Some of the vocabulary words from Lessons 10 through 12 have related meanings. Complete the following sentences by choosing the word that best fits the context, based on information you infer from the use of the italicized word. Some word pairs will be antonyms, some will be synonyms, and some will simply be words often used in the same context.

1. Before the citizens had a chance to _____ in having a brand new seaport, a horde of raiders descended from their mountain hideout and *depredated* the village, leaving it in shambles.
    A. condescend
    B. wont
    C. perambulate
    D. indolent
    E. revel

2. The supermodel's apparent _____ was, in actuality, a *veneer* of heavy makeup and photo-editing software.
    A. compunction
    B. propensity
    C. sepulcher
    D. pulchritude
    E. physiognomy

3. Though he was the head butler of the estate, Claude felt more like a[n] _____ than a *majordomo* because his employer demanded large-scale parties featuring popular entertainers at least a few times a year.
    A. solecism
    B. cortege
    C. impresario
    D. canard
    E. etymology

4. Meagan's _____ for solitude made her *wont* to turn down invitations to big parties.
    A. propensity
    B. pulchritude
    C. sepulcher
    D. crescendo
    E. malaise

5. Making an *assiduous* effort to save lives was part of the firefighter's job description, but not one of the _____ rescuers was expected to charge into the fiery derelict from which escape was unlikely.
   A. intransigent
   B. dogged
   C. disingenuous
   D. requisite
   E. tacit

6. The talkshow host likes to _____ about a controversial topic at the start of the show, and then invite guests who disagree with him to argue on the air, creating *polemical* entertainment.
   A. depredate
   B. perambulate
   C. rhapsodize
   D. perquisite
   E. revel

7. Mayor Owen began to miss the simplicity and anonymity of his former _____ life, before fame and publicity had forced him to make *circuitous* statements about his opinions, lest he offend someone and appear on the front page of tomorrow's newspaper.
   A. assiduous
   B. voluble
   C. condescending
   D. demotic
   E. bellicose

8. Among the many _____ of the princess's royal status was a *cortege* of lady's maids to attend her every need.
   A. propensities
   B. compunctions
   C. sepulchers
   D. pulchritudes
   E. perquisites

9. The _____ stock broker offered a *canard* about crop failures to explain why his investors had lost money for the second year in a row.
   A. disingenuous
   B. condescending
   C. bellicose
   D. intransigent
   E. dogged

10. Thurston's _____ for having lived so many years in decadence and luxury inspired his *largesse* later in life, when he used his fortune to build schools and hospitals in the poorest cities.
    A. circumlocution
    B. compunction
    C. majordomo
    D. veneer
    E. perquisite

Exercise III

Deeper Meanings

Choose a word to replace the italicized word in each sentence. All of the possible choices for each sentence have similar definitions, but the correct answer will have a connotation that best suits the context. For example, the words "delete," "destroy," and "obliterate" all mean "to remove or wipe out," but no one would ever say, "I destroyed the name from the document." The correct choice will be the word that has the best specific meaning and does not render the sentence awkward in tone or content. When choices seem close, look for a clue in the context that makes one choice better than the other.

Note that the correct answer is not always the primary vocabulary word from the lesson.

lying	illness	umbrage	silent	stressed
bellicose	plague	hurt	tacit	calculating

1. Although there was no specific rule about parking spaces, there was a[n] *secret* understanding that the manager got to park in the spot closest to the front door.

    Better word: _____

2. The governor warned the public that if the deadly virus were not contained through quarantine, the ensuing *malaise* could wipe out half the population.

    Better word: _____

3. Bridget was the daughter of immigrants, so she took *sadness* at the comedian's joke about foreigners.

    Better word: _____

4. The *uptight* spectators at the boxing match screamed insults at the referee.

    Better word: _____

5. The *disingenuous* suspect in the robbery case told the police that he had been out of town, but it was clearly his face on the surveillance camera footage.

    Better word: _____

Exercise IV

Crossword Puzzle

Use the clues to complete the crossword puzzle. The answers consist of vocabulary words from Lessons 10 through 12.

Across

4. like air, food, and water is to survival, for example
5. a real like of an activity
7. like giving to charity
10. too many words; not enough info
13. eyes, ears, nose, mouth, eyebrows, etc.
14. spending hours on the phone
15. never giving up
16. like King Kong

Down

1. around and around
2. how a mummy looks
3. where you might find a mummy
6. not doing anything but sleeping on the couch
8. what you do if you run out of gasoline
9. Let him manage it!
10. It grows louder and louder.
11. like a full moon at night
12. followers who help you
13. a so-called "wonder drug"

Exercise V

Subject Prompts

Here is a writing prompt similar to the one you will find on the writing portion of an assessment test. Follow the instructions below and write a brief, efficient essay.

It is no secret that cigarette smoke is not good for you. Recent years have seen smoking bans *instituted* in bars, restaurants, and even public parks and sidewalks in some areas. As anti-tobacco groups continue to press governments to enact further bans, however, even nonsmokers are beginning to show signs of resistance, asking whether the bans are exceeding the primary purpose of protecting nonsmokers and instead are becoming a way to enforce the will of nonsmokers upon smokers. If smokers are hurting no one but themselves, then who has the right to make them stop?

Similarly, if it is acceptable to protect smokers from themselves, where do the bans end? Does alcohol get banned next? Processed sugar? Fried food? All these things have a deleterious effect on health. Neither do the bans need to end with food and drugs: many communities ban what they label as risky behavior, such as riding motorcycles without helmets, or not wearing seatbelts while driving cars.

Sometimes, bans are justified as necessary in order to save money for everyone by preventing situations requiring chronic medical care that cumulatively drive up the cost of health insurance. Is that the type of cost, though, that should be regulated on behalf of stakeholders? Does it intrude upon basic freedoms, or, specifically, everyone's right to the pursuit of happiness?

Is it good sense or is it tyranny to restrict freedom in order to protect people from themselves? Think of a ban on a food, drug, activity, or behavior that you feel is either vital to the community or entirely unnecessary. Write a letter to your local representative explaining your position. Your letter should identify the ban or proposed ban and present an argument as to whether or not the ban is a waste of taxpayer resources. Use examples, scenarios, experiences, or your own observations to support your argument.

Thesis: Write a *one-sentence* response to the above assignment. Make certain this single sentence offers a clear statement of your position.

Example: Motorcycle helmet laws are well intended, but laws that absolve people of responsibility for themselves are unrealistic demands for obedience by lawmakers.

_____

_____

Organizational Plan: List at least three subtopics you will use to support your main idea. This list is your outline.

1. _____

2. _____

3. _____

Draft: Following your outline, write a good first draft of your essay. Remember to support all of your points with examples, facts, references to reading, etc.

Review and Revise: Exchange essays with a classmate. Using the scoring guide for Sentence Formation and Variety on page 274, score your partner's essay (while he or she scores yours). Focus on sentence structure and the use of language conventions. If necessary, rewrite your essay to improve the sentence structure and/or your use of language.

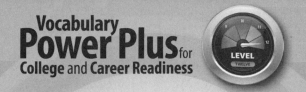
Lesson Thirteen

1. **discretionary** (di skresh´ ə ner ē) *adj.* left to one's own judgment
   Part of the grant included funds to be used specifically for research, but the
   remainder of the funds were for *discretionary* use.
   syn: elective; nonobligatory; unrestricted   *ant: mandatory; obligatory*

2. **flummox** (flum´ uks) *v.* to confuse; to perplex
   The student's profound question *flummoxed* both the professor and the class.
   syn: bewilder; baffle   *ant: clarify; simplify*

3. **punctilious** (pɔnk til´ ē əs) *adj.* attentive to details in conduct or action
   The *punctilious* reader frequently contacted publishers to point out typographical
   errors in books.
   syn: conscientious; particular; meticulous   *ant: careless; inattentive*

4. **turpitude** (tûr´ pi tōōd) *n.* wickedness; vileness
   In the lawless frontier town, newcomers were often shocked by the *turpitude* of the
   residents and patrons.
   syn: depravity; wantonness; decadence   *ant: purity; goodness*

5. **implicate** (im´ pli kāt) *v.* to involve or connect unfavorably
   Jeff *implicated* his friend in the crime by hiding in the friend's basement.
   syn: entangle; incriminate   *ant: extricate; dissociate*

6. **florid** (flôr´ id) *adj.* rosy or red in color
   His face turned a *florid* shade when he became angry.
   syn: ruddy; reddish; flushed

7. **conflagration** (kon flə grā´ shən) *n.* a large, destructive fire
   The *conflagration* that began with a scented candle reduced the entire city block to
   ashes.
   syn: blaze; inferno

8. **draconian** (drā kō´ nē ən) *adj.* extremely harsh; very severe
   The *draconian* rules and punishments at the prison are intended to prevent violence.
   syn: callous; merciless   *ant: lenient*

9. **unpalatable** (un pal´ ə tə bəl) *adj.* unpleasant to the taste or the mind
   The movie director deleted a scene that he thought would be *unpalatable* to certain
   audiences.
   syn: displeasing; objectionable; offensive   *ant: pleasing; agreeable*

10. **analgesic** (an əl jē´ zik) *n.* a medication to reduce or eliminate pain
I took an *analgesic* to relieve my headache.
syn: painkiller   *ant: irritant*

11. **moribund** (môr´ ə bund) *adj.* near death; about to die
The *moribund* patient asked his niece to come closer to hear his last request.
syn: dying; perishing   *ant: thriving; flourishing*

12. **histrionics** (his trē on´ iks) *n.* exaggerated emotional behavior
Jane was prepared for her parents' *histrionics* when she announced her engagement
to a man they detested.
syn: theatrics; dramatics; hysterics

13. **noisome** (noi´ səm) *adj.* disgusting; offensive to the senses
Despite its *noisome* odor, the imported cheese is supposedly very tasty.
syn: nauseating; fetid   *ant: delightful; pleasing*

14. **veritable** (ver´ i tə bəl) *adj.* authentic; genuine
The apple tree was a *veritable* feast for the hungry deer.
syn: indubitable; bona fide   *ant: bogus; counterfeit*

15. **fractious** (frak´ shəs) *adj.* unruly; disruptive
The *fractious* man always had something to complain about during town meetings.
syn: stubborn; difficult   *ant: temperate*

Exercise I

Words in Context

From the list below, supply the words needed to complete the paragraph. Some words will not be used.

veritable   implicate   histrionics   unpalatable
florid   punctilious   turpitude

1. Two consecutive nights of Shakespearean theater was a[n] _____ prize for Winona, who prefers the realism of classical actors to the _____ of most television actors. _____ members of the audience, such as Winona, noticed that good actors can even make their faces turn _____ with rage or great sadness. Winona often wonders if actors rely upon _____ personal memories to fuel the negative emotions they portray on the stage.

From the list below, supply the words needed to complete the paragraph. Some words will not be used.

veritable   discretionary   moribund   draconian
analgesic   flummox   noisome

2. Randy's decision to go camping was entirely _____, but after the experience, he knew that he wouldn't be returning to the great outdoors again in the near future. On the first day, a bee stung him near his eye and caused it to swell shut. That night, as he applied a topical _____ to reduce the pain of the sting, he was overwhelmed by the _____ odor of a skunk—a skunk in his tent.

    Once he'd taken an emergency bath in the river, after being sprayed by the skunk, Randy helped his family pack up the car and leave, three days early. Randy's bad luck on the trip _____ him; he had never had such a miserable time in the wilderness. He thought that the trip might have renewed his _____ sense of adventure after working eight years in an office cubicle as a computer network administrator, but instead, it caused him to think of how great it would be to go home to a clean shower, relax on the sofa, and maybe watch a movie in his skunk- and insect-free living room.

From the list below, supply the words needed to complete the paragraph. Some words will not be used.

implicate   florid   conflagration   fractious
turpitude   draconian   discretionary

3. Police suspected arson as the cause of the _____ that destroyed the apartment building, and they were thankful that the criminal's _____ had not killed anyone. A massive investigation quickly produced several suspects in the case, one of whom was _____ in the crime by mysterious burns on his hands, as though he had been too close to open flames. When the name of the suspect leaked to the general public, police had to restrain a[n] _____ mob from destroying his house in an attempt to inflict some sort of _____ justice on the man.

Exercise II

Sentence Completion

Complete the sentence in a way that shows you understand the meaning of the italicized vocabulary word.

1. You can inadvertently start a *conflagration* if you…

2. Few people were capable of surviving the *draconian* conditions of…

3. The wine had a deep, *florid* color resembling that of…

4. The *punctilious* artist was famous for his tiny…

5. The *turpitude* of a few elected officials has the potential to…

6. The previously calm peace talks turned into a *veritable* shouting match when…

7. Jason winced at the *noisome* sight of…

8. The school will provide sports equipment, but players have the *discretionary* option to…

9. "This is *unpalatable*," gasped the chef after…

10. The teacher asked the angry drama student to save her *histrionics* for…

11. The boss assumed full responsibility for the mistake even though he could have *implicated*…

12. Some say that publishing books on paper is a *moribund* practice because digital texts will…

13. The *fractious* patrons of the tavern near the wharf were known to…

14. Jokingly, the identical twins sometimes *flummoxed* their parents by…

15. The doctor prescribed an *analgesic* to…

Exercise III

Roots, Prefixes, and Suffixes

Study the entries and answer the questions that follow.

The root *hib* means "have" or "hold."
The roots *cept* and *capt* mean "to take" or "to seize."
The prefix *in–* means "in."
The prefix *ex–* means "out."
The prefix *de–* means "away from."
The prefix *pre–* means "before."
The prefix *re–* means "back" or "again."
The prefix *con–* means "together."

1. Using *literal* translations as guidance, define the following words without using a dictionary.

    A. except   D. deception
    B. inhibit   E. exhibition
    C. precept   F. reception

2. What word comes from the *hib* root and means "to forbid"?

3. If you _____ someone's mail, then you bolde it before that person receives it; however, it is illegal to take someone's mail, so the police might attempt to _____ you and put you in jail.

4. After you pay a bill, you might *take back* a document that proves that you paid. This document is called a[n] _____.

5. List as many words as you can think of that contain the prefix *pre–*.

Exercise IV

Inference

Complete the sentence by inferring information about the italicized word from its context.

1. If the concert crowd becomes *fractious*, the police might…

2. The Joneses knew that their son needed discipline, but they were afraid that the *draconian* rules at the military academy would…

3. Some people believe that wearing a helmet when riding a motorcycle should be *discretionary* for riders, but others believe that…

Exercise V

Writing

Here is a writing prompt similar to the one you will find on the writing portion of an assessment test.

Plan and write an essay based on the following statement:

> The superior man understands what is right; the inferior man understands what will sell.
>
> —Confucius (551–479 B.C.)

Assignment: The Chinese philosopher Confucius was said to have knowledge beyond the ages. In an essay, explain the meaning of the quotation and how it might apply to a modern situation or person. Support your essay using evidence from your reading, studies, or observations and experience.

Thesis: Write a *one-sentence* response to the above assignment. Make certain this single sentence offers a clear statement of your position.

Example: Though Confucius lived long before modern philosophies involving enterprise and entrepreneurship, he knew that financial success is not always a measure of moral or spiritual status.

_____

_____

Organizational Plan: List at least three subtopics you will use to support your main idea. This list is your outline.

1. _____

2. _____

3. _____

Draft: Following your outline, write a good first draft of your essay. Remember to support all of your points with examples, facts, references to reading, etc.

Review and Revise: Exchange essays with a classmate. Using the scoring guide for Development on page 272, score your partner's essay (while he or she scores yours). Focus on the development of ideas and the use of language conventions. If necessary, rewrite your essay to incorporate more (or more relevant) support and/or improve your use of language.

Exercise VI

English Practice

Identifying Sentence Errors

Identify the grammatical error in each of the following sentences. If the sentence contains no error, select answer choice E.

1. Many students <u>look much</u> different <u>than</u> they did last <u>semester; it's</u> probably because
         (A)   (B)   (C)
    of <u>their new outfits.</u>   <u>No error</u>
         (D)   (E)

2. Both my <u>brother-in-laws</u> <u>work</u> at the same <u>company, and</u> they are trying to get me
              (A)   (B)   (C)
    <u>an interview</u> for a job there.   <u>No error</u>
       (D)   (E)

3. <u>Would you please</u> tell the delivery <u>person to sit</u> the packages on the <u>kitchen table?</u>
        (A)   (B)   (C)
    <u>I'll pay him after I find my purse.</u>   <u>No error</u>
          (D)   (E)

4. <u>All members of the volunteer</u> fire company, and even their dog, <u>received a</u>
           (A)   (B)
    commendation from the mayor for <u>its enormous</u> efforts during the <u>fund-raising drive.</u>
                                          (C)   (D)
    <u>No error</u>
      (E)

5. If I <u>had brought</u> enough money, I definitely <u>would have purchased</u> the car I wanted
          (A)   (B)
    at last <u>week's auction</u> in <u>Marvell, New York.</u>   <u>No error</u>
          (C)   (D)   (E)

Improving Sentences

The underlined portion of each sentence below contains some flaw. Select the answer choice that best corrects the flaw.

6. If you pay close attention to what I actually say, <u>you will be able to understand my instructions more perfectly.</u>
    A. you might be able to understand my instructions more perfectly.
    B. it will be an easy time understanding my instructions.
    C. you will understand my instructions perfectly and ably.
    D. you will be able to understand my instructions perfectly.
    E. my instructions will be able to be understood by you perfectly.

7. <u>My father objects to me playing football because of the dangers</u> inherent in any contact sport.
    A. My father objects to my playing football because of the dangers
    B. My father objects to playing football because of the dangers
    C. My father objects to me playing because of the dangers in football, which are
    D. Because of the dangers, my father objects to me playing football
    E. My father objects to football because of the dangers

8. The coach awarded the "Most Improved Player" award to both of the seniors on the <u>team, my cousin and I.</u>
    A. team, I and my cousin.
    B. team my cousin and me.
    C. team, my cousin and me.
    D. team: my cousin and I.
    E. team, meaning me and my cousin.

9. <u>The principal said that everyone, who is going on the trip to New York, must have a signed parent-permission slip.</u>
    A. The principal said that everyone who is going on the trip to New York, must have a signed parent-permission slip.
    B. The principal said that everyone, who is going on the trip to New York must have a signed parent-permission slip.
    C. The principal said, "Everyone, who is going on the trip to New York, must have a signed parent permission slip."
    D. The principal said that everyone who is going on the trip to New York must have a signed parent permission slip.
    E. In order to go on the trip to New York, the principal said that everybody needed a signed parent permission slip.

10. The physician says that <u>there is always the possibility that the cancer might return, but so far, there has been no signs of a recurrence.</u>
    A. there was always the possibility that the cancer might return, but so far, there has been no signs of a recurrence.
    B. there is always the possibilities that the cancer might return, but so far, there has been no signs of any recurrence.
    C. there is always the possibility that the cancer might return, but so far, there was no signs of a recurrence.
    D. there is always the possibility that the cancer might return, but so far, there have been no signs of a recurrence.
    E. there always is the possibility that the cancer might return but so far there has been not any sign of it recurring.

Lesson Fourteen

1. **virulent** (vir´ yə lənt) *adj.* extremely infectious or poisonous
   The hospital used an incinerator to destroy any *virulent* waste.
   syn: venomous; toxic   *ant: harmless*

2. **artisan** (är´ ti zən) *n.* a skilled manual worker; a craftsperson
   Mike hired *artisans* from the welder's union to make repairs to the steel holding tanks.

3. **phlegmatic** (fleg mat´ ik) *adj.* calm and unemotional
   The *phlegmatic* man didn't even smile when he saw that he had a winning lottery ticket.
   syn: apathetic; cold; unfeeling   *ant: lively; excited*

4. **moiety** (moi´ ə tē) *n.* a portion or part of something
   Each of the heirs received a *moiety* of his uncle's large estate.
   syn: division; piece

5. **opprobrium** (ə prō´ brē əm) *n.* disgrace; extreme dishonor
   The vandals who desecrated the church were regarded with *opprobrium* in the years following the crime.
   syn: obloquy; ignominy; shame   *ant: esteem; honor; respect*

6. **reciprocate** (ri sip´ rə kāt) *v.* to give in response to receiving something
   The teacher explained that he would *reciprocate* good classroom behavior by grading on a curve.
   syn: match

7. **curmudgeon** (kər muj´ ən) *n.* a stubborn, ill-tempered person
   The old *curmudgeon* sat on the bench at the mall and complained to any one who would listen.
   syn: grouch; bellyacher; killjoy

8. **potentate** (pōt´ ən tāt) *n.* a monarch; one who has great power
   Diamond Jim, a real estate *potentate*, is said to own half of the state.
   syn: sovereign; magnate; king   *ant: peasant; plebian; serf*

9. **tenable** (ten´ ə bəl) *adj.* rationally defensible
   After hearing the defendant's *tenable* reason for stealing the car, the jury found him not guilty.
   syn: sound; viable; credible   *ant: questionable; unbelievable*

10. **indiscernible** (in di sûr´ nə bəl) *adj.* difficult or impossible to discern or perceive
The flaw in the paint was *indiscernible* unless you knew where to look.
syn: imperceptible; indistinguishable; subtle   *ant: evident; noticeable; obvious*

11. **fiduciary** (fə dōō´ shē er ē) *adj.* relating to the governing of property or
estate on behalf of others
Mr. Montaire has the *fiduciary* duty of controlling the family fortune until his nephew
turns eighteen.

12. **protégé** (prō´ tə zhā) *n.* a person under the guidance or training of another
When the famous artist died, his young *protégé* began a long and successful career.
syn: apprentice   *ant: mentor*

13. **boondoggle** (bōōn´ dôg əl) *n.* an unnecessary, wasteful project
Some people believe that building a space station is a *boondoggle* because any
resulting advancements will not offset the cost of construction.

14. **inculcate** (in kəl´ kāt) *v.* to impress upon or teach someone by repetition
The chemistry teacher *inculcated* atomic mass values into her students until they
could recite the numbers without looking at a chart.

15. **repugnant** (ri pug´ nənt) *adj.* offensive; repulsive
The *repugnant* comedian depended on shock, not talent, to make a living.
syn: abhorrent; obnoxious   *ant: appealing; enjoyable; nice*

Exercise I

Words in Context

From the list below, supply the words needed to complete the paragraph. Some words will not be used.

virulent	artisan	protégé	reciprocate
inculcate	fiduciary	indiscernible	

1. To some, Kurt was a simple stonemason who built fireplaces or walls next to driveways, but James, Kurt's young __protégé__, recognized that the aging man was a[n] __artisan__ who worked with natural stones as an artist would work with paint. James had been Kurt's assistant for several years, and during that time, Kurt __inculate__ James's fingers with the many tricks and techniques for creating impressive masonry. In time, James was able to stack and chisel stones and make the natural flaws __indiscernive__ just as Kurt had done for nearly fifty years. Before Kurt passed away, he gave James __fiduciary__ responsibility of the business, pleased that the ancient craft would last for another generation.

From the list below, supply the words needed to complete the paragraph. Some words will not be used.

repugnant	protégé	reciprocate	boondoggle
phlegmatic	tenable	curmudgeon	

2. Agnes scolded her husband of sixty years for being such a[n] __curmudgeon__ "Your constant griping is __repugnant__. We're lucky to have any friends at all, now you wonder why people come to our house but don't bother to __reciprocate__ with invitations of their own."

   Harold didn't look away from the television set. "Yes, dear, you argue logically, and make many __tenable__ points, but sometimes you need to be more tactful." Briefly __phlegmatic__ and unresponsive, Harold exhaled in antipathy, and continued to watch a rerun of his favorite television game show until bursting forth with "You idiot!" at the contestant he knew would lose the big prize at the end.

From the list below, supply the words needed to complete the paragraph. Some words will not be used.

curmudgeon	virulent	boondoggle	moiety
potentate	tenable	opprobrium	

3. P. J. Tucker, the __potentat__ at the helm of the twelfth-largest corporation on Earth, squinted when he saw the company's fiscal data for the quarter. A recent series of acquisitions had turned into a[n] __boondoggle__ because two of the newly acquired companies had failed miserably. P. J. knew that when hints of the loss got out, a[n] __virulent__ rumor would spread through the corporation like a disease. Despite Tucker's willingness to contribute ten million dollars, only a small __moiety__ of his many billions, to his employees as severance pay, the men and women who no longer worked there would view him with __opprobrium__ for years as the wealthy executive who fired thousands just to protect his own fortune.

Exercise II

Sentence Completion

Complete the sentence in a way that shows you understand the meaning of the italicized vocabulary word.

1. The scientist's young *protégé* quickly learned…

2. The piano teacher *inculcated* the major musical scales into her students by…

3. During construction of the mansion, woodworking *artisans* were hired to…

4. Half of Congress felt that the nation had a *tenable* reason for…

5. Mortimer has *fiduciary* responsibility for the charitable organization, so he decides…

6. The nearly *indiscernible* stain on the carpet is noticeable only if you…

7. Kim felt that she deserved at least a *moiety* of credit for the team's championship season because…

8. The *curmudgeon* frequently wrote letters to the editor of the newspaper demanding…

9. During the hurricane, the *phlegmatic* ship captain showed…

10. When George refused to curb his *repugnant* language at work,…

11. Jerry, the spatula *potentate* of the kitchen utensil industry, had…

12. The government quarantined anyone with a *virulent* strain of anthrax because…

13. Constructing a new warehouse while sales were floundering proved to be a *boondoggle* that caused…

14. When his neighbor shovels snow from Joe's sidewalk, Joe *reciprocates* by…

15. Though the man was found innocent in court, he lived in *opprobrium* for years because…

Exercise III

Roots, Prefixes, and Suffixes

Study the entries and answer the questions that follow.

The root *pugn* means "fight."
The root *bell* means "war."
The root *pac* means "peace."
The suffix *–ious* means "full of."
The suffix *–ose* means "full of."
The prefix *re–* means "back" or "again."
The prefix *ante–* means "before."

1. Using *literal* translations as guidance, define the following words without using a dictionary.

    A. repugnant   D. antebellum
    B. pacify   E. pugnacious
    C. belligerent   F. pact

2. The prefix *im–* means "against," so what do you think it means to *impugn* someone's claim?

3. How do you think the Pacific Ocean got its name?

4. Someone who fights back against the rules might be called a[n] _____.

5. List as many words as you can think of that contain the root *pac*.

Exercise IV

Inference

Complete the sentence by inferring information about the italicized word from its context.

1. Customers complained about Jake's *repugnant* behavior at the upscale restaurant when he...

2. If you fail to *reciprocate* when someone treats you well, then that person...

3. Someone who has a *virulent* cold should not...

Exercise V

Critical Reading

Below is a reading passage followed by several multiple-choice questions. Carefully read the passage and choose the best answer for each of the questions.

Joseph Conrad wrote the classic novella Heart of Darkness *in 1899, during the peak of the British Empire. In the story, Marlow, a steamboat captain and the narrator of the tale, recounts his voyage deep into the Congo, which was a Belgian territory at the time. Marlow's mission is to contact Kurtz, an ivory trader who works for the Belgian company at the "inner station." The following excerpt from* Heart of Darkness *begins with Marlow's arrival at a Belgian station thirty miles from the mouth of the Congo.*

    "There's your company's station," said the Swede, pointing to three wooden barrack-like structures on the rocky slope. "I will send your things up. Four boxes did you say? So. Farewell."

    I came upon a boiler wallowing in the grass, then found a path leading up the hill. It turned aside for the boulders, and also for an undersized railway truck lying there on its back with its
5 wheels in the air. One was off. The thing looked as dead as the carcass of some animal. I came upon more pieces of decaying machinery, a stack of rusty rails. To the left a clump of trees made a shady spot, where dark things seemed to stir feebly. I blinked, the path was steep. A horn tooted to the right, and I saw the black people run. A heavy and dull detonation shook the ground, a puff of smoke came out of the cliff, and that was all. No change appeared on the face of the rock.
10 They were building a railway. The cliff was not in the way or anything; but this objectless blasting was all the work going on.

    A slight clinking behind me made me turn my head. Six black men advanced in a file, toiling up the path. They walked erect and slow, balancing small baskets full of earth on their heads, and the clink kept time with their footsteps. Black rags were wound round their loins,
15 and the short ends behind waggled to and fro like tails. I could see every rib, the joints of their limbs were like knots in a rope; each had an iron collar on his neck, and all were connected together with a chain whose bights swung between them, rhythmically clinking. Another report from the cliff made me think suddenly of that ship of war I had seen firing into a continent. It was the same kind of ominous voice; but these men could by no stretch of imagination be called
20 enemies. They were called criminals, and the outraged law, like the bursting shells, had come to them, an insoluble mystery from the sea. All their meager breasts panted together, the violently dilated nostrils quivered, the eyes stared stonily uphill. They passed me within six inches, without a glance, with that complete, death-like indifference of unhappy savages. Behind this raw matter one of the reclaimed, the product of the new forces at work, strolled despondently, carrying a rifle
25 by its middle. He had a uniform jacket with one button off, and seeing a white man on the path, hoisted his weapon to his shoulder with alacrity. This was simple prudence, white men being so much alike at a distance that he could not tell who I might be. He was speedily reassured, and with a large, white, rascally grin, and a glance at his charge, seemed to take me into partnership in his exalted trust. After all, I also was a part of the great cause of these high and just proceedings.
30 Instead of going up, I turned and descended to the left. My idea was to let that chain gang get out of sight before I climbed the hill. You know I am not particularly tender; I've had to strike and to fend off. I've had to resist and to attack sometimes—that's only one way of resisting—without counting the exact cost, according to the demands of such sort of life as I had blundered into. I've seen the devil of violence, and the devil of greed, and the devil of hot desire; but, by
35 all the stars! these were strong, lusty, red-eyed devils, that swayed and drove men—men, I tell you. But as I stood on this hillside, I foresaw that in the blinding sunshine of that land I would become acquainted with a flabby, pretending, weak-eyed devil of a rapacious and pitiless folly. How insidious he could be, too, I was only to find out several months later and a thousand miles farther. For a moment I stood appalled, as though by a warning. Finally I descended the hill,
40 obliquely, towards the tree I had seen.

I avoided a vast artificial hole somebody had been digging on the slope, the purpose of which I found it impossible to divine. It wasn't a quarry or a sandpit, anyhow. It was just a hole. It might have been connected with the philanthropic desire of giving the criminals something to do. I don't know. Then I nearly fell into a very narrow ravine, almost no more than a scar in the
45 hillside. I discovered that a lot of imported drainage pipes for the settlement had been tumbled in there. There wasn't one that was not broken. It was a wanton smashup. At last I got under the trees. My purpose was to stroll into the shade for a moment; but no sooner within than it seemed to me I had stepped into the gloomy circle of some inferno. The rapids were near, and an uninterrupted, uniform, headlong, rushing noise filled the mournful stillness of the grove, where
50 not a breath stirred, not a leaf moved, with a mysterious sound—as though the tearing pace of the launched earth had suddenly become audible.

Black shapes crouched, lay, sat between the trees leaning against the trunks, clinging to the earth, half coming out, half effaced within the dim light, in all the attitudes of pain, abandonment, and despair. Another mine on the cliff went off, followed by a slight shudder of the soil under my
55 feet. The work was going on. The work! And this was the place where some of the helpers had withdrawn to die.

They were dying slowly—it was very clear. They were not enemies, they were not criminals, they were nothing earthly now, nothing but black shadows of disease and starvation, lying confusedly in the greenish gloom. Brought from all the recesses of the coast in all the legality of
60 time contracts, lost in uncongenial surroundings, fed on unfamiliar food, they sickened, became inefficient, and were then allowed to crawl away and rest. These moribund shapes were free as air—and nearly as thin. I began to distinguish the gleam of the eyes under the trees. Then, glancing down, I saw a face near my hand. The black bones reclined at full length with one shoulder against the tree, and slowly the eyelids rose and the sunken eyes looked up at me,
65 enormous and vacant, a kind of blind, white flicker in the depths of the orbs, which died out slowly. The man seemed young—almost a boy—but you know with them it's hard to tell. I found nothing else to do but to offer him one of my good Swede's ship's biscuits I had in my pocket. The fingers closed slowly on it and held—there was no other movement and no other glance. He had tied a bit of white worsted round his neck—Why? Where did he get it? Was it a badge—an
70 ornament—a charm—a propitiatory act? Was there any idea at all connected with it? It looked startling round his black neck, this bit of white thread from beyond the seas.

1A. As used in paragraph 3, *raw matter* refers to people who
   A. are new criminals.
   B. are strong.
   C. are well trained.
   D. are broken in spirit.
   E. are angry.

1B. Which phrase from the context of *raw matter* best supports your answer to question 1A?
   A. "death-like indifference"
   B. "connected together with a chain"
   C. "balancing small baskets of earth on their heads"
   D. "violently dilated nostrils quivered…eyes stared stonily uphill"
   E. "advanced in a file, toiling up the path"

2A. The narrator of the passage is probably
    A.   one of the enslaved workers.
    B.   a white newcomer to the station.
    C.   an official of the colony that he is describing.
    D.   a high-ranking native worker for the station.
    E.   the Swedish captain.

2B. Choose the statement that best describes the implication of the following line, as it applies to the prisoners.

"They were called criminals, and the outraged law, like the bursting shells, had come to them, an insoluble mystery from the sea."

    A.   The prisoners are a sacrifice to the gods of the sea.
    B.   No one is innocent at the inner station.
    C.   The men are labeled criminals but might be innocent.
    D.   Foreigners govern the native people from ships at sea.
    E.   The law is as destructive to the native people as artillery shells are.

3A. Which choice best describes the author's purpose for including the following line?

"After all, I also was a part of the great cause of these high and just proceedings."

    A.   He is demonstrating his own nationalism.
    B.   He is suggesting his relief that the colony is now civilized.
    C.   He is sarcastically criticizing the jurisprudence of the colonies.
    D.   He is mocking the prisoners.
    E.   He is boasting about his high status in the Congo.

3B. Which phrase from lines 32-40 best supports your answer to question 3A?
    A.   "...blinding sunshine of that land..."
    B.   "...these were strong...red-eyed devils..."
    C.   "I've had to resist and to attack sometimes..."
    D.   "...descended the hill..."
    E.   "How insidious he could be..."

4A. As used in line 35, *swayed* most nearly means
    A.   spoke to.
    B.   governed.
    C.   timed.
    D.   staggered.
    E.   hired.

4B. Choose the answer that best explains why the author emphasizes "men" in line 35.
    A.   It implies the lack of women and children at the station.
    B.   The author discriminates based on race.
    C.   It is verbal irony in which the author mocks the will of the enslaved.
    D.   It suggests that there are more prisoners at the station than can be seen.
    E.   It emphasizes the power of the "devils" in charge.

5. The author suggests that the "flabby" devil of "folly" is responsible for the miseries occurring throughout the station. Consider the pointless blasting, the discarded building materials, and the slow deaths of the workers, and choose the "sin" that seems to be the defining characteristic of the "flabby" devil.
    A. murder
    B. laziness
    C. disease
    D. lying
    E. waste

6A. In his use of physical description, the author of the passage suggests that eyes
    A. are often symbolic in literature.
    B. show man's inner nature.
    C. are unimportant to laborers.
    D. reveal one's sins.
    E. require special care in the jungle.

6B. Choose the line from the passage that best supports your answer to question 6A.
    A. "…almost no more than a scar in the hillside."
    B. "…blind, white flicker in the depths of the orbs, which died out slowly."
    C. "…that ship of war I had seen firing into a continent."
    D. "They were dying slowly—it was very clear."
    E. "…blinding sunshine of that land…"

7A. As used in line 42, *divine* most nearly means
    A. mistake.
    B. bless.
    C. deny.
    D. determine.
    E. believe.

7B. How does the artificial hole on the hillside most resemble the blasting of the cliff?
    A. It is an inherently dangerous project.
    B. The foremen do not allow outsiders near the areas.
    C. It was completed for no obvious reason.
    D. Both are objects of greed, according to Marlow.
    E. Only selected prisoners are allowed to perform the work.

8A. In the final paragraph, the narrator declares that the people beneath the trees are not criminals because
    A. they did not have proper trials.
    B. they are political enemies, not criminals.
    C. most of them are from other nations.
    D. the narrator recognizes one of them, and he is not a criminal.
    E. they do not even appear to be people.

8B. Choose the term used to refer to the prisoners (lines 52-62) that best supports your answer to question 8A.
   A. helpers
   B. shapes
   C. moribund
   D. They
   E. earthly

9A. According to the passage, which word best describes the narrator's feelings about the scenes he witnesses?
   A. fear
   B. indifference
   C. pride
   D. horror
   E. confusion

9B. Choose the line from the passage that best supports your answer to question 9A.
   A. "...each had an iron collar on his neck..."
   B. "...made me think suddenly of that ship of war I had seen firing..."
   C. "For a moment I stood appalled, as though by a warning."
   D. "...I found it impossible to divine."
   E. "You know I am not particularly tender..."

10A.Consider the details of the wool scarf worn by the dying prisoner. Based on evidence from the passage, the scarf would be a likely symbol for
   A. the pride that resulted in the prisoner's mistakes.
   B. the Belgians' control over the natives in the African colony.
   C. the prisoner's undying allegiance to his captors.
   D. the prisoner's native culture.
   E. Marlow's misgivings about his trip to the inner station.

10B.Which detail about the scarf best supports your answer to question 10A?
   A. "a badge"
   B. "a bit"
   C. "a propitiatory act"
   D. "an ornament"
   E. "from beyond the sea"

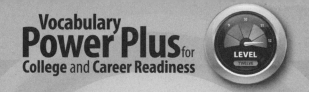
Lesson Fifteen

1. **chthonian** (thō′ nē ən) *adj.* pertaining to the underworld; dwelling in or beneath the surface of the earth
The *chthonian* engraving in the tomb featured a lion guarding the gates of the netherworld.

2. **autonomy** (ô tän′ ə mē) *n.* independence
Vicky enjoys the *autonomy* of being self-employed as a freelance writer.
syn: self-rule; license; sovereignty   *ant: subordination*

3. **puissance** (pwē′ səns) *n.* power; might
You'll need considerable *puissance* to win the game tomorrow, so get plenty of rest.
syn: strength; vigor   *ant: frailty; weakness*

4. **tutelary** (tōōt′ ə ler ē) *adj.* pertaining to guardianship
Donald had enough *tutelary* experience to be a good foster father.
syn: custodial; guardian

5. **malevolent** (mə lev′ ə lənt) *adj.* having ill-will; wishing harm; evil
The burglar turned and ran when he met the *malevolent* stare of a large guard dog.
syn: malicious; sinister; menacing   *ant: benevolent*

6. **peripatetic** (per ə pə tet′ ik) *adj.* traveling, especially by foot
The *peripatetic* wanderer seldom passed through the same town twice.
syn: ambulant; vagabond; nomadic   *ant: stationary*

7. **prominent** (prom′ ə nənt) *adj.* very noticeable or obvious
The trunk is a *prominent* feature of an elephant.
syn: conspicuous; clear   *ant: inconspicuous*

8. **extirpate** (ek′ stər pāt) *v.* to root out or eradicate; to destroy completely
New weeds sprouted faster than Bob could *extirpate* them.
syn: expunge; uproot; exterminate   *ant: generate; propagate*

9. **misanthrope** (mis′ ən thrōp) *n.* one who hates or mistrusts humankind
The *misanthrope* never travels far from his remote cabin, and he threatens anyone who wanders near it.
                                        ant: samaritan

10. **supercilious** (sōō pər sil′ ē əs) *adj.* contemptuous; arrogant
The *supercilious* widow raised her eyebrows and looked away when I greeted her.
syn: haughty; condescending; conceited   *ant: modest; humble*

11. **appellation** (ap ə lā´ shən) *n.* a name, title, or designation
The pre-med student hoped to earn the *appellation* of "Doctor."
syn: denomination; classification

12. **gustatory** (gus´ tə tôr ē) *adj.* relating to the sense of taste
The gourmet dinner lacked the *gustatory* appeal that Julie expected.

13. **coagulate** (kō ag´ yə lāt) *v.* to change or be changed from liquid into a thickened
or solid mass
You should clean the spilled cooking grease before it *coagulates* on the floor.
syn: congeal; solidify; curdle   *ant: liquefy*

14. **scion** (sī´ ən) *n.* descendant; heir
The *scions* of the wealthy industrialist quickly squandered the family fortune.
syn: successor; progeny   *ant: predecessor; ancestor*

15. **jurisprudence** (joor is prōōd´ əns) *n.* the science, philosophy, and application of
the law
The judge had to dismiss the case because of the prosecutor's faulty *jurisprudence*.

Exercise I

Words in Context

From the list below, supply the words needed to complete the paragraph. Some words will not be used.

> gustatory   extirpate   autonomy   misanthrope
> peripatetic   malevolent   chthonian

1. The old _____, convinced that everyone he met had _____ intentions meant to harm him, relocated his home to a remote mountain cabin, far from the civilization he loathed. With the exception of his tools, clothing, rifle, and ammunition, he _____ every possible trace of the outside world from his cabin. Other than his _____ foraging in the wilderness for food or firewood, the hermit never again left the valley or visited the small town eight miles south of the cabin. In a short time, his _____ preferences changed from those of average, domestic meals to the tastes of nuts, berries, and wild game.

From the list below, supply the words needed to complete the paragraph. Some words will not be used.

> puissance   scion   misanthrope   prominent
> autonomy   supercilious   appellation

2. After three years of working at the department store, Mark was the _____ candidate for the promotion to manager. He eagerly anticipated the _____ that accompanied the high-ranking position; there would be no more punch clocks and time cards, and no more _____ boss to belittle or second-guess Mark's decisions. Mark had always been certain that he had the _____ to work his way to the top of the company and eventually become a[n] _____ to the corporate dynasty despite not being a relative of the owner.

From the list below, supply the words needed to complete the paragraph. Some words will not be used.

> peripatetic   chthonian   puissance   coagulate
> tutelary   jurisprudence   appellation

3. Audrey looked at an old photograph of her recently deceased grandfather, taken when he had been a coal miner. Blackened with coal dust and squinting at the sun, her grandfather looked like a[n] _____ creature emerging from its subterranean lair. Audrey, who called her grandfather by the _____ "Papa," missed the wise old man's _____ guidance. Before law school, she and her grandfather had often discussed the way in which _____ had changed from one generation to the next. In the days following the funeral, Audrey's fond memories seemed to _____ into a lump of sadness that weighed heavily on her being.

Exercise II

Sentence Completion

Complete the sentence in a way that shows you understand the meaning of the italicized vocabulary word.

1. When experiencing their first taste of *autonomy*, many young adults…

2. Gina thought that her neighbor was some kind of *misanthrope* because he…

3. The hot, melted candle wax will *coagulate* when…

4. The explorer was surprised to find that the *gustatory* preferences of the natives were…

5. Nancy preferred *peripatetic* vacations to…

6. It took weeks for Wendy to learn everyone's proper *appellation* after she…

7. During a secret meeting in the underground headquarters, the evil genius outlined his *malevolent* plan to…

8. American *jurisprudence* prohibits a person from being permanently imprisoned without…

9. The dictator attempted to *extirpate* any dissidents from the ranks of his army by…

10. The *supercilious* waiter didn't want to serve us because…

11. Millionaires with humble beginnings resented the *scions* of the railroad magnate because they…

12. Donald developed a *tutelary* relationship with his niece because…

13. Jane braved the snowstorm, but she didn't know if she would have the *puissance* to…

14. The ancient Greeks carved a *chthonian* deity into the prow of their warship in order to…

15. One of the most *prominent* factors in identifying the criminal…

Exercise III

Roots, Prefixes, and Suffixes

Study the entries and answer the questions that follow.

The roots *mit* and *miss* mean "send."
The root *duct* means "to lead."
The prefix *dis–* means "away."
The prefix *ad–* means "toward."
The prefix *ab–* means "away from."
The prefix *in–* means "into."
The prefix *trans–* means "across."

1. Using *literal* translations as guidance, define the following words without using a dictionary.

A.	dismiss	D.	abduct
B.	remit	F.	induct
C.	admit	F.	transmission

2. The prefix *per–* means "through," so what does the word *permit* literally mean?

3. The prefix *de–* means "from." If your process of reasoning leads you to an idea, you might call that idea a[n] _____.

4. An *emissary* is someone sent out to deliver a specific message, and a lamp _____, or "sends out" light. We can assume that the *e–* prefix means _____.

5. Iron and copper are good _____ because they can be used to lead electrical current from one place to another.

6. What do you think the word *missile* literally means?

7. List as many words as you can think of that contain the prefix *trans–*.

Exercise IV

Inference

Complete the sentence by inferring information about the italicized word from its context.

1. A *misanthrope* who avoids contact with people might not appreciate it if you...

2. If you fail to *extirpate* the bamboo shoots in your lawn, the plants might...

3. If you underestimate the *puissance* of your enemy, you might...

Exercise V

Writing

Here is a writing prompt similar to the one you will find on the writing portion of an assessment test.

Plan and write an essay based on the following statement:

> "Far better it is to dare mighty things, to win glorious triumphs, even though checkered by failure, than to take rank with those poor spirits who neither enjoy much nor suffer much, because they live in the gray twilight that knows not victory nor defeat."
>
> —Theodore Roosevelt

Assignment: Decide whether you agree or disagree with President Roosevelt's suggestion that it is better to fail than it is never to have tried. In an essay, explain why Roosevelt's statement is realistic or not, and support your argument using an example from history, current events, literature, or your experience or observation.

Thesis: Write a *one-sentence* response to the above assignment. Make certain this single sentence offers a clear statement of your position.

Example: In his bold suggestion to "dare mighty things," Roosevelt wrongly implies that it is shameful to live in timid, "gray twilight"; most people strive to lead lives without extremes because they cannot live comfortably while enduring the constant peril that "glorious triumphs" might induce.

_____

_____

Organizational Plan: List at least three subtopics you will use to support your main idea. This list is your outline.

1. _____

2. _____

3. _____

Draft: Following your outline, write a good first draft of your essay. Remember to support all of your points with examples, facts, references to reading, etc.

Review and Revise: Exchange essays with a classmate. Using the scoring guide for Sentence Formation and Variety on page 274, score your partner's essay (while he or she scores yours). Focus on sentence structure and the use of language conventions. If necessary, rewrite your essay to improve the sentence structure and/or your use of language.

Exercise VI

Improving Paragraphs

Read the following passage and then answer the multiple-choice questions that follow. The questions will require you to make decisions regarding the revision of the reading selection.

1   (1) The yawn—that irritating, ungainly, impolite disruption in board meetings, classrooms, and assembly lines all over the world—is but one of the great mysteries of humankind. (2) Despite centuries of research, not one scientist can say with certainty why, exactly, people yawn. (3) Oh, yes, they theorize; lines of physiologists spout their suppositions: "Excessive carbon dioxide in the lungs!" "Under-stimulated brains!" "A primal response to ward off predators!" (4) Unfortunately, while it would be fantastic if a simple yawn could frighten away a saber-toothed tiger, the real reason for yawning is anyone's guess.

2   (5) People begin expressing their boredom very early in life—even before their born. (6) The fact that fetuses yawn tells researchers that yawning is both involuntary and not due to a general lack of oxygen, since babies in utero do not breath oxygen as adults do. (7) Now, simply determining why babies yawn has become a part of the quest to solve the riddle of yawns. (8) One theory that currently holds water is that yawning releases a chemical called surfactant, a substance that ensures that the alveoli, or tiny air pockets in the lungs, stay open. (9) The production of surfactant is critical to development because it ensures that the lungs of a newborn will be ready to survive outside the womb; however, as everyone knows, the yawning continues well beyond birth.

3   (10) Boring classes, office meetings, lectures, seminars, and traffic jams take quite a toll on brains, and yawning does help to revive brains to better cope with the drudgery of staying awake; however, yawning often strikes at seemingly arbitrary times. (11) Stressful situations often beget yawns, as do colds, allergies, and sinus problems, even strenuous activity can spark excessive yawning. (12) Experts agree that the lungs stretch during yawning, and the stretching prevents the collapse of tiny airways. (13) This might help to explain why yawning that accompanies periods of shallow breathing, such as before and after sleeping, helps more air to enter the respiratory system. (14) More air is good.

4   (15) The seemingly arbitrary nature of yawning has prompted many scientists to suggest that yawning is actually a form of involuntary communication. (16) Both human beings are creatures of imitation and quite receptive to suggestion; fifty-five percent of all people, in fact, will yawn within five minutes after seeing someone else yawn. (17) Reading about yawns also has this effect, as well as talking about them and even thinking about them. (18) Yawns also can express strong antisocial messages. (19) Yawns are widely perceived as rude gestures. (20) They frequently imply boredom, but yawns often accompany feelings of rejection or even anger. (21) Some medical professionals claim that yawning is stimulated by the same chemicals in the brain that effect emotions, moods, and appetites, so perhaps to ancient ancestors, yawns were involuntary, visual signals that alerted people that it was time to seek shelter for the night, which therefore synchronized sleeping patterns. (22) Humans are, after all, social beings.

5   (23) Perhaps someday scientists will find the proper combination of theories that explains yawning once and for all. (24) There seems to be a connection between prenatal yawns producing surfactant and adult yawns filling tiny airways in the lungs, but the ease with which humans will yawn simply because they saw someone else yawn suggests that the act is purely psychosomatic. (25) Despite the many theories and facts pertaining to its origins, the mysterious act of yawning must join the tailbone and the appendix on the list of human anatomical conundrums.

1. Which choice best describes an error in the first sentence of paragraph 2?
   A. subject-verb agreement
   B. unnecessary commas
   C. misuse of *ensures*
   D. incorrect pronoun
   E. double negative

2. Which choice would improve the following sentence from paragraph 2?

   "One theory that currently holds water is that yawning releases a chemical called *surfactant*, a substance that ensures that the alveoli, or tiny air pockets in the lungs, stay open."

   A. Rewrite the sentence to omit the cliché.
   B. Make two sentences out of the original sentence.
   C. Use the sentence as the introduction of the paragraph.
   D. Change *yawning* to *a yawn*.
   E. Place a semicolon after *surfactant*.

3. Which sentence should be deleted from paragraph 3?
   A. sentence 10
   B. sentence 11
   C. sentence 12
   D. sentence 13
   E. sentence 14

4. Correcting which error would fix the second sentence of paragraph 4?
   A. semicolon use
   B. use of *both*
   C. the hyphen in *fifty-five*
   D. missing linking verb
   E. *else* not possessive

5. Which redundant sentence should be removed from paragraph 4?
   A. sentence 15
   B. sentence 16
   C. sentence 17
   D. sentence 19
   E. sentence 20

Vocabulary
PowerPlus for
College and Career Readiness

LEVEL
TWELVE

Review Lessons 13-15

Exercise I

Inferences

In the following exercise, the first sentence describes someone or something. Infer information from the first sentence, and then choose the word from the Word Bank that best completes the second sentence.

moiety	noisome	peripatetic	prominent
artisans	analgesic	indiscernible	autonomy

1. At the height of his sinus infection, Jeremy's headache throbbed so much that he could barely keep his eyes open.

    From this sentence, we can infer that Jeremy could probably use a[n] _____ to alleviate his headache.

2. The company found itself with too many managers and not enough skilled, talented crafters who created new products to sell.

    From this sentence, we can infer that the company needs more _____.

3. Chris does not like working in groups, so he found a job as a forest ranger at a remote outpost, where he operates on his own and makes his own schedule.

    From this sentence, we can infer that Chris enjoys the _____ of his isolated job.

4. Tail fins on the rear fenders of American cars reached their maximum height with the '59 Cadillac Eldorado, which had the tallest fins on a production car.

    From this sentence, we can infer that tall tail fins are a[n] _____ feature of the 1959 Eldorado.

5. A local community group formed in order to fight the construction of a new sewage treatment facility just down the street from a large residential neighborhood.

    From this sentence, we can infer that residents did not welcome the _____ waste plant so close to the neighborhood.

Exercise II

Related Words

Some of the vocabulary words from Lessons 13 through 15 have related meanings. Complete the following sentences by choosing the word that best fits the context, based on information you infer from the use of the italicized word. Some word pairs will be antonyms, some will be synonyms, and some will simply be words often used in the same context.

1. The rocket fuel factory exploded with such _____ that train cars were thrown hundreds of feet from the blast, and it took two weeks for firefighters to extinguish the subsequent *conflagration*.
   A. analgesic
   B. turpitude
   C. puissance
   D. histrionics
   E. opprobrium

2. Mary Lou, a skilled pianist, held a _____ role as a foster mother, and she *inculcated* musicianship in her children by ensuring that they practiced the instruments of their choice every day.
   A. tutelary
   B. supercilious
   C. malevolent
   D. prominent
   E. chthonian

3. The wait staff argued over whose turn it was to attend to the _____ customer who made *supercilious* comments about the food and the service.
   A. prominent
   B. peripatetic
   C. fiduciary
   D. repugnant
   E. virulent

4. The _____ calligrapher adorned documents in beautiful script and ornate flourishes befitting a true *artisan*, though it was not a fast process.
   A. indiscernible
   B. phlegmatic
   C. tenable
   D. unpalatable
   E. punctilious

5. The wealthy family's lawyer maintained _____ control of the estate until the *scions* of the Internet giant reached the age of twenty-one.
   A. fiduciary
   B. repugnant
   C. indiscernible
   D. virulent
   E. tenable

6. General *jurisprudence* mandates the right for even the worst criminals to be defended at trial, but defense lawyers are often received with _____ for doing the job.
   A. protégé
   B. artisan
   C. boondoggle
   D. potentate
   E. opprobrium

7. The students enjoyed their _____ during the class trip to London, where they followed *discretionary* schedules of sightseeing and museum tours at their own leisure.
   A. moiety
   B. curmudgeon
   C. potentate
   D. autonomy
   E. appellation

8. The king ordered his guard to find the rebellious author whose _____ writings had a chance to further incite the *fractious,* starving subjects of the realm.
   A. peripatetic
   B. gustatory
   C. virulent
   D. tutelary
   E. supercilious

9. Pure *turpitude* drove Forrest to do whatever was necessary to get the office promotion, even if it meant spreading _____ rumors about his rivals.
   A. tutelary
   B. supercilious
   C. prominent
   D. malevolent
   E. chthonian

10. Though once she was sociable and beloved by the community, the _____ woman became a cynical *misanthrope* in the last days of her illness, speaking to or trusting no one.
    A. peripatetic
    B. gustatory
    C. moribund
    D. prominent
    E. supercilious

Exercise III

Deeper Meanings

Choose a word to replace the italicized word in each sentence. All of the possible choices for each sentence have similar definitions, but the correct answer will have a connotation that best suits the context. For example, the words "delete," "destroy," and "obliterate" all mean "to remove or wipe out," but no one would ever say, "I destroyed the name from the document." The correct choice will be the word that has the best specific meaning and does not render the sentence awkward in tone or content. When choices seem close, look for a clue in the context that makes one choice better than the other.

Note that the correct answer is not always the primary vocabulary word from the lesson.

liberty	tyrannical	unpalatable	autonomy
malevolent	bad	repugnant	rigid
rotten	mischievous		

1. The teacher had *draconian* rules about turning in assignments on time, but she worked with anyone who truly needed extra help.

    Better word: _____

2. The man's *lame* T-shirt had a vulgar phrase printed on the front; it was a truly terrible choice of shirt to wear to a birthday party for a six-year-old.

    Better word: _____

3. The toddler hatched a[n] *evil* plan to get to the cookies stored above the refrigerator.

    Better word: _____

4. Though he must still report to his boss once a month, Rob enjoys the *sovereignty* of working alone in a remote, Arctic research outpost.

    Better word: _____

5. Too many hot peppers will cause the chili to go from spicy to *gross* because no one will be able to eat it.

    Better word: _____

Exercise IV

Crossword Puzzle

Use the clues to complete the crossword puzzle. The answers consist of vocabulary words from Lessons 13 through 15.

Across

8. a billion dollar study on the effect of music on squirrels
9. what the Colonies wanted from England
10. what Robin is to Batman
11. like activities that wear out shoes
13. personality trait of a villain
14. opposite of a people-person
15. the real thing
16. difficult to tell if it's there or not
17. what a drama queen might display

Down

1. horrible, distasteful
2. the boss's boss
3. two of these for a headache
4. like Ebola, radiation, or snake venom
5. Sure tastes great!
6. guilty or innocent
7. the Chicago Fire
10. plenty of this in a barrel of dynamite
12. like cutting hands off for stealing, just as a warning to others

Exercise V

Subject Prompts

Here is a writing prompt similar to the one you will find on the writing portion of an assessment test. Follow the instructions below and write a brief, efficient essay.

Even during the economic recession toward the end of the first decade of the millennium, the amount of money the United States doled out to foreign nations increased to over $43 billion annually. This increase occurred against a setting of rising unemployment rates, a floundering housing market, heavy US military spending, and declining US manufacturing.

Is it rational to send the money of US taxpayers abroad to assist other nations while unemployed US citizens barely manage to pay mortgages or buy groceries? Should we be helping other nations become more economically competitive, while US schools, plagued with decreasing performance, are forced to cut academic budgets and school programs?

Take a position on whether or not the taxes you pay should be spent for the improvement of foreign nations. Before you decide, consider the benefits of foreign assistance in addition to the detriments; foreign assistance, ideally, is intended to be an investment. Investing in developing nations has the potential to yield economic allies and trading partners. Assisting young governments can prevent political instability and subsequent wars, which are always costly for anyone involved.

Imagine that you have been elected to the office of US senator, and that you have been appointed to the Senate Foreign Relations Committee. You have an opportunity to reform US foreign assistance, but you will need to explain your recommendation. Identify where you stand on the issue and argue for or against increasing foreign spending. Support your argument using at least one example, experience, or observation.

Thesis: Write a *one-sentence* response to the above assignment. Make certain this single sentence offers a clear statement of your position.

Example: Foreign assistance is necessary to the development of young nations, which, in turn, will create a better world and global economy.

_____

_____

Organizational Plan: List at least three subtopics you will use to support your main idea. This list is your outline.

1. _____

2. _____

3. _____

Review and Revise: Exchange essays with a classmate. Using the Holistic scoring guide on page 276, score your partner's essay (while he or she scores yours). If necessary, rewrite your essay to correct the problems noted by your partner.

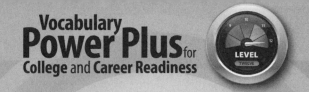
Lesson Sixteen

1. **paladin** (pal´ lə dən) *n.* a heroic champion or leader
   Though he was nothing more than a fictional cartoon character, Captain Justice was an inspiring *paladin* to children everywhere.
   syn: hero   *ant: villain*

2. **nascent** (nā´ sənt) *adj.* emerging; coming into existence
   Jill attributed her *nascent* interest in sailing to her discovery of her seafaring ancestors.
   syn: blooming; fledgling   *ant: dying; withering*

3. **tangential** (tan jen´ shəl) *adj.* merely touching or slightly connected; digressing from the main point
   The chairman asked the board to avoid *tangential* issues during the important meeting.
   syn: nonessential; peripheral   *ant: vital; crucial; relevant*

4. **vicissitude** (vi sis´ i tōōd) *n.* a sudden change or shift in one's life or circumstances
   She claimed that her many *vicissitudes* throughout life had made her a stronger person.
   syn: alteration; variation

5. **matriculate** (mə trik´ yə lāt) *v.* to admit or be admitted into a group or a college
   Sam's grades were high enough for him to *matriculate* at State in the fall.

6. **salubrious** (sə lōō´ brē əs) *adj.* healthful
   Each day, after lunch, Tammy took a *salubrious* walk through the park.
   syn: salutary; wholesome   *ant: harmful; useless*

7. **sine qua non** (sin i kwä nän´) *n.* something essential; a prerequisite
   Good communication is the *sine qua non* of a productive workplace.
   syn: must; requirement; necessity   *ant: option*

8. **bourgeois** (boor zhwä´) *adj.* relating to the middle class
   Adam hoped to become wealthy and abandon his *bourgeois* life.

9. **arcane** (är kān´) *adj.* known or understood by only a few; mysterious
   The alchemist claimed to know an *arcane* formula for turning iron into gold.
   syn: secret; obscure; esoteric   *ant: famous; obvious; exoteric*

10. **squelch** (skwelch) *v.* to suppress; squash
The candidate desperately tried to *squelch* rumors that he had once been arrested.
syn: extinguish; muffle; thwart   *ant: promote; support; enact*

11. **trenchant** (tren´ chənt) *adj.* effectively keen and forceful in thought or expression
The expert's *trenchant* comments silenced his critics.
syn: cutting; forthright   *ant: ambiguous; lenient; insipid*

12. **indefeasible** (in di fē´ zə bəl) *adj.* not capable of being undone or voided
When times were rough, Teresa found comfort in the *indefeasible* love of her parents.
syn: immutable; unremitting; constant   *ant: varying; irregular;*
                                                      temporary

13. **mercurial** (mər kyōōr´ ē əl) *adj.* quickly changing; volatile
Frank acted like an entirely different person sometimes because of his *mercurial* personality.
syn: fickle; unstable   *ant: unchanging; stable*

14. **exculpate** (ek´ skəl pāt) *v.* to clear of guilt; to declare innocent
The judge dismissed the case when new evidence *exculpated* the defendant.
syn: exonerate; acquit; vindicate   *ant: condemn; accuse; indict*

15. **tyro** (tī´ rō) *n.* a beginner; novice
Until he learned the trade, the *tyro* was advised to keep his ears open and his thoughts to himself.
syn: amateur; neophyte; rookie   *ant: expert; master; guru*

Exercise I

Words in Context

From the list below, supply the words needed to complete the paragraph. Some words will not be used.

tyro	arcane	nascent	sine qua non
vicissitude	matriculate	bourgeois	

1. Steve cannot complain about where the _____ of life led him. His excellent academic record allowed him to _____ into the university of his choice, and he now enjoys a[n] _____, almost upper-class lifestyle, despite having grown up in abject poverty. Steve earns his living as an anthropologist studying the _____ data of lost civilizations, though a few of his recent finds have been worth millions and have given him a[n] _____ interest in treasure hunting.

From the list below, supply the words needed to complete the paragraph. Some words will not be used.

vicissitude	tangential	tyro	squelch
exculpate	trenchant	paladin	

2. Debbie had the _____ qualities of a good leader, but she was still a[n] _____ at charity work and never expected to become the prime _____ of any specific cause. It was true that she had always had _____ interests in eliminating poverty in underdeveloped nations, but until she realized how rewarding the work was, she had _____ any interest in making a career out of it.

From the list below, supply the words needed to complete the paragraph. Some words will not be used.

indefeasible	arcane	sine qua non	mercurial
exculpate	salubrious	bourgeois	

3. "An extra pair of socks is a[n] _____ in making it to the end of this hike," said Mr. Bronson, the wilderness guide. "Your feet will be your greatest asset when we're twenty miles from civilization, and you'll need to exercise _____ habits to keep them in good shape for the duration of the week. Saying 'I forgot to pack them,' if you run out of socks or, 'They're new,' if your boots are too tight will not _____ you on this hike. You will have to continue walking!" The group understood the guide's concern; there were enough natural hazards to worry about, such as the _____ weather and poisonous snakes, without complicating matters more by making _____ mistakes on the trail.

Exercise II

Sentence Completion

Complete the sentence in a way that shows you understand the meaning of the italicized vocabulary word.

1. The prestigious university refused to *matriculate* the student until...

2. Denny is a *tyro* at riding a bicycle, so he...

3. The princess, detained deep within the castle, hoped that someday a *paladin* would...

4. Some people prefer a *bourgeois* life to a wealthy life because they do not...

5. The reporter wanted a straight answer, but the public relations clerk gave only *tangential* statements that...

6. According to the Declaration of Independence, life, liberty, and the pursuit of happiness are *indefeasible* rights that cannot...

7. The doctor told Phil to find a *salubrious* hobby that...

8. A healthy breakfast is a *sine qua non* for...

9. The eccentric professor took pride in his *arcane* knowledge that included...

10. Our increasingly technological society must protect itself against *nascent* threats of...

11. The old storyteller had such a *trenchant* way of speaking that...

12. To limit media interference during the investigation, the police *squelched*...

13. On some days, the *mercurial* teacher was pleasant and soft spoken, but...

14. Despite experiencing the *vicissitudes* of life during the war, every member of the family...

15. After the court *exculpated* Jack of any wrongdoing, he...

Roots, Prefixes, and Suffixes

Study the entries and answer the questions that follow.

The root *path* means "feel" or "suffer."
The root *pass* means "endure" or "suffer."
The prefix *in*– means "not."
The prefix *syn*– means "together with."
The prefix *com*– means "together with."
The prefix *tele*– means "across."
The prefix *a*– means "not" or "none."
The suffix *–ic* means "pertaining to."

1. Using *literal* translations as guidance, define the following words without using a dictionary.

   A. compassion   D. telepathy
   B. impassive   E. apathy
   C. sympathy   F. passive

2. The prefix *en*– or *em*– means "in" or "into," and the suffix *–y* means "a state, condition, or quality." What does the word *empathy* mean?

3. The word *pathetic* literally means _____.

4. *Passion* is another word for a strong _____.

5. List as many words as you can think of that contain the root *path*.

Inference

Complete the sentence by inferring information about the italicized word from its context.

1. If you are still a *tyro* at swimming long distances, you might think twice about…

2. Tom's personality changed with each *vicissitude* he endured because he…

3. A *nascent* way of doing something will probably not become popular until…

Exercise V

Critical Reading

Below is a pair of reading passages followed by several multiple-choice questions. Carefully read the passages and choose the best answer for each of the questions.

The authors of the following passages comment on the way in which technology influences the study of literature.

Passage 1

"Kids don't read enough" might sound like the anthem of any given English teacher, but suspend your bias for a few minutes and consider the facts. You might soon agree that television, movies, and other electronic media are, indeed, imperiling the critical thinking skills that only the study of literature affords.

5   The average American child spends between 22 and 28 hours a week watching television; that's four hours a day, every day, and that exempts factors that might increase viewing, such as unfavorable weather. Four hours of television—this is the daily diet of the average American TV watcher. It's enough to be a part-time job! When you throw in all the other electronic media, such as movies, games, chatting, etc., the number climbs to a brain-rotting six hours a day—six hours

10   and nothing to show for it.

    As people vegetate for increasingly long periods each day, the popularity of reading, of course, lags. Children under eighteen spend, on average, less than one hour a day reading, and behold, reading assessment scores are plummeting! Coincidence?

    The insidiousness of television can be attributed to its many attractions—perpetual

15   action, simple story lines, and neat endings that reinforce expectations of quick and complete gratification. It is not surprising that the young hedonists in the making find it difficult to progress through a substantial work of literature, whether it's a classic novel assigned in high school or a chapter book written for young students. It is becoming dangerously routine for writers to cater to diminished attention spans by "dumbing down" literature, thus giving it the effect of television

20   commercials or erratic web pages. Internet summaries of novels are replacing the actual stories; after all, the authors obviously didn't mean to include all that extra nonsense when they wrote the books.

    Watching television requires only a passive role from the viewer. Providing all the imagery **squelches** the viewer's imagination. The mental process by which readers internalize and interpret

25   literature must be developed through use, one book at a time. Developing the **tangential** skills to understand texts—increased vocabulary, orthography, interpretation—takes practice, and that means more reading. These fundamental skills eventually coalesce into critical-thinking skills and grant readers the ability to anticipate, infer, and understand arguments and ideas in both texts and in any other form of communication.

30   Without the skills to interpret their own written language, people walk through a hazy world in which there are even fewer certainties than there are for people who do understand parts of it; they are like earthworms trying to understand the cackling of birds—hungry birds, perhaps. Oblivious people, in turn, make bad decisions in life. The paragons of literature—those books, stories, and novels that have inspired great people to do great things—are simply unavailable to

35   those who cannot read them. So please, turn off the television, even if it's for only one of the four nightly hours, and read something. **Matriculate** to the thinking world; your brains will thank you one day.

Passage 2

Don't waste your time reading books—or, at least, don't pass up a great movie in order to read Tolstoy on a Friday night. In the present age, television, videos, and movies deliver literature twenty-four hours a day, and with all the immediacy of a newscast and the colors of a pageant.

5 The stories that have withstood the test of time—the classics—did so because they tell **trenchant**, age-old human stories. "Man-versus-nature," "Man-versus-self," and "Man-versus-man" have been told and retold in so many thousands of ways that it's almost ridiculous even to create any new literature, let alone disallow the incorporation of these age-old themes into motion pictures that tell the same stories in much better ways than books do. The film versions of *Ben-Hur, Antony and Cleopatra,* and *Lord of the Flies* excited people just as the novels did when they 10 were first released, and they eliminated the ponderous, literature-imposed obligation of having to sort out and understand characters without visual representation. Costumes, music, and visual clues in movies help viewers to differentiate characters, and convoluted stories told with **arcane** ideas or language are easier to follow.

A transcendent acting performance can make a film version of a literary work much more 15 memorable than the original printed version, and movies are often superior to texts because the language of the original is modernized. This opens a door through which even **nascent** thinkers can experience the great classics, which previously were only understandable to those people fluent in specialized languages and dialects. Few children can tackle *The Lord of the Rings,* for example, but they can enjoy a great introduction to the work by watching the film version.

20 Publishers and booksellers will rarely, if ever, complain about movies reviving the popularity of certain books; they cash in on movie-based versions of books. Sometimes, these movie-books help original works to achieve a popularity that they never experienced on their own. Successful movies might line pockets in Hollywood, but they certainly also create a **salubrious** boost to the publishing industry.

25 With more than 98 percent of American homes owning at least one television set, the TV has replaced the book as a source of literature, and rightly so; by offering hundreds of channels, networks and cable companies are offering Americans a rich array of novels, drama, and nonfiction that's available all day, every day. Made-for-TV movies, archived classics, and documentaries about movies ensure that a plethora of cultural knowledge is available to viewers 30 everywhere.

Some critics worry that the transfer of literature from books to movies or equivalent electronic media will diminish thinking skills, but the concern is unnecessary because in most movie adaptations, clever scripts and subtle acting skills help viewers to understand the plot. How were Shakespeare's plays administered? They weren't read! Who would call Shakespeare 35 an impediment to learning? Television can only enhance vocabulary skills because most scripts maximize the use of mainstream words that represent the widest possible cross-section of American English dialect, which is what people need to know in order to function in society.

The literature that we know originated in oral tradition, by which stories were relayed from one generation to the next. To make the stories memorable, storytellers, bards, and poets sang, 40 acted-out, or narrated dramatically, all of which ensured the perpetuation of their important messages. The modern film has taken the place of those itinerant storytellers in the mead halls of Europe, and it guarantees that the great legends will continue to entertain and educate indefinitely.

1A. The tone of passage 1 is best described as

- A. doubtful.
- B. animated.
- C. detached.
- D. scholarly.
- E. troubled.

1B. Which words from passage 1 best support your answer to question 1A?
    A. anthem, gratification, tangential
    B. imperiling, plummeting, please
    C. electronic, brain-rotting, vocabulary
    D. exempts, dumbing down, hazy
    E. critical thinking, summaries, interpretation

2A. As used in line 6 of passage 1, *exempts* most nearly means
    A. includes.
    B. divides.
    C. accounts.
    D. excludes.
    E. determines.

2B. According to passage 1, lines 5-10, the estimate of how much television is watched accounts for
    A. indirect viewing, such as on televisions in cafeterias or waiting rooms.
    B. educational videos and documentaries.
    C. distance or online learning programs.
    D. pure entertainment.
    E. work-related communication.

3A. The *hedonists* mentioned in passage 1, paragraph 4, are people who
    A. learn quickly.
    B. seek pleasure.
    C. read profusely.
    D. debate television.
    E. play sports.

3B. Choose the sentence that best explains the author's intent in lines 20-22 (passage 1).
    A. Reading has become a much more efficient process.
    B. Novelists expect too much from publishers.
    C. The line suggests that lengthy texts are becoming obsolete.
    D. The author means the opposite of what he writes.
    E. Digital publishing is just as valid as traditional publishing.

4A. The simile in line 32 of passage 1 suggests that
    A. a lack of language skills can be dangerous.
    B. insects are higher-order animals than birds.
    C. mastering language skills is hard for some people.
    D. bird calls are a form of language.
    E. language skills are for those who want them.

4B. Which of the following best describes the cause of people becoming like "earth-worms" (line 32), according to passage 1?
    A. failure to develop critical thinking skills
    B. overdependence on simplified literature
    C. poor recall skills, due to the overuse of digital media
    D. failure to adapt to new technologies
    E. the lack of role models who advocate reading

5A. In passage 2, paragraph 2, "Man-versus-nature," "Man-versus-self," and "Man-versus-man" are
   A.   television shows about literature.
   B.   categories for use by movie critics.
   C.   ways for the author to express his misogyny.
   D.   common thematic conflicts in literature.
   E.   literary character types.

5B. Choose the statement about stories that can be inferred from the author's inclusion of the story types in lines 4-13, passage 2.
   A.   Readers might like books better than movies, but movies are almost as good.
   B.   Writers should focus on telling a new type of story.
   C.   Film adaptations never match the quality of original novels.
   D.   All stories are essentially the same; only the details change.
   E.   There are thousands of themes in literature, and film can accommodate some of them.

6A. In line 14 of passage 2, *transcendent* means
   A.   ridiculous.
   B.   inspiring.
   C.   transparent.
   D.   ubiquitous.
   E.   timeless.

6B. According to passage 2, lines 14-19, the positive result of *transcendent* acting is that
   A.   it helps viewers retain what they see.
   B.   it causes resurgence in book popularity.
   C.   it changes how the viewers perceive themselves.
   D.   it makes the original story obsolete.
   E.   the actor becomes well respected in the industry.

7A. Which choice best describes the author's intent in the following quotation from passage 2?

"Television can only enhance vocabulary skills because most scripts maximize the use of mainstream words that represent the widest possible cross-section of American English dialect, which is what people need to know in order to function in society."

   A.   It portrays television's lack of challenging vocabulary words as a positive characteristic.
   B.   It favorably describes the relationship between cable programming and current trends in education.
   C.   It negatively portrays educators who rely upon literature-based films for classroom teaching.
   D.   It supports the author's argument that literary works often share similar themes.
   E.   It suggests that the author is a movie producer.

7B. Choose the alternate, positive interpretation of the quotation from question 7A.
    A.   People should aspire to speak mainstream language.
    B.   People without a television are limited to vocabularies they learn from books.
    C.   Society would collapse if television did not exist.
    D.   The vocabulary of television is better than that of mainstream American English.
    E.   Television helps people develop vocabularies they will actually use in life.

8A. The purpose of lines 38-42, passage 2, is
    A.   to inform about the history of drama.
    B.   to suggest that television will soon replace books entirely.
    C.   to create an emotional connection between readers and the cause of television.
    D.   to determine whether readers benefit most from books or from television.
    E.   to suggest that film is responsible for the continuation of literature.

8B. According to the author of passage 2, film most resembles which genre of literature?
    A.   poetry
    B.   novels
    C.   drama
    D.   myths
    E.   short stories

9A. The authors of both passages would agree that
    A.   reading is extremely popular.
    B.   movies are more entertaining than books.
    C.   books are more entertaining than movies.
    D.   television is extremely popular.
    E.   educators should use television more often.

9B. The author of passage 1 would most likely say that
    A.   movie adaptations of stories give new perspectives of old material.
    B.   watching television is never more valuable than reading a classic novel.
    C.   people worry too much about the overuse of visual media.
    D.   television provides more information than people can process during one viewing.
    E.   the skills one gains from analyzing literature are useful, but considered luxuries.

10A. On which topic do the two passages directly conflict?
    A.   the importance of vocabulary skills
    B.   the prevalence of television viewers
    C.   the effect of television on critical thinking skills
    D.   challenges for educators teaching literature
    E.   the history of literature

10B. According to the author of passage 1, the ultimate consequence of not reading can be summarized as "Oblivious people…make bad decisions in life." What is the ultimate consequence of indulging in non-print media, according to the author of passage 2?
    A.   "…language of the original is modernized."
    B.   "…great legends will continue to entertain and educate indefinitely."
    C.   "…nascent thinkers can experience the great classics…"
    D.   "…boost to the publishing industry."
    E.   "…stories…are easier to follow."

Lesson Seventeen

1. **megalomania** (meg ə lō mā´ nē ə) *n.* having delusions of grandeur; an obsession with grandiose things
Bill's actual-sized wood reproduction of the Great Pyramid is said to be the result of the unemployed carpenter's *megalomania*.

2. **discourse** (dis´ kôrs) *n.* a discussion; a conversation
The suspect refused to engage in any *discourse* about the crime until his lawyer arrived.
syn: communication

3. **ethereal** (i thēr´ ē əl) *adj.* light or airy; intangible; heavenly
The subjects of Michelangelo's paintings often have an *ethereal* beauty.
syn: celestial; impalpable; unearthly   *ant: heavy; thick; substantial*

4. **depravity** (di prav´ i tē) *n.* moral corruption; perversion
Megan was shocked by the *depravity* occurring on the reputable college's campus.
syn: immorality; debauchery; vice   *ant: virtue; goodness; decency*

5. **congenital** (kən jen´ i təl) *adj.* dating from birth; inherent or natural
The child's *congenital* heart condition was minor, but it had to be monitored for the rest of her life.
syn: inborn   *ant: acquired; contracted*

6. **encomium** (en kō´ mē əm) *n.* formal praise; a tribute
The publisher hoped that the author's first novel would receive an *encomium* from the demanding critic.
syn: acclaim; endorsement; commendation   *ant: insult; condemnation*

7. **ascetic** (ə set´ ik) *n.* a person who renounces material comforts and practices extreme self-denial
The ancient fortune-teller was an *ascetic* who often abstained from food for days without complaint.

8. **attenuate** (ə ten´ ū āt) *v.* to reduce, weaken, or lessen
Disease *attenuated* the crops until the fields were brown and barren.
syn: diminish; shrink   *ant: strengthen; increase; intensify*

9. **alimentary** (a lə men´ tə rē) *adj.* pertaining to food, nutrition, or digestion
The doctor questioned Missy about her *alimentary* habits when she complained of frequent indigestion.
syn: dietary; nutritive

10. **attribute** (ə trib´ yōŏt) *v.* to relate to a particular cause; to ascribe
Tim, partially deaf at twenty-one, *attributes* his hearing loss to his loud car stereo.
syn: credit; blame; impute   *ant: dismiss; absolve*

11. **primordial** (prī môr´ dē əl) *adj.* first in time; original
Long before the appearance of life, *primordial* Earth had a poisonous atmosphere
and widespread volcanic activity.
syn: primeval; prehistoric   *ant: recent; current*

12. **celerity** (sə ler´ i tē) *n.* swiftness of action; speed
The factory lost money every second it was shut down, so the engineers worked
with great *celerity* to repair the huge machine on the assembly line.
syn: haste; rapidity; alacrity   *ant: delay; procrastination*

13. **remuneration** (ri myōō nə rā´ shən) *n.* compensation; payment
Clark demanded *remuneration* for having been brought to trial on false charges.
syn: recompense; restitution; reimbursement

14. **mutable** (myōō´ tə bəl) *adj.* subject to change
Pack an assortment of clothes, because the weather in the mountains is *mutable*.
syn: variable; inconstant; unstable   *ant: consistent; constant; steady;*
                                                                    immutable

15. **tactile** (tak´ təl, tīl) *adj.* pertaining to the sense of touch
Roger still had *tactile* sensations in his paralyzed legs, indicating that he had a good
chance of walking again.

Exercise I

Words in Context

From the list below, supply the words needed to complete the paragraph. Some words will not be used.

attenuate	depravity	remuneration	primordial
encomium	discourse	ethereal	

1. Paige, a researcher who had earned a[n] _____ from the pharmaceutical industry for her accomplishments, frequently traveled to the jungles of Peru in pursuit of a natural compound thought to _____ the torturous side effects of chemotherapy. The jungle fascinated Paige; its thick vegetation and enormous plants gave her a sense of what the _____ forests of Earth must have looked like when dinosaurs grazed on treetops and the ground rumbled with volcanic activity. In the evenings, Paige usually sat quietly at her camp and watched as the fog crept slowly down the verdant hills and settled in the valley, blanketing the old forest in a[n] _____ haze, like something out of a dream. To Paige, witnessing such natural beauty was ample _____ for her hard work.

From the list below, supply the words needed to complete the paragraph. Some words will not be used.

ethereal	ascetic	congenital	depravity
attribute	megalomania	mutable	

2. During the new mayor's campaign, he claimed to be a "political _____," who had the goal of reducing all wasteful government spending and ending financial _____ and rampant corruption within the ranks of the city government; however, his promises proved to be easily _____ because his first action as mayor was to approve the construction of an unnecessary, million-dollar park named after him. Critics _____ the expensive project to the new mayor's _____, which was proven correct when the mayor published his autobiography, a book that was filled with exaggerated claims of his accomplishments.

From the list below, supply the words needed to complete the paragraph. Some words will not be used.

remuneration	celerity	alimentary	congenital
attribute	discourse	tactile	

3. All of Mike's _____ senses were still numb after the surgery, but he was able to hear the _____ between his wife and the surgeon. The _____ stomach condition that had interfered with Mike's _____ processes since he was a baby had been corrected, but Mike would simply need plenty of rest if he expected to heal with _____.

Exercise II

Sentence Completion

Complete the sentence in a way that shows you understand the meaning of the italicized vocabulary word.

1. Kristen was awed by the *ethereal* sight of…

2. Dave, who frequently ate three desserts, called his wife an *ascetic* because…

3. The part of the tactile toy that the baby seemed to like the most was…

4. After the recall, the automobile manufacturer said that *remunerations* would be provided for anyone who…

5. The high rate of *congenital* birth defects in the area…

6. Lisa enjoyed the *encomium* from all the townspeople for…

7. The rising costs of building supplies *attenuated* the couple's desire to…

8. Tim's *megalomania* makes life difficult for his friends because he is constantly…

9. *Discourse* among the students suddenly stopped when…

10. *Depravity* in the cult eventually caused…

11. The plans are *mutable*, so be prepared to…

12. The archaeologist found fossils of *primordial* microorganisms when she…

13. *Celerity* of work was important to the construction crew because…

14. Logan *attributes* crop circles to UFOs, but…

15. An earthworm's *alimentary* process is…

| | | Exercise III | | |

Roots, Prefixes, and Suffixes

Study the entries and answer the questions that follow.

The roots *grad* and *gress* mean "step."
The roots *ced* and *cess* mean "go."
The prefix *de–* means "down."
The prefix *pro–* means "forward."
The prefix *re–* means "back."
The prefix *di–* means "apart" or "away from."
The prefix *trans–* means "across" or "through."

1. Using *literal* translations as guidance, define the following words without using a dictionary.

A.	regression	D.	recede
B.	procession	E.	degrade
C.	digress	F.	progression

2. The prefix *se–* means "away." In the 1860s, the Confederate States tried to _____ (literally, "go away") from the Union.

3. A synonym for the word *sin* that literally means "stepping across the line" is

   _____.

4. If the prefix *ex–* means "outside," what does the word *exceed* literally mean?

5. List as many words as you can think of that contain the roots *ced* or *cess*.

6. List as many words as you can think of that contain the roots *grad* or *gress*.

| | | Exercise IV | | |

Inference

Complete the sentence by inferring information about the italicized word from its context.

1. The fire chief *attributed* the blaze to faulty wiring, so the police had no need to…

2. If father refuses to partake in any further *discourse* on the subject, then he does not want to…

3. An *ascetic* who eats roots, sleeps on the floor, and drinks only water, would probably decline an invitation to…

Exercise V

Writing

Here is a writing prompt similar to the one you will find on the writing portion of an assessment test.

Plan and write an essay based on the following statement:

> Virtue is like a rich stone, best plain set.
> —Francis Bacon (1561–1626)

Assignment: Francis Bacon suggests that virtue, like a fine diamond, requires no decorative enhancement. In an essay, explain the purpose of Francis Bacon's statement, identify whether you agree or disagree with it, and include an example of the behavior that Bacon alludes to. Support your essay using an example from literature, history, current events, or your experience or observation.

Thesis: Write a *one-sentence* response to the above assignment. Make certain this single sentence offers a clear statement of your position.

Example: Advertising one's virtue, or demonstrating it unnecessarily, can diminish its value.

_____

_____

Organizational Plan: List at least three subtopics you will use to support your main idea. This list is your outline.

1. _____

2. _____

3. _____

Draft: Following your outline, write a good first draft of your essay. Remember to support all of your points with examples, facts, references to reading, etc.

Review and Revise: Exchange essays with a classmate. Using the scoring guide for Word Choice on page 275, score your partner's essay (while he or she scores yours). Focus on word choice and the use of language conventions. If necessary, rewrite your essay to improve word choice and/or your use of language.

| Exercise VI |

English Practice

Identifying Sentence Errors

Identify the grammatical error in each of the following sentences. If the sentence contains no error, select answer choice E.

1. We <u>saved enough money</u> from the previous <u>three month's paychecks,</u> and we can
             (A)   (B)
    <u>finally afford</u> to <u>go on a long vacation to</u> Rome.   <u>No error</u>
          (C)   (D)   (E)

2. Last <u>April, members</u> of the <u>senior class took</u> a trip from
              (A)   (B)
    <u>Buffalo to Niagara Falls New York,</u> and then across the border to <u>Toronto, Canada.</u>
                        (C)   (D)
    <u>No error</u>
       (E)

3. We <u>visited Tom</u> in the hospital after his <u>car accident;</u> he <u>seemed good,</u> and the
           (A)   (B)   (C)
    broken bones <u>are almost completely healed.</u>   <u>No error</u>
                              (D)   (E)

4. <u>Although</u> the elderly King James died last week after a long <u>illness, his</u> son
        (A)   (B)
    <u>will legally</u> become <u>the new ruler of the country.</u>   <u>No error</u>
          (C)   (D)   (E)

5. Jeremy, <u>the person</u> with <u>whom</u> I've been <u>carpooling, wrecked</u> his <u>car yesterday.</u>
                  (A)   (B)   (C)   (D)
    <u>No error</u>
       (E)

Improving Sentences

The underlined portion of each sentence below contains some flaw. Select the answer choice that best corrects the flaw.

6. <u>Neither Charlotte nor her sisters is going to the mall.</u>
    A. Neither Charlotte or her sisters is going to the mall.
    B. Neither Charlotte nor her sisters are going to the mall.
    C. Charlotte and her sisters are not going to the mall.
    D. Neither Charlotte, nor her sisters, are going to the mall.
    E. Neither of Charlotte's sisters are going to the mall.

7. The assistance of two electricians, one network administrator, an information technology specialist, and three helpers <u>were necessary to fix all the computer errors that had caused the crash.</u>
    A. was necessary to fix all the computer errors that had caused the crash.
    B. were necessary to fix the computer errors that caused the crash.
    C. were necessary to fix all the computer errors, which had caused the crash.
    D. was necessary to fix each and every one of the errors that had caused the computer to crash.
    E. fixed all the computer errors that crashed.

8. <u>One thing I know that will keep me from traveling abroad, and those are the high costs of flying.</u>
    A. I know one thing that will keep me from traveling abroad—the high cost of flying.
    B. One thing that I know that will keep me from traveling overseas are the high costs of flying.
    C. I know one thing that is keeping me from traveling abroad, and that is the costs of flying.
    D. Flying and the high costs of doing so are some of the major things I know that will keep me from traveling abroad.
    E. Traveling abroad, with its high cost, will keep me from flying, that is one thing I know.

9. He is <u>as strong, if not stronger than his father.</u>
    A. as strong as if not stronger than his father.
    B. strong, as is his father.
    C. as strong, if not more strong than his father.
    D. stronger than his father, if not as strong.
    E. as strong as his father, if not stronger.

10. An aspiring pianist should spend hours <u>practicing; otherwise you will never be successful.</u>
    A. practicing otherwise you will never be successful.
    B. practicing because otherwise, you will never be successful.
    C. practicing; otherwise, he or she will never be successful.
    D. in practicing; otherwise they will never be a success.
    E. practicing, otherwise, he or she will never be successful.

Vocabulary Power Plus for College and Career Readiness

LEVEL TWELVE

Lesson Eighteen

1. **satiate** (sā´ shē āt) *v.* to satisfy fully
No amount of riches could *satiate* the greedy baron.
syn: gratify; suit

2. **vituperative** (vī tōō´ pə rə tiv) *adj.* fault-finding; verbally abusive
The *vituperative* drill instructor screamed at the new recruit for not having shiny boots and a pressed uniform.
syn: castigating; derisive; scathing   *ant: flattering; sweet; kind*

3. **poignant** (poin´ yənt) *adj.* very moving; touching
The movie would be simply mediocre if it didn't contain an especially *poignant* scene.
syn: emotional; affecting; sentimental   *ant: unemotional; cold*

4. **pundit** (pun´ dĭt) *n.* a critic
The political *pundit* commented on government actions each morning on a radio show.
syn: commentator; reviewer; analyzer

5. **surfeit** (sûr´ fit) *n.* an excessive amount
A *surfeit* of oranges this year drove the price down.
syn: excess; overabundance; surplus   *ant: shortage; dearth; deficiency*

6. **lithe** (līth) *adj.* graceful in motion; moving and bending with ease
The *lithe* gymnast's movements were graceful and seemingly effortless.
syn: agile; flowing; supple   *ant: rigid; clumsy; awkward*

7. **trite** (trīt) *adj.* overused; hackneyed; clichéd
I could tell by my agent's *trite* reply that she hadn't actually read my manuscript.
syn: banal; routine; timeworn   *ant: fresh; provocative; original*

8. **propriety** (prə prī´ i tē) *n.* proper behavior; appropriateness
The man carried himself with such *propriety* that few would have guessed he was homeless.
syn: decency; etiquette; seemliness   *ant: rudeness; indecency*

9. **cumulative** (kyōō´ myə lə tiv) *adj.* resulting from accumulation; increasing
Her *cumulative* grade point average, from the ninth grade to the present, is 3.7.
syn: aggregate; summative; collective   *ant: decreasing; subtracting*

10. **venial** (vē´ nē əl) *adj.* easily excused or forgiven
A *venial* offense such as jaywalking usually bears little or no fine.
syn: pardonable; remittable; excusable   *ant: inexcusable; unforgivable*

11. **exhilaration** (ig zil´ ə rā´ shən) *n.* thrill; invigoration
A sense of *exhilaration* overwhelmed me as I reached the summit and looked down at the forest far below.
syn: excitement; elation   *ant: boredom; apathy; ennui*

12. **goad** (gōd) *v.* to urge forward; to prod
The kids in the schoolyard *goaded* the boy into sticking his tongue to the frozen flagpole.
syn: spur; press; incite   *ant: deter; discourage; dissuade*

13. **impunity** (im pyōō´ ni tē) *n.* freedom from punishment, penalty, or harm
No one can speak against the king with *impunity*.
syn: immunity; liberty   *ant: vulnerability; risk*

14. **extricate** (ek´ stri kāt) *v.* to release; to disentangle
In less than one minute, the escape artist *extricated* himself from the chains holding him underwater.
syn: free; deliver; liberate   *ant: entangle; hinder*

15. **superfluous** (sōō pûr´ flōō əs) *adj.* unnecessary; excessive
The new luxury SUV had many *superfluous* options, including two televisions.
syn: exorbitant; gratuitous; extravagant   *ant: essential; necessary;*
                                                    imperative

Exercise I

Words in Context

From the list below, supply the words needed to complete the paragraph. Some words will not be used.

surfeit   lithe   superfluous   satiate
pundit   trite   vituperative   goad

1. Robert knew that his novel was far from great, but according to the _____ reviews by numerous _____, the book was simply awful. Most critics noted that the detective thriller contains a _____ of _____ expressions that could have been stolen from the script of any low-budget action film, and that the author used little creativity in allowing the hero of the novel, Lance Driver, to solve most of his problems through _____ and graphic violence. Robert swore that no one would ever _____ him into writing another mystery.

From the list below, supply the words needed to complete the paragraph. Some words will not be used.

extricate   pundit   venial   exhilaration
poignant   goad   lithe

2. Two months after the tragic bridge collapse, the lone survivor told her _____ tale to a newspaper reporter. Sharon had been injured when the roadway surface of the bridge fell more than sixty feet to the water, but luckily she was _____ enough to _____ herself from the mangled wreckage of the bridge and her car. Feeling the pain of multiple fractures, Sharon crawled up a fallen steel girder. She recalled the _____ she felt when she first saw the rescue helicopter approaching; however, the feeling was short-lived because Sharon quickly passed out from shock.

From the list below, supply the words needed to complete the paragraph. Some words will not be used.

vituperative   cumulative   impunity   satiate
propriety   exhilaration   venial

3. To Randy's parents, wasting hard-earned money was no _____ crime. When Randy was six years old, his parents opened a savings account for him. Over the years, the _____ balance rose to thousands of dollars, but Randy could not touch it unless he proved that he would demonstrate _____ in handling the money. On occasion, Randy was allowed to use some of it to help _____ his "need" to increase the size of his baseball card collection, but he was certainly never allowed to go to the mall and spend with _____; the money was meant to pay for college, after all.

Exercise II

Sentence Completion

Complete the sentence in a way that shows you understand the meaning of the italicized vocabulary word.

1. Every time Roslyn watches that *poignant* black-and-white movie, she...

2. Frank harvested a *surfeit* of tomatoes from his garden this year, so he...

3   The supervisor didn't mind if workers committed *venial* errors, but if they made mistakes that cost the company money, she...

4. After twenty years of working with uranium, Steve's *cumulative* radiation exposure finally...

5. Each morning, the *pundit* scanned the newspaper to find...

6. The cover of the greeting card featured a *trite* expression about...

7. The *lithe* ballet dancer made...

8. Shannon had to avoid any *superfluous* expenses until she...

9. Craig had never been swimming, so his parents had to *goad* him to...

10. Cal stopped allowing his dog to run free in the woods after he had to *extricate* the animal from...

11. The mobsters operated the illegal casino with *impunity* until...

12. When a bowling ball fell on Dad's foot after he opened the closet door, he broke into a series of *vituperative* screams about...

13. Before the field trip, the teacher warned the students that anyone who failed to represent the school with *propriety* would...

14. Ben didn't eat enough to *satiate* himself because he didn't...

15. Brad lived for experiencing the *exhilaration* of...

Exercise III

Roots, Prefixes, and Suffixes

Study the entries and answer the questions that follow.

The roots *ag* and *act* mean "to do" or "drive."
The roots *mov* and *mot* mean "to move."
The prefix *de–* means "down."
The prefix *in–* means "not."
The prefix *pro–* means "forward."

1. Using *literal* translations as guidance, define the following words without using a dictionary.

    A. promote   D. proactive
    B. inactive   E. immovable
    C. demote   F. agitate

2. The prefix *com–* means "together." What does the word *commotion* literally mean?

3. If a story *moves* you, then it might cause you to experience a particular _____, or feeling.

4. *Mob* is another form of the root *mov*. List as many words as you can think of that contain the root *mob*.

5. List as many words as you can think of that contain the roots *mov* or *mot*.

Exercise IV

Inference

Complete the sentence by inferring information about the italicized word from its context.

1. Ambassadors must demonstrate great *propriety* while meeting with foreign officials because...

2. If the fishermen have to *extricate* a dolphin from the fishing net, then the dolphin must be...

3. A teacher might overlook a student's *venial* faults if the student...

Exercise V

Critical Reading

Below is a reading passage followed by several multiple-choice questions. Carefully read the passage and choose the best answer for each of the questions.

The following passage is an excerpt from Jane Eyre, *an extremely popular book by Victorian author Charlotte Brontë (1816–1855).* Jane Eyre, *written in 1847, is fiction, but it contains significant autobiographical elements.*

Ere the half-hour ended, five o'clock struck; school was dismissed, and all were gone into the refectory to tea. I now ventured to descend: it was deep dusk; I retired into a corner and sat down on the floor. The spell by which I had been so far supported began to dissolve; reaction took place, and soon, so overwhelming was the grief that seized me, I sank prostrate with my
5   face to the ground. Now I wept: Helen Burns was not here; nothing sustained me; left to myself I abandoned myself, and my tears watered the boards. I had meant to be so good, and to do so much at Lowood: to make so many friends, to earn respect and win affection. Already I had made visible progress: that very morning I had reached the head of my class; Miss Miller had praised me warmly; Miss Temple had smiled approbation; she had promised to teach me drawing, and to let
10 me learn French, if I continued to make similar improvement two months longer: and then I was well received by my fellow-pupils; treated as an equal by those of my own age, and not molested by any; now, here I lay again crushed and trodden on; and could I ever rise more?

"Never," I thought; and ardently I wished to die. While sobbing out this wish in broken accents, some one approached: I started up—again Helen Burns was near me; the fading fires just
15 showed her coming up the long, vacant room; she brought my coffee and bread.

"Come, eat something," she said; but I put both away from me, feeling as if a drop or a crumb would have choked me in my present condition. Helen regarded me, probably with surprise: I could not now abate my agitation, though I tried hard; I continued to weep aloud. She sat down on the ground near me, embraced her knees with her arms, and rested her head upon
20 them; in that attitude she remained silent as an Indian. I was the first who spoke.

"Helen, why do you stay with a girl whom everybody believes to be a liar?"

"Everybody, Jane? Why, there are only eighty people who have heard you called so, and the world contains hundreds of millions."

"But what have I to do with millions? The eighty, I know, despise me."
25 "Jane, you are mistaken: probably not one in the school either despises or dislikes you: many, I am sure, pity you much."

"How can they pity me after what Mr. Brocklehurst has said?"

"Mr. Brocklehurst is not a god: nor is he even a great and admired man: he is little liked here; he never took steps to make himself liked. Had he treated you as an especial favorite, you would
30 have found enemies, declared or covert, all around you; as it is, the greater number would offer you sympathy if they dared. Teachers and pupils may look coldly on you for a day or two, but friendly feelings are concealed in their hearts; and if you persevere in doing well, these feelings will ere long appear so much the more evidently for their temporary suppression. Besides, Jane"— she paused.
35 "Well, Helen?" said I, putting my hand into hers: she chafed my fingers gently to warm them, and went on.

"If all the world hated you, and believed you wicked, while your own conscience approved you, and absolved you from guilt, you would not be without friends."

"No; I know I should think well of myself; but that is not enough: if others don't love me
40 I would rather die than live—I cannot bear to be solitary and hated, Helen. Look here; to gain some real affection from you, or Miss Temple, or any other whom I truly love, I would willingly submit to have the bone of my arm broken, or to let a bull toss me, or to stand behind a kicking

horse, and let it dash its hoof at my chest—"

"Hush, Jane! You think too much of the love of human beings; you are too impulsive, too
45 vehement; the sovereign hand that created your frame, and put life into it, has provided you
with other resources than your feeble self, or than creatures feeble as you. Besides this earth, and
besides the race of men, there is an invisible world and a kingdom of spirits: that world is round
us, for it is everywhere; and those spirits watch us, for they are commissioned to guard us; and if
we were dying in pain and shame, if scorn smote us on all sides, and hatred crushed us, angels see
50 our tortures, recognize our innocence (if innocent we be: as I know you are of this charge which
Mr. Brocklehurst has weakly and pompously repeated at second-hand from Mrs. Reed; for I read
a sincere nature in your ardent eyes and on your clear front), and God waits only the separation
of spirit from flesh to crown us with a full reward. Why, then, should we ever sink overwhelmed
with distress, when life is so soon over, and death is so certain an entrance to happiness—to
55 glory?"

I was silent; Helen had calmed me; but in the tranquility she imparted there was an alloy
of inexpressible sadness. I felt the impression of woe as she spoke, but I could not tell whence it
came; and when, having done speaking, she breathed a little fast and coughed a short cough, I
momentarily forgot my own sorrows to yield to a vague concern for her.

60 Resting my head on Helen's shoulder, I put my arms round her waist; she drew me to her,
and we reposed in silence. We had not sat long thus, when another person came in. Some heavy
clouds, swept from the sky by a rising wind, had left the moon bare; and her light, streaming in
through a window near, shone full both on us and on the approaching figure, which we at once
recognized as Miss Temple.

65 "I came on purpose to find you, Jane Eyre," said she; "I want you in my room; and as Helen
Burns is with you, she may come too."

We went; following the superintendent's guidance, we had to thread some intricate passages,
and mount a staircase before we reached her apartment; it contained a good fire, and looked
cheerful. Miss Temple told Helen Burns to be seated in a low armchair on one side of the hearth,
70 and herself taking another, she called me to her side.

"Is it all over?" she asked, looking down at my face. "Have you cried your grief away?"

"I am afraid I never shall do that."

"Why?"

"Because I have been wrongly accused; and you, ma'am, and everybody else, will now think
75 me wicked."

"We shall think you what you prove yourself to be, my child. Continue to act as a good girl,
and you will satisfy us."

"Shall I, Miss Temple?"

"You will," said she, passing her arm round me. "And now tell me who is the lady whom Mr.
80 Brocklehurst called your benefactress?"

"Mrs. Reed, my uncle's wife. My uncle is dead, and he left me to her care."

"Did she not, then, adopt you of her own accord?"

"No, ma'am; she was sorry to have to do it: but my uncle, as I have often heard the servants
say, got her to promise before he died that she would always keep me."

85 "Well now, Jane, you know, or at least I will tell you, that when a criminal is accused, he
is always allowed to speak in his own defense. You have been charged with falsehood; defend
yourself to me as well as you can. Say whatever your memory suggests is true; but add nothing
and exaggerate nothing."

I resolved, in the depth of my heart, that I would be most moderate—most correct; and,
90 having reflected a few minutes in order to arrange coherently what I had to say, I told her all
the story of my sad childhood. Exhausted by emotion, my language was more subdued than
it generally was when it developed that sad theme; and mindful of Helen's warnings against
the indulgence of resentment, I infused into the narrative far less of gall and wormwood than
ordinary. Thus restrained and simplified, it sounded more credible: I felt as I went on that Miss
95 Temple fully believed me.

In the course of the tale I had mentioned Mr. Lloyd as having come to see me after the fit:

for I never forgot the, to me, frightful episode of the red-room: in detailing which, my excitement was sure, in some degree, to break bounds; for nothing could soften in my recollection the spasm of agony which clutched my heart when Mrs. Reed spurned my wild supplication for pardon, and
100 locked me a second time in the dark and haunted chamber.

    I had finished: Miss Temple regarded me a few minutes in silence; she then said, "I know something of Mr. Lloyd; I shall write to him; if his reply agrees with your statement, you shall be publicly cleared from every imputation; to me, Jane, you are clear now."

1A. The narrator of this passage is
    A. Jane, a school-aged girl.
    B. Mrs. Reed, Jane's aunt.
    C. Helen, a student.
    D. Mr. Brocklehurst, the schoolmaster.
    E. Miss Temple, the superintendent.

1B. As it is used in line 3, the word *spell* is most synonymous with
    A. curse.
    B. time.
    C. emotion.
    D. trance.
    E. expression.

2A. Helen Burns is probably
    A. Jane's guardian.
    B. Jane's sister.
    C. Jane's counselor.
    D. Jane's friend.
    E. Jane's tutor.

2B. Helen warns Jane about befriending Mr. Brocklehurst because
    A. Mr. Brocklehurst is the superintendent.
    B. it would cause people to dislike Jane.
    C. Mr. Brocklehurst does not like Helen.
    D. he is an acquaintance of Jane's family.
    E. Mr. Brocklehurst is the schoolmaster.

3A. Which statement best demonstrates the intended idea of the following quotation?

"If all the world hated you, and believed you wicked, while your own conscience approved you, and absolved you from guilt, you would not be without friends."

    A. Friends will always believe you, as long as you believe yourself.
    B. No one needs friends because they can turn on you.
    C. You always have a friend in yourself.
    D. You cannot count on friends to bail you out of a bad situation.
    E. Only what you think is important, unless you think yourself to be guilty.

3B. According to the passage, Jane was
    A.   caught in a lie.
    B.   stealing supplies from a classroom.
    C.   fighting with someone in the hall.
    D.   accused of something that she did not do.
    E.   accused of something that Helen did.

4A. Choose the statement that best summarizes Helen's answer to the injustice imposed upon Jane in lines 44-55.
    A.   Some people are simply meant to suffer.
    B.   Misery on Earth doesn't matter; you'll be happy when you're dead.
    C.   Your nature is unimportant; it is your actions that matter most.
    D.   The people who wrongly accuse you will experience retribution.
    E.   Heaven is on Earth, and those who deceive cannot experience it.

4B. Who witnesses and attests to the pain and misery of life on Earth, according to Helen, in lines 47-50?
    A.   angels
    B.   enemies
    C.   good people
    D.   God
    E.   the accused

5A. As used in line 56, *alloy* most nearly means
    A.   abundance.
    B.   blending.
    C.   metal.
    D.   truce.
    E.   contaminant.

5B. Jane describes the sadness as an *alloy* because
    A.   the sadness overpowers and ruins the tranquility Jane feels.
    B.   the sadness is a part of the tranquility Helen imparts.
    C.   the sadness is cold, like bronze or steel.
    D.   she is unsure what the source of the sadness is.
    E.   the sadness combines with Jane's other feelings, turning them sad as well.

6A. Which choice best paraphrases the following quotation?

"…mindful of Helen's warnings against the indulgence of resentment, I infused into the narrative far less of gall and wormwood than ordinary."

    A.   Being mindful of Helen's warning about spite, I focused on positive things during my explanation.

    B.   I left out the bad things during my explanation because it is not good to be resented.

    C.   The resentment that I felt did not stop me from infusing my usual dramatics into my story.

    D.   Heeding Helen's warning about being resentful, I made my account less spiteful than it might have typically been.

    E.   Helen's warning about resentment allowed me to be polite, as usual, during my narrative.

6B. Per Helen's suggestion, Jane suspects that people are more likely to believe a story that is

    A.   exceptionally emotional.

    B.   confirmed by adults.

    C.   a call for sympathy.

    D.   free of hostility.

    E.   embellished with gall.

7.   The story in this passage takes place

    A.   in the morning, before school begins.

    B.   at lunchtime, while Jane and Helen are waiting for their next class.

    C.   in the early afternoon, before Mr. Brocklehurst returns from vacation.

    D.   at night, after school has let out for the day.

    E.   on Saturday, while Jane is in detention for lying on Friday.

8A. As used in line 80, the word *benefactress* most nearly means

    A.   caregiver.

    B.   enemy.

    C.   relative.

    D.   friend.

    E.   neighbor.

8B. Which line from the passage seems to contradict Mrs. Reed's role as *benefactress* to Jane?

    A. "…my uncle…got her to promise before he died that she would always keep me."

    B. "Teachers and pupils may look coldly on you for a day or two…"

    C. "…Mrs. Reed…locked me a second time in the dark and haunted chamber."

    D. "…I would willingly submit to have the bone of my arm broken…"

    E. "Mr. Brocklehurst has…pompously repeated at second-hand from Mrs. Reed…"

9A. Based on the point of view alone, the passage is described best as

    A. biographical.

    B. fictional.

    C. nonfictional.

    D. humorous.

    E. historical.

9B. Choose the statement that best describes the central conflict, or problem, experienced by the main character as described in the passage.

    A. Helen is near death and cannot find her family.

    B. Mrs. Reed is abusive to Jane, who must return to Mrs. Reed's custody.

    C. Jane has been wrongly accused of deviant behavior.

    D. Miss Temple is being forced to transfer to a new school.

    E. Mr. Brocklehurst wants to expel Jane.

10. The most appropriate title for this passage would be

    A. The Liar's Club.

    B. Worry Not, Jane.

    C. Being the New Girl.

    D. Miss Temple's Mistake.

    E. White Lies.

Review Lessons 16-18

Exercise I

Inferences

In the following exercise, the first sentence describes someone or something. Infer information from the first sentence, and then choose the word from the Word Bank that best completes the second sentence.

extricate	remuneration	matriculate	alimentary
propriety	exculpated	mercurial	impunity

1. The DNA evidence from a recent crime matched the DNA from a crime twenty years ago, which meant that the wrong man had been convicted and sent to prison.

   From this sentence, we can infer that the DNA evidence _____ the innocent man.

2. The author had dozens of great ideas, but they were strangled by chapters filled with poorly written scenes and unrealistic dialogue.

   From this sentence, we can infer that a good editor might be able to _____ the author's good ideas from the bad writing.

3. Unopposed, well-armed, and unwed to any particular nation, the pirates attacked foreign ships without worry of reprisal and simply disappeared with the loot.

   From this sentence, we can infer that the pirates operated with _____.

4. Fiona was sure that she was sick with the flu, but her doctor ignored her theory and instead asked her for a list of foods that she had eaten during the last three days.

   From this sentence, we can infer that the doctor suspects that Fiona's illness has a[n] _____ cause.

5. After fighting off the barbarian hordes in defense of an allied city in their territory, the defenders wondered whether they should demand crops, spices, or treasure as payment for their services.

   From this sentence, we can infer that the defending army expected _____ for their services rendered in defense of the city.

Exercise II

Related Words

Some of the vocabulary words from Lessons 16 through 18 have related meanings. Complete the following sentences by choosing the word that best fits the context, based on information you infer from the use of the italicized word. Some word pairs will be antonyms, some will be synonyms, and some will simply be words often used in the same context.

1. To the *ascetic*, anything of this world that wasn't directly necessary for staying alive was simply _____.
   A. superfluous
   B. trenchant
   C. bourgeois
   D. arcane
   E. tangential

2. The chef's unparalleled _____ knowledge helped her create *salubrious* gourmet meals at little cost.
   A. congenital
   B. primordial
   C. mutable
   D. alimentary
   E. ethereal

3. Regan wanted her career to be _____ until she narrowed her interests, so she refused to sign the *indefeasible* contract to be a doctor for the Navy.
   A. tactile
   B. ethereal
   C. mutable
   D. primordial
   E. alimentary

4. During the council's formal _____, the chairperson quickly dismissed any *tangential* topics and steered the conversation back to the central matter.
   A. exhilaration
   B. discourse
   C. pundit
   D. propriety
   E. impunity

5. At first, Carla loved television shows about the _____ history of lost nations, but after a single year, every network had similar shows adhering to the same *trite* format.
   A. arcane
   B. poignant
   C. vituperative
   D. cumulative
   E. indefeasible

6. Rising tuition costs *attenuated* enrollment numbers at the university, so the college board allowed more applicants to _____ the following year.
   A. exculpate
   B. squelch
   C. attribute
   D. goad
   E. matriculate

7. The _____ lecturer could have even the toughest audience sobbing after telling one of his *poignant* stories.
   A. arcane
   B. tangential
   C. trenchant
   D. mercurial
   E. salubrious

8. The _____ act of changing one's mind after bidding on an item defies any sense of *propriety* at an auction, and the bidder will still be liable for the purchase.
   A. salubrious
   B. mercurial
   C. trenchant
   D. indefeasible
   E. arcane

9. The television political _____ seizes upon the latest news with *celerity* in order to be the first to comment on or criticize the information.
   A. pundit
   B. sine qua non
   C. paladin
   D. vicissitude
   E. tyro

10. The king's depravity and arrogance repulsed the *paladin* who had mistakenly sworn himself to a life of honor and service to this undeserving _____.
    A. tyro
    B. encomium
    C. ascetic
    D. megalomaniac
    E. remuneration

Exercise III

Deeper Meanings

Choose a word to replace the italicized word in each sentence. All of the possible choices for each sentence have similar definitions, but the correct answer will have a connotation that best suits the context. For example, the words "delete," "destroy," and "obliterate" all mean "to remove or wipe out," but no one would ever say, "I destroyed the name from the document." The correct choice will be the word that has the best specific meaning and does not render the sentence awkward in tone or content. When choices seem close, look for a clue in the context that makes one choice better than the other.

Note that the correct answer is not always the primary vocabulary word from the lesson.

old	decimated	uncommon	squelched	yanked
extricated	unique	superfluous	weird	prehistoric

1. Lloyd wanted a hot rod with a[n] *arcane*, custom paint job, but he could not afford one yet.

   Better word: _____

2. The quaint cottage would have blended right in with the pretty environment if it were not for the *optional* lawn decorations out front—especially the pink flamingos.

   Better word: _____

3. The *primordial* man next door remembers the time before television was invented.

   Better word: _____

4. In a ten-hour surgery, doctors slowly and carefully *pulled* the metal fragments from the tissue surrounding the soldier's spinal cord.

   Better word: _____

5. A court order *quieted* the Internet bulletin board on which people had dishonestly defamed a local business.

   Better word: _____

Exercise IV

Crossword Puzzle

Use the clues to complete the crossword puzzle. The answers consist of vocabulary words from Lessons 16 through 18.

Across

1. far from the original topic
5. like the weather, from one day to the next
9. a quick-change specialist
11. "I'd like to thank a special person for making this all possible..."
13. I dare you to!
15. It all adds up.
16. like a freshman
17. What a thrill!
18. getting away with it

Down

2. without running water, a TV, or electricity
3. just a little wrong
4. not the upper, not the lower
6. "He was out bowling with me when the store was robbed."
7. don't need it
8. good pay for good work
10. had it from birth
12. low in fat, salt, sugar, etc.
14. Let's eat!

Exercise V

Subject Prompts

Here is a writing prompt similar to the one you will find on the writing portion of an assessment test. Follow the instructions below and write a brief, efficient essay.

The long term health of a generation is at risk in America, not because of floods or locusts or global warming, but because of simple overindulgence. America is at the height of an obesity epidemic.

Previous generations who, in youth, lacked the many technological distractions that the present generation enjoys, tend to blame sedentary lifestyles and self-indulgence for obesity. Children once explored nature freely and walked or bicycled daily from one end of town to the next. Children now spend a mind-numbing seven hours a day surfing the Internet, watching television, and playing video games. Roaming forests and fields simply isn't a realistic alternative when tracts of wilderness post *NO TRESPASSING* signs, or when the land around the old fishing hole has become host to a housing development. New roads and neighborhoods often lack sidewalks for easy foot or bicycle travel.

The contradictory part of the epidemic is that we know more now about human physiology and the benefits of diet and exercise than at any other time in human history. Forcing people to diet and exercise would be tyranny, but there is little doubt that people now, more than ever, need motivation to spend less time on the couch and more on their feet.

What incentives would entice the youth of America to turn off the television, abandon social networking sites, and get back outside to do real, healthy things? Has something changed during the last few decades, other than necessity, that has caused so many people to become digital hermits?

Pinpoint your feelings on the general health of your generation and whether it is a legitimate problem. Write a speech to be delivered at a youth exposition that describes why Americans' lack of fitness is a problem and whether or not it is related to the plugged-in status of so many people. Most importantly, include a minimum of one detailed solution, or a well-developed argument as to why no solution is necessary.

Thesis: Write a *one-sentence* response to the above assignment. Make certain this single sentence offers a clear statement of your position.

Example: The waning physical health of a generation leads to decreased mental heath, and the only solution will be to mandate activity through school programs.

_____

_____

Organizational Plan: List at least three subtopics you will use to support your main idea. This list is your outline.

1. _____

2. _____

3. _____

Draft: Following your outline, write a good first draft of your essay. Remember to support all of your points with examples, facts, references to reading, etc.

Review and Revise: Exchange essays with a classmate. Using the scoring guide for Organization on page 271, score your partner's essay (while he or she scores yours). Focus on the organizational plan and the use of language conventions. If necessary, rewrite your essay to improve the organizational plan and/or your use of language

Lesson Nineteen

1. **propitious** (prō pish´ əs) *adj.* promising; auspicious
    The gold doubloon was a *propitious* discovery for the explorers because it meant that the treasure was nearby.
    syn: favorable; advantageous; beneficial   *ant: ominous; harmful; unfortunate*

2. **utilitarian** (yōō til ə târ´ ē ən) *adj.* useful; practical
    The hermit's *utilitarian* cabin provided shelter from the weather and a place to store food, but little else.
    syn: functional   *ant: useless*

3. **inchoate** (in kō´ ət, kō´ āt) *adj.* not yet complete; undeveloped
    He thought that with a little refining, his *inchoate* idea could easily become the invention of the century.
    syn: rudimentary; preliminary; unformed   *ant: refined; shaped; developed*

4. **inveterate** (in vet´ ər it) *adj.* habitual; continuing
    The *inveterate* criminal didn't retire until he was incarcerated.
    syn: chronic

5. **spurious** (spyŭr´ ē əs) *adj.* possible but ultimately false; not genuine
    The evidence did not comply with the defendant's *spurious* testimony.
    syn: counterfeit; bogus   *ant: legitimate; genuine; authentic*

6. **schism** (siz´ əm, skiz´) *n.* a separation or division
    The political party experienced a severe *schism* when members disagreed about how best to distribute the funds.
    syn: break; estrangement; split   *ant: unification; merger; alliance*

7. **tremulous** (trem´ yə ləs) *adj.* timid; fearful
    Afraid of being rejected, he asked her out on a date in a *tremulous* voice.
    syn: anxious; sheepish; nervous   *ant: brave; confident; bold*

8. **dissipate** (dis´ ə pāt) *v.* to waste recklessly; to exhaust
    It took only one month for the irresponsible son to *dissipate* his inheritance.
    syn: squander; misuse   *ant: save; conserve*

9. **rescind** (ri sind´) *v.* to repeal; to make void
    Congress was forced to *rescind* the unconstitutional law.
    syn: recall; nullify   *ant: adopt; enact; promote*

233

10. **transient** (tran´ zē ənt) *adj.* remaining only a short time
The restaurant owner treated the regular customers better than she did the *transient* customers, who probably wouldn't return.
syn: temporary; fleeting; provisional *ant: permanent; enduring*

11. **stentorian** (sten tôr´ ē ən) *adj.* extremely loud
The lieutenant repeated the general's orders in a *stentorian* voice that could be heard by the entire regiment.
syn: blaring; booming; roaring *ant: quiet; muted*

12. **fulsome** (fŏŏl´ səm) *adj.* offensively flattering; insincere
The driver smirked and made a *fulsome* compliment to his opponent before the race.
syn: unctuous; ingratiating; fawning *ant: sincere; heartfelt*

13. **extant** (ek´ stənt, stânt) *adj.* still in existence
Despite the effectiveness of modern medicine, home remedies and the use of healing herbs are still *extant*.
syn: existent; present; remaining *ant: extinct; dead; gone*

14. **unwieldy** (un wēl´ dē) *adj.* not easily carried because of size, shape, or complexity
It took an hour to carry the *unwieldy* couch up the stairs to the apartment.
syn: awkward; cumbersome; ungainly *ant: convenient; manageable*

15. **abjure** (ab jōōr´) *v.* to renounce or recant
During a public rally, the dictator forced the writer to *abjure* his criticism of the government.
syn: retract; revoke *ant: assert; maintain; endorse*

Exercise I

Words in Context

From the list below, supply the words needed to complete the paragraph. Some words will not be used.

dissipate	**inchoate**	**propitious**	**rescind**
extant	**transient**	**unwieldy**	

1.   The tropical storm struck with swift fury; a rogue wave had destroyed the tiny ship's wheelhouse and pulled both the skipper and the first mate overboard into the raging sea. The engine and radio had been rendered inoperable, and the only _____ supplies consisted of a single case of bottled water and a small cooler containing sandwiches.
      "We don't know how long we'll be adrift, so we cannot foolishly _____ our limited food supply," said the only remaining officer as the passengers stared horrified at the broken glass lying on the deck where the wheelhouse once stood. Jack, a sailor who at least had a[n] _____ knowledge of mechanics, fiddled with the engine in an attempt to get it to run. That night, passengers helplessly watched the _____ lights of ships passing in the distance, but had no means of signaling them. Early the next morning, though, they awoke to the _____ sound of the ship's engine sputtering, coughing, clanging, and then, miraculously, running.

From the list below, supply the words needed to complete the paragraph. Some words will not be used.

dissipate	**spurious**	**unwieldy**	**schism**
inveterate	**abjure**	**stentorian**	

2.   Bill and Ted had been friends for twenty years, until falling in love with the same woman caused a[n] _____ that drove them apart. Though the woman had no interest in either of the men and had long ago departed the small town, a[n] _____ contempt remained between the former pals for years. When they inadvertently crossed paths with one another around town or at the grocery store, Bill and Ted exchanged _____ greetings that did little to hide their mutual scorn. It took twelve years for the two men to _____ their dislike for each other and cast off the ridiculous and _____ grudge that had burdened them throughout their lives.

From the list below, supply the words needed to complete the paragraph. Some words will not be used.

rescind	**extant**	**fulsome**	**stentorian**
utilitarian	**tremulous**	**schism**	

3.   Ryan was just about to doze off when a[n] _____ announcement blasted over the intercom, causing some of his more _____ fellow travelers to sit up straight in their coach-class seats. In his most _____ voice, the captain thanked the passengers for flying the airline and then _____ his previous estimate that the flight would be late; passengers could expect to arrive in Anchorage in less than one hour. The news pleased Ryan; if the flight arrived early, he would have ample time to prepare for his important business meeting. He smiled as he slipped his notebook computer into a[n] _____ leather briefcase and buckled his seatbelt.

Exercise II

Sentence Completion

Complete the sentence in a way that shows you understand the meaning of the italicized vocabulary word.

1. Jill wants a *utilitarian* family car, but her husband wants…

2. Vicky replaced her *unwieldy* purse with one that…

3. The corporation hired a lobbyist to convince the government to *rescind* legislation that…

4. The *tremulous* man could not bring himself to…

5. The supports of the century-old railroad bridge are still *extant*, despite…

6. Phil had only *transient* exposure to the contagious patients, so he didn't…

7. The campers could not *dissipate* their supplies because they…

8. During the questioning, the captured soldier created a *spurious* story that…

9. Mike, an *inveterate* joker, constantly thinks about…

10. The boss hated hearing the *fulsome* comments of employees who were simply trying to…

11. When a *schism* resulted over the best way to find the trail, half of the lost hikers…

12. The angry teacher made a *stentorian* request for the students to…

13. To the crew of the marooned ship, a bird carrying nesting materials was a *propitious* sign that…

14. When new discoveries proved him wrong, the scientist was driven to *abjure*…

15. The novel will remain *inchoate* until the author…

Exercise III

Roots, Prefixes, and Suffixes

Study the entries and answer the questions that follow.

The root *mis* means "hatred."
The root *bio* means "life."
The root *morph* means "shape."
The root *anthrop* means "human."
The suffix *–logy* means "study of."
The prefix *meta–* means "change."
The prefix *anti–* means "against."
The prefix *a–* means "not" or "none."

1. Using *literal* translations as guidance, define the following words without using a dictionary.

    A.   anthropomorphic   D.   antibiotic
    B.   metamorphosis   E.   biology
    C.   anthropology   F.   amorphous

2. The root *graph* means "writing." What does the word *biography* literally mean?

3. There is a special branch of linguistics (the study of language) called *morphology*. Explain the probable purpose of this branch.

4. A[n] _____ has a hatred for his or her fellow human beings.

5. List as many words as you can think of that contain the root *bio*.

Exercise IV

Inference

Complete the sentence by inferring information about the italicized word from its context.

1. Your current jacket might look nice on you in the Arctic, but you'll need to replace it with a *utilitarian* coat that...

2. Someone who has an *inchoate* understanding of electricity should not...

3. To get the *unwieldy* box from the store to your home, you might need to...

Exercise V

Writing

Here is a writing prompt similar to the one you will find on the writing portion of an assessment test.

Plan and write an essay based on the following statement:

> Let us honor if we can
> The vertical man,
> Though we value none
> But the horizontal one.

> –W. H. Auden, *Shorts*

Assignment: Do you agree or disagree with Auden's suggestion about how and when people are appreciated by others? In an essay, use your own language to translate Auden's statement, and explain why you do or do not agree with it. Support your essay using examples from literature, history, current events, or your experience or observation.

Thesis: Write a *one-sentence* response to the above assignment. Make certain this single sentence offers a clear statement of your position.

Example: Auden appropriately suggests that great people are seldom appreciated while they are alive, but there are many exceptions to this practice.

_____

_____

Organizational Plan: List at least three subtopics you will use to support your main idea. This list is your outline.

1. _____

2. _____

3. _____

Draft: Following your outline, write a good first draft of your essay. Remember to support all of your points with examples, facts, references to reading, etc.

Review and Revise: Exchange essays with a classmate. Using the Holistic scoring guide on page 276, score your partner's essay (while he or she scores yours). If necessary, rewrite your essay to correct the problems noted by your partner.

Exercise VI

Improving Paragraphs

Read the following passage and then choose the best revision for the underlined portions of the paragraph. The questions will require you to make decisions regarding the revision of the reading selection. Some revisions are not of actual mistakes, but will improve the clarity of the writing.

[1]

(1) Any day of the week, between 10am to 11pm, drop by a major bookstore. (2) You will see why movies and television will never replace written <u>literature, people</u>[2] simply love to hold a book. (3) They find excitement, comfort, <u>an adventure, and</u>[3] familiarity in both handling and reading books.

1. Which choice best corrects an error in sentence 1?
   A. Remove the comma after *week*.
   B. Remove the comma after *11pm*.
   C. Replace *drop* with *stop*.
   D. Replace *to* with *and*.

2. F. NO CHANGE
   G. literature: people
   H. literature people
   J. literature because people

3. A. NO CHANGE
   B. adventure, and also a
   C. adventure, and
   D. an adventure and

[2]

(4) Holding a book transports the reader to earlier times, even to the happiness of childhood, when we snuggled up for that last story before bedtime. (5) Bedtime stories taught us to associate the closeness of a parent, the safety of home, and the joy of a story; on the contrary, some remnant of this satisfaction carries over to our more mature encounters with books. (6) The physicality of those experiences is somehow enclosed within the covers of every new book we touch.

4. In sentence 5, *on the contrary* should be replaced with
   F. indeed.
   G. even so.
   H. after all.
   J. in simpler terms.

[3]

(7) Even the look and the smell of a book can be captivating. (8) The <u>memories contained in a book that have old photographs take</u>[5] us back to the time when we pored over pictures, trying to imagine the motion of Willie Mays making "The Catch," or searching the faces of soldiers to understand their feelings before they landed on the <u>beaches of normandy</u>.[6] (9) The pulp-smell of an old book can also bring back the memories of discovering classics like *Jane Eyre*, *Wuthering Heights*, or *Pride and <u>Prejudice books</u>*[7] that carried us through long summers at a grandmother's house. (10) The same smell, though, reminds us of finally being forced to open up a copy of *David Copperfield* to fulfill a summer reading list assignment, so it is not always a pleasant experience. (11) Connecting books with sight and smell is only natural; smell is, <u>after-all</u>[8] the most memorable sense for humans, and sight is the most used.

5. A. NO CHANGE
   B. memories contained in a book that have old photographs takes
   C. memories contained in a book that has old photographs takes
   D. memories contained in a book that has old photographs take

6. F. NO CHANGE
   G. Beaches of Normandy
   H. beaches of Normandy
   J. Normandy's Beaches

7. A. NO CHANGE
   B. *Prejudice*, these books
   C. *Prejudice,* books
   D. *Prejudice* the books

8. F. NO CHANGE
   G. after all
   H. afterall
   J. after all,

9. Which sentence of paragraph 3 is antithetical to the intent of the passage?
   A. sentence 7
   B. sentence 8
   C. sentence 9
   D. sentence 10

[4]

(12) While very few people read reference books for fun, many researchers prefer <u>paper books versus online</u>[10] databases, which are usually inundated with pop-up windows and advertisements. (13) With **utilitarian** books, readers can use paper bookmarks to easily compare several sources simultaneously. (14) Advanced publishing technology have shortened the time required to print new books, giving many reference books faster production cycles and making them easier to update frequently. (15) While some material may be more current on the Internet, the intricacies of computer-based research <u>were daunting</u>[12] for many researchers; the ability to make textual comparisons is circumscribed, and the problems of documenting source material are multiplied.

10. F. NO CHANGE
    G. paperback books versus online
    H. paper books from online
    J. paper books to online

11. Which choice best describes a grammatical error in sentence 14?
    A. subject-verb agreement error
    B. run-on sentence
    C. improper capitalization
    D. comma splice

12. F. NO CHANGE
    G. was daunting
    H. had been daunting
    J. can be daunting

[5]

(16) The peculiar relationship between writer and reader is best felt through the medium of a book. (17) A book, sometimes even a particular edition, casts a spell on the reader by which he or she can <u>literally explore</u>[13] the mind or heart of the author. (18) The relationship is apparent in the way that a child reads and deeply experiences a picture book<u>, to return to</u> it[14] repeatedly and treasuring the experience for years. (19) This experience melds the intellectual with the tactile, the cognitive with the emotional, and the personal with the universal; it is unique to the reader, the author, and the book that ties them together.

13. A. NO CHANGE
    B. literarily explore
    C. virtually explore
    D. explore

14. F. NO CHANGE
    G. , returning to it
    H. to returning to it
    J. , return to it

15. If one paragraph had to be deleted from this passage, which one could be deleted without affecting the author's main idea?
    A. paragraph 1
    B. paragraph 2
    C. paragraph 3
    D. paragraph 4

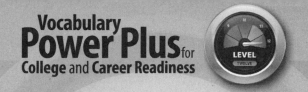
Lesson Twenty

1. **waive** (wāv) *v.* to relinquish something voluntarily; to refrain from enforcing
   Before testing the new medicine, he *waived* his right to sue the drug company.
   syn: forfeit; cede; defer   *ant: demand; enforce; impose*

2. **discerning** (di sûr´ ning) *adj.* having keen perception
   The *discerning* hunter spotted a deer hundreds of yards away.
   syn: perceptive; sharp; astute

3. **cerebral** (ser ə´ brəl) *adj.* favoring intelligence over emotions or instinct
   The dry novel had more *cerebral* appeal than it had displays of drama.
   syn: intellectual; rational; logical   *ant: intuitive; instinctive*

4. **punitive** (pyōō´ ni tiv) *adj.* punishing; pertaining to punishment
   The government enacted *punitive* trade restrictions on any nation that refused to comply with new environmental laws.
   syn: disciplinary; corrective; retaliatory

5. **conundrum** (kə nun´ drəm) *n.* a difficult problem
   The police officer faced quite a *conundrum* when he caught his own son shoplifting.
   syn: quandary; predicament

6. **relegate** (rel´ i gāt) *v.* to place in an unfavorable place or position
   The tsar *relegated* his political enemies to the freezing tundra of Siberia.
   syn: demote; displace; exile

7. **echelon** (esh´ ə lon) *n.* a level of authority or responsibility; a rank
   Workers in the management *echelon* of the company were happy, but the laborers were about to go on strike.
   syn: level

8. **idyllic** (īdil´ ik) *adj.* simple and carefree; delightfully serene
   A hurricane ruined our plans for an *idyllic* vacation at the beach house.
   syn: charming; picturesque; pleasant   *ant: unpleasant; oppressive; dire*

9. **soluble** (sol´ yə bəl) *adj.* easily dissolved
   The packets contain *soluble* powder for making iced tea.
   ant: insoluble

10. **hypocrisy** (hi pok′ ri sē) *n.* professing beliefs, feelings, or values that one does
     not have or practice
     In an act of complete *hypocrisy*, the actress who complains about the overuse of
     fossil fuels bought a second private jet.
     syn: insincerity; duplicity   *ant: sincerity; earnestness*

11. **serendipity** (ser ən dip′ i tē) *n.* the occurrence of a fortunate, accidental event
     or discovery
     The discovery of penicillin is attributed to *serendipity* because the mold's properties
     were first observed when it was inadvertently allowed to contaminate a different
     experiment.
     syn: luck

12. **nondescript** (non di skript′) *adj.* lacking individual or distinct characteristics
     The private investigator drove a *nondescript* car so she could keep a low profile.
     syn: uninteresting; common; ordinary   *ant: unusual; unique;*
                                                                          extraordinary

13. **acme** (ak′ mē) *n.* the highest point
     Winning the championship game was the *acme* of the season.
     syn: pinnacle; climax; peak   *ant: nadir*

14. **malinger** (mə ling′ gər) *v.* to feign illness to avoid work
     Scott *malingered* so often that no one believed him when he was actually ill.
     syn: shirk

15. **deleterious** (del i tēr′ ē əs) *adj.* having a harmful effect; injurious
     Many people simply ignore the *deleterious* effects of prolonged exposure to the sun.
     syn: destructive; pernicious; damaging   *ant: beneficial; harmless; benign*

Exercise I

Words in Context

From the list below, supply the words needed to complete the paragraph. Some words will not be used.

soluble	echelon	punitive	waive
idyllic	discerning	deleterious	

1. Their garage contained three generations of family junk, but Carla's _____ eye easily noticed the broken antique thermometer on the floor. She carefully picked it up, balancing the exposed blob of mercury on the top of the thermometer's tin backing. She knew that mercury fumes were _____ to good health, but she didn't realize that gold is _____ in liquid mercury until a drop of the substance dissolved a portion of her wedding ring. As she stared in disbelief at her ring, Carla easily thought of a few _____ chores for her son, who had knocked the old thermometer to the floor, ignored it, and left to enjoy a[n] _____ summer day with his friends.

From the list below, supply the words needed to complete the paragraph. Some words will not be used.

cerebral	relegate	echelon	serendipity
conundrum	malinger	nondescript	

2. Newman faced a[n] _____ at work. He had to inform the higher _____ that what began as a[n] _____ typographical error in the company's software was now threatening the stability of the entire company network; however, Newman himself was responsible for the error. He assumed that management, upon hearing the bad news, would _____ him to a demeaning job in the mail room, but to his surprise, the bosses were overjoyed that Newman had spotted the error before any major damage had been done. Newman decided not to inform them that his catch was pure _____; he had found the error only because he had accidentally selected the wrong software to edit that day.

From the list below, supply the words needed to complete the paragraph. Some words will not be used.

acme	malinger	cerebral	punitive
hypocrisy	nondescript	waive	

3. Tension at the civic association reached its _____ when Fred accused the governing council of _____. Fred claimed that the charter members _____ their own membership fees, and most of them _____ when the organization conducted activities that did not directly benefit its leaders. Council members accused Fred of making false accusations, but he said that it didn't take a[n] _____ giant to figure out that the leaders had been engaging in crooked practices.

Exercise II

Sentence Completion

Complete the sentence in a way that shows you understand the meaning of the italicized vocabulary word.

1. Sam, orphaned since the age of four, did not have the *idyllic*...

2. The college might *waive* the requirement to take English 101 if you can prove that...

3. When the upper *echelon* of the company noticed Sandra's talent for eliminating unnecessary expenses, the board of directors...

4. After an hour of reading the *cerebral* articles in the textbook, Matt just wanted to...

5. Paul always *malingers* on days when...

6. The adventurers found themselves in a *conundrum* when they encountered...

7. The politician's *hypocrisy* became apparent when she made a speech about protecting wildlife and then approved...

8. A *discerning* collector will be able to...

9. That car's leaking radiator is *deleterious* to...

10. Meeting his former teacher was *serendipitous* because...

11. In addition to fines and court costs, the company had to pay *punitive* damages meant to...

12. Discovering the ancient treasure was the *acme* of...

13. After several disciplinary problems, Adam's parents decided to *relegate* their son to...

14. Sugar is *soluble* in water, so if it gets damp,...

15. The police wanted the van to appear *nondescript*, so...

Exercise III

Roots, Prefixes, and Suffixes

Study the entries and answer the questions that follow.

The root *pol* means "city."
The root *civ* means "citizen."
The root *urb* means "city."
The prefix *mega–* means "large."
The prefix *sub–* means "under."

1. Using *literal* translations as guidance, define the following words without using a dictionary.

A. suburban	D. megalopolis
B. civic	E. civilian
C. urbanize	F. civil

2. The word *urbane* means "smooth," "polished," or "charming." Explain the possible reason for this word containing the root *urb*.

3. During a city council election, _____ might go door-to-door and ask you for your vote; however, if they refuse to leave your property, you might need to call the _____.

4. The prefix *metro–* means "mother." What, literally, is a *metropolis*?

5. List as many words as you can think of that contain the prefix *sub–*.

Exercise IV

Inference

Complete the sentence by inferring information about the italicized word from its context.

1. If Bill *waives* his rights of ownership in order to have his manuscript published, then he will not…

2. A scientist might attribute his or her success to *serendipity* if he or she did not intentionally…

3. A person who prefers *cerebral* books about philosophy or science would probably not…

Exercise V

Critical Reading

Below is a pair of reading passages followed by several multiple-choice questions. Carefully read the passages and choose the best answer for each of the questions.

Victor Hugo, famous for works such as Les Miserables, *which depicts life during the French Revolution, had a son, Charles, who was accused of criticizing a public execution—a punishable offense in Paris at the time. In passage 1, delivered in 1851, Hugo entreats the court to grant mercy in sentencing his son.*

Socrates, one of the greatest philosophers in world history, was executed in 399 B.C. Passage 2 recounts parts of Socrates' last speech before the judges of the Greek court condemned him to death.

Passage 1

GENTLEMEN OF THE JURY:—If there is a culprit here, it is not my son—it is myself—it is I!—I, who for these last twenty-five years have opposed capital Punishment—have contended for the inviolability of human life—have committed this crime, for which my son is now arraigned. Here I denounce myself, Mr. Advocate General! I have committed it under all aggravated
5   circumstance—deliberately, repeatedly, tenaciously. Yes, this old and absurd lex talionis—this law of blood for blood—I have combated all my life—all my life, gentlemen of the jury! And, while I have breath, I will continue to combat it, by all my efforts as a writer, by all my words and all my votes as a legislator! I declare it before the crucifix; before that victim of the penalty of death, who sees and hears us; before that gibbet, to which, two thousand years ago, for the eternal instruction
10 of the generations, the human law nailed the Divine!

In all that my son has written on the subject of capital punishment—and for writing and publishing which he is now before you on trial—in all that he has written, he has merely proclaimed the sentiments with which, from his infancy, I have inspired him. Gentlemen jurors, the right to criticize a law, and to criticize it severely—especially a penal law—is placed beside
15 the duty of amelioration, like a torch beside the work under the artisan's hand. This right of the journalist is as sacred, as necessary, as imprescriptible, as the right of the legislator.

What are the circumstances? A man, a convict, a sentenced wretch, is dragged, on a certain morning, to one of our public squares. There he finds the scaffold! He shudders, he struggles, he refuses to die. He is young yet—only twenty-nine. Ah! I know what you will say—"He is a
20 murderer!" But hear me. Two officers seize him. His hands, his feet, are tied. He throws off the two officers. A frightful struggle ensues. His feet, bound as they are, become entangled in the ladder. He uses the scaffold against the scaffold! The struggle is prolonged. Horror seizes on the crowd. The officers—sweat and shame on their brows—pale, panting, terrified, despairing—despairing with I know not what horrible despair—shrinking under that public reprobation which ought
25 to have visited the penalty, and spared the passive instrument, the executioner—the officers strive savagely. The victim clings to the scaffold and shrieks for pardon. His clothes are torn—his shoulders bloody—still he resists.

At length, after three-quarters of an hour of this monstrous effort, of this spectacle without a name, of this agony—agony for all, be it understood—agony for the assembled spectators as well
30 as for the condemned man—after this age of anguish, gentlemen of the jury, they take back the poor wretch to his prison. The people breathe again. The people, naturally merciful, hope that the man will be spared. But no—the guillotine, though vanquished, remains standing. There it frowns all day in the midst of a sickened population. And at night, the officers, reinforced, drag forth the wretch again, so bound that he is but an inert weight—they drag him forth, haggard, bloody,
35 weeping, pleading, howling for life—calling upon God, calling upon his father and mother—for like a very child had this man become in the prospect of death—they drag him forth to execution. He is hoisted on to the scaffold, and his head falls! And then through every conscience runs a shudder.

Passage 2

FOR the sake of no long space of time, O Athenians, you will incur the character and reproach at the hands of those who wish to defame the city, of having put that wise man, Socrates, to death. For those who wish to defame you will assert that I am wise, tho I am not. If, then, you had waited for a short time, this would have happened of its own accord; for observe my age, that
5 it is far advanced in life, and near death. But I say this not to you all, but to those only who have condemned me to die. And I say this too to the same persons. Perhaps you think, O Athenians, that I have been convicted through the want of arguments, by which I might have persuaded you, had I thought it right to do and say anything so that I might escape punishment. Far otherwise: I have been convicted through want indeed, yet not of arguments, but of audacity and impudence,
10 and of the inclination to say such things to you as would have been most agreeable for you to hear, had I lamented and bewailed and done and said many other things unworthy of me, as I affirm, but such as you are accustomed to hear from others.

But neither did I then think that I ought, for the sake of avoiding danger, to do anything unworthy of a freeman, nor do I now repent of having so defended myself; but I should much
15 rather choose to die having so defended myself than to live in that way. For neither in a trial nor in battle is it right that I or any one else should employ every possible means whereby he may avoid death; for in battle it is frequently evident that a man might escape death by laying down his arms and throwing himself on the mercy of his pursuers. And there are many other devices in every danger, by which to avoid death, if a man dares to do and say everything.
20 But this is not difficult, O Athenians, to escape death, but it is much more difficult to avoid depravity, for it runs swifter than death. And now I, being slow and aged, am overtaken by the slower of the two; but my accusers, being strong and active, have been overtaken by the swifter, wickedness. And now I depart, condemned by you to death; but they condemned by truth, as guilty of iniquity and injustice: and I abide my sentence and so do they. These things, perhaps,
25 ought so to be, and I think that they are for the best.

In the next place, I desire to predict to you who have condemned me, what will be your fate: for I am now in that condition in which men most frequently prophesy, namely, when they are about to die. I say then to you, O Athenians, who have condemned me to death, that immediately after my death a punishment will overtake you, far more severe, by Jupiter, than that which you
30 have inflicted on me. For you have done this thinking you should be freed from the necessity of giving an account of your life. The very contrary however, as I affirm, will happen to you. Your accusers will be more numerous, whom I have now restrained, though you did not perceive it; and they will be more severe, inasmuch as they are younger and you will be more indignant. For, if you think that by putting men to death you will restrain any one from upbraiding you because
35 you do not live well, you are much mistaken; for this method of escape is neither possible nor honorable, but that other is most honorable and most easy, not to put a check upon others, but for a man to take heed to himself, how he may be most perfect. Having predicted thus much to those of you who have condemned me, I take my leave of you.

But with you who have voted for my acquittal, I would gladly hold converse on what has
40 now taken place, while the magistrates are busy and I am not yet carried to the place where I must die. Stay with me then, so long, O Athenians, for nothing hinders our conversing with each other, whilst we are permitted to do so; for I wish to make known to you, as being my friends, the meaning of that which has just now befallen me. To me then, O my judges—and in calling you judges I call you rightly—a strange thing has happened. For the wonted prophetic voice of
45 my guardian deity, on every former occasion, even in the most trifling affairs, opposed me, if I was about to do anything wrong; but now, that has befallen me which ye yourselves behold, and which any one would think and which is supposed to be the extremity of evil, yet neither when I departed from home in the morning did the warning of the god oppose me, nor when I came up here to the place of trial, nor in my address when I was about to say anything; yet on
50 other occasions it has frequently restrained me in the midst of speaking. But now it has never throughout this proceeding opposed me, either in what I did or said. What then do I suppose to be the cause of this? I will tell you: what has befallen me appears to be a blessing; and it is

impossible that we think rightly who suppose that death is an evil. A great proof of this to me is
the fact that it is impossible but that the accustomed signal should have opposed me, unless I had
55 been about to meet with some good.

You, therefore, O my judges, ought to entertain good hopes with respect to death, and to
meditate on this one truth, that to a good man nothing is evil, neither while living nor when
dead, nor are his concerns neglected by the gods. And what has befallen me is not the effect of
chance; but this is clear to me, that now to die, and be freed from my cares, is better for me. On
60 this account the warning in no way turned me aside; and I bear no resentment toward those who
condemned me, or against my accusers, although they did not condemn and accuse me with this
intention, but thinking to injure me: in this they deserve to be blamed.

Thus much, however, I beg of them. Punish my sons, when they grow up, O judges, paining
them as I have pained you, if they appear to you to care for riches or anything else before virtue,
65 and if they think themselves to be something when they are nothing, reproach them as I have
done you, for not attending to what they ought, and for conceiving themselves to be something
when they are worth nothing. If ye do this, both I and my sons shall have met with just treatment
at your hands.

But it is now time to depart,—for me to die, for you to live. But which of us is going to a
70 better state is unknown to every one but God.

1A. Choose the statement that best rephrases the argument Hugo establishes in the first
sentence of passage 1.
  A. The courts of Paris are corrupt.
  B. Hugo will die before he agrees with the court.
  C. The death penalty is morally wrong.
  D. Hugo is responsible for his son's misdeed.
  E. Too many people blindly adhere to the law.

1B. The intended audience of passage 1 is
  A. Hugo's opponents.
  B. government legislators.
  C. a courtroom.
  D. the French public.
  E. the world at large.

2A. Which choice best paraphrases the following quotation from passage 1?

"Gentlemen jurors, the right to criticize a law, and to criticize it severely—especially
a penal law—is placed beside the duty of amelioration, like a torch beside the work
under the artisan's hand."

  A. Unrestricted criticism is essential to the improvement of law.
  B. Legislation should not be criticized without a solution.
  C. Gentlemen must criticize, as an artisan must work.
  D. The penal law cannot be harmed by constructive criticism.
  E. Criticism is even more important than duty to uphold the law.

2B. Based on your answer to question 2A, *amelioration* most nearly means
  A.   interpreting.
  B.   obstructing.
  C.   fighting.
  D.   understanding.
  E.   helping.

3A. Paragraph 3, passage 1, is best described as portraying
  A.   the population's demand for public executions.
  B.   the spectacle caused by a fear-stricken condemned prisoner.
  C.   Hugo's first-hand observation of an execution.
  D.   the public's judgmental attitude toward the prisoner.
  E.   the abusive treatment by the officers during the execution.

3B. In paragraphs 3 and 4, passage 1, Hugo suggests that witnesses to an execution are most likely to react with feelings of
  A.   rage.
  B.   panic.
  C.   smugness.
  D.   indifference.
  E.   mercy.

4A. The author personifies the guillotine in the final paragraph of passage 1 by suggesting that
  A.   the condemned man has escaped the guillotine before.
  B.   the guillotine knows it will claim another victim soon.
  C.   the public disapproves of a killing device in the square.
  D.   the guillotine is sympathetic to the criminal's misfortune.
  E.   the guillotine is angry for having to wait for the execution.

4B. Choose the phrase from passage 1, paragraph 4, that best supports your answer to question 4A.
  A.   "frowns all day"
  B.   "drag forth the wretch"
  C.   "prospect of death"
  D.   "howling for life"
  E.   "age of anguish"

5A. As used in lines 7 and 9 of passage 2, *want* most nearly means
  A.   desire.
  B.   lack.
  C.   famine.
  D.   choice.
  E.   like.

5B. According to lines 1-25, Socrates suggests that he could have avoided trial by
   A.   firmly adhering to his own beliefs.
   B.   providing better arguments to support his ideas.
   C.   showing mercy to his accusers.
   D.   seeking no mercy from his judges.
   E.   telling the court officials what they wanted to hear.

6A. According to paragraph 3 of the second passage, the accusers are guilty of
   A.   theft.
   B.   revenge.
   C.   mercy.
   D.   corruption.
   E.   rejection.

6B. Socrates would agree with which one of the following statements?
   A.   Saying nothing is the greatest defense.
   B.   It is better to die with integrity than to live a lie.
   C.   Death is the only way the council can silence detractors.
   D.   Court officials usually represent the best citizens of society.
   E.   Survival dictates that one must compromise at times.

7A. How do the passages differ regarding how the authors' sons are included?
   A.   Hugo uses his son as an example of decency, while Socrates accuses his sons of corruption.
   B.   Hugo compares his son to the jurors, unlike Socrates.
   C.   Hugo attempts to justify his son's actions, while Socrates prescribes a tentative punishment for his sons.
   D.   Socrates seeks mercy for his sons, unlike Hugo.
   E.   Socrates takes more responsibility for his son's crimes than Hugo does for his son.

7B. Socrates requests that his sons be punished if they
   A.   become government officials.
   B.   take too much interest in wealth.
   C.   refuse to attend their father's burial.
   D.   do not follow the teachings of Plato.
   E.   speak out against the government.

8A. Both passages involve situations in which people are put on trial for
   A.   extorting government funds.
   B.   harboring fugitives.
   C.   leading revolutions.
   D.   communicating with the enemy.
   E.   subversive speech.

8B. The narrators of each passage are different in that
    A. one is a philosopher, and the other is a soldier.
    B. one defends capital punishment, and the other condemns it.
    C. one is defending himself, while the other is defending his son.
    D. one has two sons being tried, and the other has only one.
    E. one appears to be relieved, while the other is horrified.

9. The two authors might *disagree* with each other about which one of the following statements?
    A. Capital punishment can have negative effects upon the public.
    B. Citizens must be watchful of the government.
    C. One should be free to speak out against government policies.
    D. One should attempt every possible option to escape death.
    E. There are problems with capital punishment.

10A. Which choice most accurately contrasts the basis of each author's argument?
    A. Hugo demands that his son be held culpable, while Socrates attempts to atone for his crimes.
    B. Passage 1 is persuasive, while passage 2 is informative.
    C. Passage 1 emphasizes rhetoric, and passage 2 contains abundant physical descriptions.
    D. Passage 1 is written in third-person point of view, and passage 2 is written in omniscient.
    E. Hugo pleads for compassion, but Socrates warns of consequences that will follow.

10B. Choose the quotation from passage 2 that best supports your answer to question 10A.
    A. "These things, perhaps, ought so to be, and I think that they are for the best." (24-25)
    B. "I have been convicted through want indeed,...of audacity and impudence..." (8-12)
    C. "...I desire to predict to you who have condemned me, what will be your fate..." (26-28)
    D. "...this method of escape is neither possible nor honorable..." (35-37)
    E. "...to a good man nothing is evil...nor are his concerns neglected by the gods." (56-58)

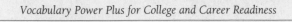

Vocabulary Power Plus for College and Career Readiness

LEVEL
TWELVE

Lesson Twenty-One

1. **prosaic** (prō zā´ ik) *adj.* straightforward and unimaginative; uninteresting
   After missing my curfew, I had to sit through yet another boring, *prosaic* speech on family rules.
   syn: banal; humdrum; monotonous   *ant: fascinating; inspiring*

2. **anomie** (an´ ə mē) *n.* societal or personal instability caused by a lack or erosion of values, standards, or ideals
   The Roman Empire ruled the world until widespread *anomie*, fueled by corruption, caused its decline.

3. **factotum** (fak tō´ təm) *n.* an employee with a variety of jobs or responsibilities
   As a *factotum* for the family business, Craig did the jobs of three employees.
   syn: workhorse; operator   *ant: principal*

4. **extrinsic** (ik strin´ sik) *adj.* not essential, extraneous
   To make the aircraft lighter, the crew removed *extrinsic* parts not required for flight.
   syn: unnecessary; adventitious   *ant: necessary; crucial; required; intrinsic*

5. **abrogate** (ab´ rə gāt) *v.* to abolish, especially by authority; to revoke formally
   The town council voted to *abrogate* the unpopular law.
   syn: annul; invalidate; repeal   *ant: establish; ratify; support*

6. **apostasy** (ə păs´ tə sē) *n.* abandonment of one's principles, faith, or religious beliefs
   Government officials doubted the genuineness of the former spy's sudden *apostasy*.
   syn: defection; disavowal; renunciation   *ant: commitment; dedication; loyalty*

7. **propinquity** (prə pink´ wi tē) *n.* nearness; proximity
   His *propinquity* to both murders made Tom a suspect.
   syn: closeness; immediacy; adjacency   *ant: distance; remoteness*

8. **outré** (ōō trā´) *adj.* extremely unconventional; bizarre
   Malcolm had an *outré* personality that made him well known for his odd behavior.
   syn: eccentric; freaky; outlandish   *ant: conforming; ordinary*

9. **magniloquent** (mag nil´ ə kwənt) *adj.* lofty in expression; pompous
   In a *magniloquent* voice, the herald announced the arrival of the royal family.
   syn: grandiloquent; grandiose; ostentatious   *ant: humble; subtle; reserved*

10. **febrile** (fe´ bril) *adj.* pertaining to fever; feverish
    The *febrile* child was sent home from school to recover.

11. **supine** (soo pīn´) *adj.* lying on one's back; lying face-up
    The hero lay helplessly *supine* in the villain's library after falling victim to the knockout gas.

    ant: prone

12. **parity** (par´ i tē) *n.* equality
    North and South Korea have no economic *parity*.
    syn: balance; equivalence; proportion   *ant: disparity; imbalance*

13. **analects** (an´ ə lekts) *n.* selections from a literary work
    The Eastern philosophy class discussed the *analects* of Confucius.

14. **surreptitious** (sûr əp tish´ əs) *adj.* accomplished through stealth and secrecy
    Smiling and nodding, the man cast a *surreptitious* glance at his watch while listening to his chatty neighbor.
    syn: furtive; sneaky; clandestine   *ant: open; candid*

15. **cognizant** (kăg´ nə zənt) *adj.* fully informed; having knowledge of
    Ben nodded his head, pretending to be *cognizant* of what the teacher was talking about.
    syn: aware; perceptive; sentient   *ant: ignorant; unaware; oblivious*

Exercise I

Words in Context

From the list below, supply the words needed to complete the paragraph. Some words will not be used.

outré	prosaic	propinquity	analects
surreptitious	cognizant	supine	

1. None of the guards noticed Alistair's _____ entry into the secret compound. The investigative reporter, known for his _____ strategies in obtaining information, had ridden through the gates beneath a supply truck, and now he lay _____ on the ground beneath the vehicle, searching for potential hiding places. He grimaced when he became _____ of the anthill directly beneath his shoulders, but he made no sound because of the _____ of the guards in front of the truck.

From the list below, supply the words needed to complete the paragraph. Some words will not be used.

factotum	cognizant	prosaic	extrinsic
magniloquent	parity	abrogate	

2. When the government _____ the use of clandestine agents as assassins and saboteurs, the CIA was forced to find new methods of dealing with foreign threats and interests. Mr. Bell was one of those methods. According to his personnel file, Mr. Bell was simply a "program manager" at the Pentagon; however, despite the bland job title, he was one of many _____ whose duty was to resolve those international problems that public diplomacy cannot solve.

    Mr. Bell, whose real name is known only to his employer, gained most of his experience during the Cold War, when his primary mission was to ensure that the United States maintained defensive _____ with the Soviet Union. The work did include rare moments of extreme stress, but the job most often involved hours of reading _____ statistical documents, most of which contained only _____ information that had little bearing on national security.

From the list below, supply the words needed to complete the paragraph. Some words will not be used.

supine	analects	febrile	magniloquent
parity	anomie	apostasy	

3. Pete regretted his _____ of the simple life and desires he had before the massive failure of his dotcom business. Like many other young entrepreneurs, Pete's _____ overtook him as he fixated on monthly profit margins, _____-sounding advertisements, and lower prices, but failed to invest in better customer service.

    At times, Pete's anger over his own poor judgment made him red-faced and nearly _____, but within a week, he had thought of a new marketing idea: He would create a best-selling book that featured the personal accounts of the hundreds of failed dotcom business owners. The _____ of the failed owners would be excellent guidance for future entrepreneurs and would probably make him rich once again.

Exercise II

Sentence Completion

Complete the sentence in a way that shows you understand the meaning of the italicized vocabulary word.

1. Madeline grew weary of being a *factotum* with the responsibilities of…

2. Young Ralphie looked *febrile* this morning, so his mother…

3. Fiction and movies often depict the American Wild West as a place of *anomie*, where…

4. The English teacher said that the *extrinsic* information in the essay merely…

5. Derek's parents *abrogated* his access to the computer after…

6. The narrator of the automobile commercial explained in a *magniloquent* voice why the featured car was…

7. The camper was not *cognizant* of the rattlesnake in her tent until…

8. There is little *parity* in the quality of the hotel rooms, since one might…

9. The man's *outré* sales pitch involved the use of…

10. When a passing policeman saw customers in the bank lying *supine*, he knew that…

11. Detective Stone of the white-collar crimes division never understood the *apostasy* that caused successful people with wonderful families to…

12. As soon as the iron filings are in *propinquity* to the magnet, they…

13. Bored after sitting in the waiting room for an hour, Lenny picked up a *prosaic* pamphlet about…

14. Under the *surreptitious* cover of night, the spy…

15. The students discussed *analects* from *The Adventures of Huckleberry Finn* while studying…

Exercise III

Roots, Prefixes, and Suffixes

Study the entries and answer the questions that follow.

The roots *cur* and *curs* mean "to run."
The root *ambul* means "to walk."
The prefix *ob–* means "in the way of" or "against."
The prefix *per–* means "through."

1. Using *literal* translations as guidance, define the following words without using a dictionary.

A.	current	D.	amble
B.	ambulatory	E.	occur
C.	cursive	F.	perambulate

2. In the sentence, "John made a *cursory* inspection of his luggage," does the word *cursory* mean "fast," or "slow"?
    Explain why the blinking prompt on the display of a computer screen is called a *cursor*.

3. The root *somn* means sleep. If a person *somnambulates*, what is he or she doing?

4. A *current* is a flowing of something, or a passing from one person to another, so it is appropriate that coin or paper money, which circulates among people, is called _____.

5. List as many words as you can think of that contain the prefix *ob–*.

Exercise IV

Inference

Complete the sentence by inferring information about the italicized word from its context.

1. In a household with many children, *parity* of parental attention might be difficult to maintain because…

2. If a religious sect experiences widespread *apostasy*, then members are probably…

3. The government might be forced to *abrogate* an unpopular law if…

Exercise V

Writing

Here is a writing prompt similar to the one you will find on the writing portion of an assessment test.

Plan and write an essay based on the following statement:

> As in political so in literary action a man wins friends for himself
> mostly by the passion of his prejudices and the consistent narrowness
> of his outlook.
>
> –Joseph Conrad (1857–1924)

Assignment: Think about qualities of famous authors and determine whether you agree or disagree with Joseph Conrad's statement. In an essay, defend or refute Conrad's suggestion that a narrow outlook might be advantageous. Support your essay with evidence from literature, history, or your experience or observation.

Thesis: Write a *one-sentence* response to the above assignment. Make certain this single sentence offers a clear statement of your position.

Example: If not for the unique, narrow outlook of writers, the world would be absent of any great literature, for it is that unique perspective that attracts and fixes the attention of both readers and critics alike.

_____

_____

Organizational Plan: List at least three subtopics you will use to support your main idea. This list is your outline.

1. _____

2. _____

3. _____

Draft: Following your outline, write a good first draft of your essay. Remember to support all of your points with examples, facts, references to reading, etc.

Review and Revise: Exchange essays with a classmate. Using the Holistic scoring guide on page 276, score your partner's essay (while he or she scores yours). If necessary, rewrite your essay to correct the problems noted by your partner.

Exercise VI

English Practice

Identifying Sentence Errors

Identify the grammatical error in each of the following sentences. If the sentence contains no error, select answer choice E.

1. None of the students in gym class were dressed for calisthenics because the teacher
         (A)   (B)   (C)
    made them exercise too many times.   No error
             (D)   (E)

2. We could not account for our loss, not even after we went over our bank statement.
       (A)   (B)   (C)   (D)
    No error
     (E)

3. We need to make a decision about which of the three plans is more advantageous.
      (A)   (B)   (C)   (D)
    No error
     (E)

4. If you have any questions, please contact myself or any other teacher on duty
                 (A)   (B)   (C)
    who can help you with the test   No error
        (D)   (E)

5. You will have to speak quick to have your message go into the company's voice mail.
      (A)   (B)   (C)   (D)
    No error
     (E)

Improving Sentences

The underlined portion of each sentence below contains some flaw. Select the answer choice that best corrects the flaw.

6. If the boys had been in the shed, they would not hear the loud explosion, but since they were in the yard, they did notice the noise.
    A. they could not hear the loud explosion, but since they were in the yard, they did notice the noise.
    B. they would not have heard the loud explosion, but since they were in the yard, they did notice the noise.
    C. they would not hear the loud explosion; since they were in the yard, they noticed the noise.
    D. they were unable to have heard the loud explosion, but since they were in the yard, they did notice the noise.
    E. they would not hear the loud explosion, since they were in the yard; they noticed the noise.

7. Many people believe <u>that the reason dinosaurs became extinct is because</u> Earth's climate changed.
   A. that the reason the dinosaurs became extinct was because
   B. the reason dinosaurs became extinct is
   C. that dinosaurs became extinct when
   D. that dinosaurs became extinct because
   E. that the reason behind dinosaurs being extinct is because

8. <u>Between the three candidates, no one achieved a majority of the votes,</u> and there was a run-off election.
   A. Between the three candidates, no one achieved a large-enough majority of the votes,
   B. The court ruled that among the three candidates, no one achieved a majority of the votes,
   C. Not one of the three candidates achieved a majority of the votes cast,
   D. Among the three candidates, no one achieved a plurality of the votes,
   E. Between the three candidates, no one achieved the plurality of the votes,

9. Either the twins, the triplets, or the baby <u>have won the prize for being the most beautiful child in the contest.</u>
   A. has won the prize of the most beautiful child in the contest.
   B. has won the prize for being the most beautiful child in the contest.
   C. has won the prize for the most beautiful child in the contest.
   D. has won the contest by winning the most beautiful child competition.
   E. wins the prize for being the most beautiful child in the contest.

10. <u>Did you hear the cry for help asked Larry</u>
    A. "Did you hear the cry for 'help'?" asked Larry.
    B. "Did you hear the cry for Help?" asked Larry.
    C. Did you hear the cry for "help!" asked Larry?
    D. "Did you hear the cry for help?" asked Larry.
    E. "Did you hear the cry for help," asked Larry.

Vocabulary Power Plus for College and Career Readiness

LEVEL TWELVE

Review Lessons 19-21

Exercise I

Inferences

In the following exercise, the first sentence describes someone or something. Infer information from the first sentence, and then choose the word from the Word Bank that best completes the second sentence.

deleterious	punitive	unwieldy	transient
echelons	factotum	propinquity	propitious

1. Since the fishing boat survived the first half of the typhoon and now bobbed in the eye of the storm, the captain and crew had hope that they might just survive the second bout.

    From this sentence, we can infer that the ship's surviving the first half of the storm was a[n] _____ sign to the crew.

2. Each second the brave nuclear engineer spent in the reactor room trying to avert a meltdown increased the probability that he would die of radiation poisoning.

    From this sentence, we can infer that large doses of radiation have a[n] _____ effect on health.

3. Sid hates moving the upright piano because it is extremely heavy and has no good places to get a grip on it.

    From this sentence, we can infer that the _____ piano is difficult to relocate.

4. Yolanda knew that the food was terrible at the restaurant where she worked, but she never mentioned it because she was friends with the owner and grateful to have a much-needed job.

    From this sentence, we can infer that Yolanda's _____ with her employer prevented her from complaining about the restaurant's failures.

5. The soldiers on the front line hated receiving orders from high-ranking desk jockeys who had no idea what conditions were like on the battlefield.

    From this sentence, we can infer that the soldiers felt the _____ above them did not fully understand the complexities of the war.

Exercise II

Related Words

Some of the vocabulary words from Lessons 19 through 21 have related meanings. Complete the following sentences by choosing the word that best fits the context, based on information you infer from the use of the italicized word. Some word pairs will be antonyms, some will be synonyms, and some will simply be words often used in the same context.

1. Because they _____ when important work needed to be done, Privates Bailey and Pile received the *punitive* duty of cleaning latrines.
   A. rescinded
   B. malingered
   C. abjured
   D. dissipated
   E. waived

2. If the guards became _____ of anything out of the ordinary, then the prisoner's *surreptitious* escape over the wall would be blown.
   A. deleterious
   B. cerebral
   C. soluble
   D. magniloquent
   E. cognizant

3. Audrey likes the _____ designs of the flamboyant fashions modeled at shows, but because she is shy, she wears only *nondescript* clothes that do not draw attention to her.
   A. outré
   B. extrinsic
   C. prosaic
   D. supine
   E. surreptitious

4. When the church elders accused the young parishioner of _____ for complaints he had made, the man accused the elders of *hypocrisy* for breaking the very rules they preached.
   A. factotum
   B. anomie
   C. apostasy
   D. propinquity
   E. parity

5. After the gambling addict *dissipated* her entire retirement fund on table games such as poker and blackjack, she was consumed with _____ and slowly let her life fall apart.
   A. analects
   B. parity
   C. propinquity
   D. anomie
   E. echelon

6. The homeless man's _____ speech led people to believe his *spurious* story that he had been an opera singer who had fallen on hard times.
   A. nondescript
   B. punitive
   C. magniloquent
   D. discerning
   E. idyllic

7. Ryan was hired as a *factotum* who would work in each of the company's divisions, seeking _____ tools and methods to reduce waste and increase production.
   A. tremulous
   B. utilitarian
   C. stentorian
   D. transient
   E. extant

8. The eastern chapter of the secret society perceived a lack of economic _____ with its West Coast counterpart, and initiated a *schism* that severed relations between the groups.
   A. propinquity
   B. analects
   C. anomie
   D. parity
   E. apostasy

9. An *inveterate* user of methamphetamine has a life expectancy of five years, owing to the especially _____ effects and addictive nature of the drug.
   A. supine
   B. deleterious
   C. extrinsic
   D. outré
   E. prosaic

10. The _____ film really made us think about our place in the universe, but the *prosaic* dialogue nearly put everyone to sleep.
    A. cerebral
    B. nondescript
    C. punitive
    D. idyllic
    E. discerning

> ### Exercise III

Deeper Meanings

Choose a word to replace the italicized word in each sentence. All of the possible choices for each sentence have similar definitions, but the correct answer will have a connotation that best suits the context. For example, the words "delete," "destroy," and "obliterate" all mean "to remove or wipe out," but no one would ever say, "I destroyed the name from the document." The correct choice will be the word that has the best specific meaning and does not render the sentence awkward in tone or content. When choices seem close, look for a clue in the context that makes one choice better than the other.

Note that the correct answer is not always the primary vocabulary word from the lesson.

exciting	extreme	utilitarian	fun	unwieldy
sneaky	acme	awkward	disguised	useful

1. The *weird* shape of the killer whale made relocating it to a new body of water very difficult.

   Better word: _____

2. The fans hoped to have a[n] *idyllic* time at the heavy metal concert, starring bands such as "Chainsaw" and "Gnash."

   Better word: _____

3. Meg hides the house key in a[n] *surreptitious* key holder that looks like one of the rocks in the flower garden.

   Better word: _____

4. The newest handheld video game is the *height* of every ten-year-old's wish list.

   Better word: _____

5. Jeremy's *functional* van dependably gets him from point A to point B; it hauls six passengers comfortably, and it will never be stolen because it is the ugliest vehicle on the street.

   Better word: _____

Exercise IV

Crossword Puzzle

Use the clues to complete the crossword puzzle. The answers consist of vocabulary words from Lessons 19 through 21.

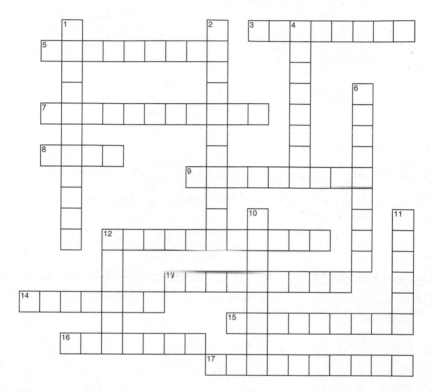

Across

3. only in the planning stages
5. understanding completely
7. just a coincidence
8. Mt. Everest's summit
9. shy and afraid
12. in the same room
13. what we don't need
14. a temperature of 103 degrees
15. use it all up
16. couldn't be better
17. hurts my ears!

Down

1. just like everything else
2. simple, plain, and cheap, but it works great
4. knows all the answers in physics class
6. just passing through
10. Grounded! Again!
11. on the couch
12. Two teams with the same record might have this.

Exercise V

Subject Prompts

Here is a writing prompt similar to the one you will find on the writing portion of an assessment test. Follow the instructions below and write a brief, efficient essay.

Imagine that a miracle spice has been recently discovered which, if ingested, adds 300 years to the average human lifespan. There is enough of the spice in existence to supply almost everyone in the nation with a single dose, rendering them virtually immortal, compared to the humans who do not receive the treatment.

The spice is too valuable a resource to simply discard—its lifesaving value alone could, temporarily at least, virtually stop death in the nation. There is no way to dilute the spice so that it can be distributed to a larger population—only the maximum dose yields the full effect.

You, as the leader of the free world, have the responsibility of deciding what to do with the existing supply of the spice. In a well-written essay, describe your plan for handling the distribution of the spice, and defend your decision. Include who will, or should, receive it, how it is to be managed, or if there should be a selection process for the recipients.

Be sure to account for many possibilities concerning the discovery: No one not yet born can receive it, other nations would want some and be willing to go to war to obtain it, people of power and money will demand greater access to it, as will the criminal element of society.

Thesis: Write a *one-sentence* response to the above assignment. Make certain this single sentence offers a clear statement of your position.

Example: Because the longevity spice is something that humans have desired for thousands of years and because of its priceless value, a selection process must be instituted to assure that those in greatest need of it—the elderly, the terminally ill, and the members of the military—receive it first.

Organizational Plan: List at least three subtopics you will use to support your main idea. This list is your outline.

1. _____

2. _____

3. _____

Draft: Following your outline, write a good first draft of your essay. Remember to support all of your points with examples, facts, references to reading, etc.

Review and Revise: Exchange essays with a classmate. Using the scoring guide for Sentence Formation and Variety on page 274, score your partner's essay (while he or she scores yours). Focus on sentence structure and the use of language conventions. If necessary, rewrite your essay to improve the sentence structure and/or your use of language.

Scoring Guide for Writing

Organization

6 = Clearly Competent

The paper is **clearly** organized **around the central point or main idea**. The organization may grow from the writer's argument or a slightly predictable structure. Ideas follow a logical order.

The work is **free of surface errors** (grammar, spelling, punctuation, etc.).

5 = Reasonably Competent

The organization of the paper is **clear, but not fully implemented**. The structure might be predictable. Ideas follow a logical order, but transitions might be simple or obvious.

Minor surface errors are present, but they **do not interfere** with the reader's understanding of the work.

4 = Adequately Competent

The organization of the paper is **apparent, but not consistently implemented**. The structure is predictable. Some ideas follow a logical order, but transitions are simple and obvious.

Surface errors are present, but they **do not severely interfere** with the reader's understanding.

3 = Nearly Competent

There **is evidence of a** simple organizational **plan**. Ideas are grouped logically in parts of the paper, but do not flow logically throughout. Transitions are needed.

Surface errors are **apparent** and **begin to interfere** with the reader's understanding of the work.

2 = Marginally Incompetent

The organizational plan of the paper is **obscured by too few details** and/or **irrelevant details**. Some of the ideas are grouped logically in parts of the paper. Transitions are needed or are incorrect.

Surface errors are **frequent and severe enough** to **interfere** with the reader's understanding of the work.

1 = Incompetent

There is **no** clear organizational **plan** and/or **insufficient material**. Ideas are not grouped logically. Transitions are absent.

Surface errors are **frequent** and **extreme**, and **severely interfere** with the reader's understanding of the work.

Scoring Guide for Writing

Development

6 = Clearly Competent
The **paper takes a position** on the issue and **offers sufficient material** (details, examples, anecdotes, supporting facts, etc.) to create a **complete discussion. Every word and sentence is relevant**. Ideas are **fully supported**.
The paper visits **different perspectives** of the argument or addresses **counterarguments** to the writer's position. The paper **focuses** on the argument evoked by the prompt. There is a **clear**, **purposed**, well-developed **introduction and conclusion**.
The work is **free of surface errors** (grammar, spelling, punctuation, etc.).

5 = Reasonably Competent
The essay **takes a position** on the issue and **offers sufficient material** for a complete discussion, but the reader is left **with a few unanswered questions**. Ideas are **supported**. The paper **partially visits different perspectives** of the argument or addresses **counterarguments. Most** of the paper **focuses** on the argument evoked by the prompt. There is **no irrelevant material**. There is a clear **introduction** and **conclusion**.
Minor surface errors are present, but they **do not interfere** with the reader's understanding of the work.

4 = Adequately Competent
The paper **takes a position** on the issue but **does not provide** enough details, examples, or supporting facts for a complete discussion, leaving a **few unanswered questions**. The paper includes **some attention** to **counterarguments** and differing perspectives. **Irrelevant material** is present. **Most** of the paper **focuses** on the topic and the specific argument.
Surface errors are present, but they **do not severely interfere** with the reader's understanding.

3 = Nearly Competent
The essay **takes a position** on the issue but **does not include** sufficient details, examples, or supporting facts for a discussion. The paper **may include incomplete or unclear counterarguments**. The paper **might repeat** details or rhetoric. The paper focuses on the topic, but **does not maintain** the specific argument.
Surface errors are **apparent** and **begin to interfere** with the reader's understanding of the work.

2 = **Marginally Incompetent**

The paper **may not take a position** on the issue, or the paper may take a position but **fail to support** it with sufficient details. Examples and ideas are **vague** and **irrelevant**. The paper might **repeat ideas extensively**. The paper **might maintain focus** on the general topic.

Surface errors are **frequent and severe enough** to **interfere** with the reader's understanding of the work.

1 = **Incompetent**

The paper **might attempt to take a position**, but it **fails to provide** examples, fact, or rhetoric to support the position. The paper may be **repetitious** with **little** or **no focus** on the general topic.

Surface errors are **frequent** and **extreme**, and **severely interfere** with the reader's understanding of the work.

Scoring Guide for Writing

Sentence Formation And Variety

6 = Clearly Competent
Sentences are **varied**, **complete**, and **assist the reader** in the flow of the discussion.
The work is **free of surface errors** (grammar, spelling, punctuation, etc.).

5 = Reasonably Competent
Sentences are **somewhat varied**, **generally correct**, and **do not distract** the reader from the flow of the discussion.
Minor surface errors are present, but they **do not interfere** with the reader's understanding of the work.

4 = Adequately Competent
Some sentences show **variety**, and **most** are **complete** and **generally correct**.
Surface errors are present, but they **do not interfere** with the reader's understanding.

3 = Nearly Competent
Sentences show a **little variety**, but the structure may be **dull**. Sentences are **generally complete** and grammatically correct, but **some errors** distract the reader.
Surface errors are **apparent** and **begin to interfere** with the reader's understanding of the work.

2 = Marginally Incompetent
Sentence Structure is **usually simple**. Problems in **sentence structure** and **grammar** distract the reader and provide **little or no variety**.
Surface errors are **frequent and severe enough** to **interfere** with the reader's understanding of the work.

1 = Incompetent
Sentence structure is **simple, generally erroneous** and **lacks variety**.
Surface errors are **frequent** and **extreme**, and **severely interfere** with the reader's understanding of the work.

Scoring Guide for Writing

Word Choice

6 = Clearly Competent

The essay shows a **good command** of language. Word choice is **specific**, **clear**, and **vivid**, favoring **powerful nouns** and **verbs** to weaker adjective and adverb phrases. **Clear, specific words** are used, instead of vague, general terms.
The work is **free of surface errors** (grammar, spelling, punctuation, etc.).

5 = Reasonably Competent

Language is **competent**. Word choice is **clear** and **accurate**. Words and phrases are **mostly** vivid, specific, and powerful.
Minor surface errors are present, but they **do not interfere** with the reader's understanding of the work.

4 = Adequately Competent

Language is **adequate**, with **appropriate** word choice. **Most** words and phrases are vivid, specific, and powerful.
Serious surface errors are present, but they **do not interfere** with the reader's understanding.

3 = Nearly Competent

Language shows a **basic control** and word choice is **usually appropriate but inconsistent**.
Surface errors are **apparent** and **begin to interfere** with the reader's understanding of the work.

2 = Marginally Incompetent

Word choice is usually **vague**.
Surface errors are **frequent** and **severe enough** to **interfere** with the reader's understanding of the work.

1 = Incompetent

Word choice is **simple**, **vague**, and **inexact**. The writer makes **no attempt** to choose the best words for the topic, audience, and purpose.
Surface errors are **frequent** and **extreme**, and **severely interfere** with the reader's understanding of the work.

Scoring Guide for Writing

Holistic

6 = Clearly Competent

The paper is **clearly organized** around the central idea. Ideas follow a **logical order**.

The paper **takes a position** on the issue and **offers sufficient material** (details, examples, anecdotes, supporting facts, etc.) to create a complete discussion. There is a **clear**, **purposed**, **well developed** introduction and conclusion.

The paper visits **different perspectives** of the argument or addresses **counterarguments** to the writer's position.

Sentences are **varied**, **complete**, and **assist the reader** in the flow of the discussion.

The paper shows a **good command** of language. Word choice is **specific**, **clear**, and **vivid**, favoring **powerful nouns** and **verbs** to weaker adjective and adverb phrases.

The work is **free of surface errors** (grammar, spelling, punctuation, etc.).

5 = Reasonably Competent

The organization of the paper is **clear**, but **not fully implemented**. Ideas follow a **logical order**, but transitions **might be simple** or obvious. The structure **might be predictable**.

The paper **takes a position** on the issue and **offers sufficient material** for a complete discussion, but the reader is left with **a few unanswered questions**. There is a clear **introduction** and **conclusion**.

The paper visits **some different perspectives** of the argument or addresses **counterarguments**.

Sentences are **somewhat varied**, **generally correct**, and **do not distract** the reader from the flow of the discussion.

Language is **competent**. Words and phrases are **mostly vivid**, **specific**, and **powerful**.

Minor surface errors are present, but they **do not interfere** with the reader's understanding of the work.

4 = Adequately Competent

The organization of the paper is **apparent**, but **not consistently** implemented. The structure is **predictable**. **Some** ideas follow a **logical order**, but transitions are **simple** and **obvious**. **Most** of the paper **focuses** on the topic and the specific argument.

The paper **takes a position** on the issue, but **does not provide** the details, examples, or supporting facts for a complete discussion, leaving **a few unanswered questions**.

The paper includes **little attention** to counterarguments and differing perspectives.

Irrelevant material is present.

Language is **adequate**, with appropriate word choice. **Most** words and phrases are vivid, specific, and powerful.

Some sentences show **variety**, and **most** are **complete** and **generally correct**.

Surface errors are present, but they **do not interfere** with the reader's understanding.

3 = Nearly Competent

There is **evidence of a simple organizational plan**. The essay **takes a position** on the issue but **does not include** sufficient details, examples, or supporting facts for a discussion. Ideas are **grouped logically** in parts of the paper, **but do not flow** logically throughout. The paper **focuses** on the topic, but **does not maintain** the specific argument.

The paper **may include incomplete** or **unclear** counterarguments.

Language shows a **basic control**, and word choice is **usually appropriate** but **inconsistent**. Sentences show a **little variety**, but the structure may be **dull**.

Sentences are **generally complete** and **grammatically correct**, but some errors **distract** the reader.

The paper might **repeat** details or rhetoric.

Surface errors are **apparent** and **begin to interfere** with the reader's understanding of the work.

2 = Marginally Incompetent

The organizational plan of the paper is **obscured by too few details** and/or **irrelevant details**. The paper **may not take a position** on the issue, or the paper may take a position but **fail to support** it with sufficient details. **Some** of the ideas are **grouped logically** in parts of the paper. The paper **generally maintains focus** on the general topic.

Examples and ideas are **vague** and **irrelevant**.

Sentence structure is **usually simple**. **Problems** in sentence structure and grammar **distract** the reader and provide **little** or **no variety**. **Word choice** is usually **vague**.

The paper might **repeat** ideas **extensively**.

Surface errors are **frequent and severe enough** to **interfere** with the reader's understanding of the work.

1 = Incompetent

There is **no clear organizational plan** and/or **insufficient material**. The paper **might attempt** to **take a position**, but it **fails** to provide examples, fact, or rhetoric to support the position. Ideas are **not grouped logically**.

The paper may be **repetitious** with little or **no focus** on the general topic.

Sentence structure is **simple** and **generally erroneous** and **lacking variety**. Word choice is **simple, vague,** and **inexact**. The writer makes **no attempt** to choose the best words for the topic, audience, and purpose.

Surface errors are **frequent** and **extreme,** and **severely interfere** with the reader's understanding of the work.

Relevant State Standards

High School - Grades 11-12

These are only the minimum standards that the product line meets; if these standards seem out of order, they typically go in "keyword" order; from the Language Usage category of standards, to Comprehension, Analysis, Writing, Research/Applied, and Technology/ Media categories. Therefore, these standards may be in a different order than the order given by your local Department of Education. Also, if one state standard meets multiple categories, that particular standard is listed the first time it appears, to reduce redundancy. Again, please refer to your local Department of Education for details on the particular standards.

Bias/Validity standards are included, as are Voice/Style standards, as both categories include use of words for different effects on the audience (connotation, denotation, distortion, formality, etc.) and, thus, are logical inclusions.

Depending on the state, standards pertaining to use of dialect and idiomatic expressions might be met by this product. Please refer to your local Department of Education for details.

Notation is as close as possible to the notation given by the Department of Education of the respective state.

States:

Alaska (GLEs only up to Grade 10; Grade 10 repeated here):
R4.1.1-4; R4.4.1-2; R4.5.1; R4.5.2-3; W4 (all); R4.1.5; R4.2.1-2; R4.3.1-4; R4.3.5-6; R4.7.1; R4.9.2; R4.9.1; R4.6.1-4; W4.2.2; W4.4.5

Indiana:
12.1.1-3; 12.3.1; 12.3.3-4; 12.4.1-6, 10-11; 12.6 (all); 12.5 (all); 12.4.12; 12.2.1; 12.2.3, 5, 6; 12.5.9; 12.3.8-9; 12.3.5,7,10; 12.5.9

Nebraska (standards set at Grade 12):
12.1.1; 12.1.5; 12.1.6

Texas (TEKS section 110.45):
b7 (all); b8 (all); b11 (all); b9 (all); b12E; b2 (all); b3 (all); b1 (all); b13 (all); b20C; B8I; B9D; B5D; B12G; B10C; B6 (entire); B1B-F

Virginia:
12.4 (all); 12.3a; 12.7 (all); 12.8b; 12.3 (entire); 12.2 (entire)

Common Core State Standards for English Language Arts

Standards	Exercises
Reading Standards for Informational Text	
Key Ideas and Details	
RI.11-12.1	Cite strong and thorough textual evidence to support analysis of what the text says explicitly as well as inferences drawn from the text.	**Critical Reading** Lessons: 2, 4, 6, 8, 10, 12, 14, 16, 18, 20
RI.11-12.2	Determine a central idea of a text and analyze its development over the course of the text, including how it emerges and is shaped and refined by specific details; provide an objective summary of the text.	**Critical Reading** Lessons: 2, 4, 6, 8, 10, 12, 14, 16, 18, 20
Craft and Structure	
RI.11-12.4	Determine the meaning of words and phrases as they are used in a text, including figurative, connotative, and technical meanings; analyze the cumulative impact of specific word choices on meaning and tone (e.g., how the language of a court opinion differs from that of a newspaper).	**Critical Reading** Lessons: 2, 4, 6, 8, 10, 12, 14, 16, 18, 20 **Inference** Lessons: 1-21
RI.11-12.6	Determine an author's point of view or purpose in a text and analyze how an author uses rhetoric to advance that point of view or purpose.	**Critical Reading** Lessons: 2, 4, 6, 8, 10, 12, 14, 16, 18, 20
Writing Standards	
Text Types and Purposes	
W.11-12.1	Write arguments to support claims in an analysis of substantive topics or texts, using valid reasoning and relevant and sufficient evidence.	**Writing** Lessons: 1, 3, 5, 7, 9, 11, 13, 15, 17, 19, 21
W.11-12.1a	Introduce precise claim(s), distinguish the claim(s) from alternate or opposing claims, and create an organization that establishes clear relationships among claim(s), counterclaims, reasons, and evidence.	**Writing** Lessons: 1, 3, 5, 7, 9, 11, 13, 15, 17, 19, 21
W.11-12.1b	Develop claim(s) and counterclaims fairly, supplying evidence for each while pointing out the strengths and limitations of both in a manner that anticipates the audience's knowledge level and concerns.	**Writing** Lessons: 1, 3, 5, 7, 9, 11, 13, 15, 17, 19, 21
W.11-12.1c	Use words, phrases, and clauses to link the major sections of the text, create cohesion, and clarify the relationships between claim(s) and reasons, between reasons and evidence, and between claim(s) and counterclaims.	**Writing** Lessons: 1, 3, 5, 7, 9, 11, 13, 15, 17, 19, 21

W.11-12.1d	Establish and maintain a formal style and objective tone while attending to the norms and conventions of the discipline in which they are writing.	**Writing** Lessons: 1, 3, 5, 7, 9, 11, 13, 15, 17, 19, 21
W.11-12.1e	Provide a concluding statement or section that follows from and supports the argument presented.	**Writing** Lessons: 1, 3, 5, 7, 9, 11, 13, 15, 17, 19, 21
W.11-12.2	Write informative/explanatory texts to examine and convey complex ideas, concepts, and information clearly and accurately through the effective selection, organization, and analysis of content.	**Writing** Lessons: 1, 3, 5, 7, 9, 11, 13, 15, 17, 19, 21
W.11-12.2a	Introduce a topic; organize complex ideas, concepts, and information to make important connections and distinctions; include formatting (e.g., headings), graphics (e.g., figures, tables), and multimedia when useful to aiding comprehension.	**Writing** Lessons: 1, 3, 5, 7, 9, 11, 13, 15, 17, 19, 21
W.11-12.2b	Develop the topic with well-chosen, relevant, and sufficient facts, extended definitions, concrete details, quotations, or other information and examples appropriate to the audience's knowledge of the topic.	**Writing** Lessons: 1, 3, 5, 7, 9, 11, 13, 15, 17, 19, 21
W.11-12.2c	Use appropriate and varied transitions to link the major sections of the text, create cohesion, and clarify the relationships among complex ideas and concepts.	**Writing** Lessons: 1, 3, 5, 7, 9, 11, 13, 15, 17, 19, 21
W.11-12.2d	Use precise language and domain-specific vocabulary to manage the complexity of the topic.	**Writing** Lessons: 1, 3, 5, 7, 9, 11, 13, 15, 17, 19, 21
W.11-12.2e	Establish and maintain a formal style and objective tone while attending to the norms and conventions of the discipline in which they are writing.	**Writing** Lessons: 1, 3, 5, 7, 9, 11, 13, 15, 17, 19, 21
W.11-12.2f	Provide a concluding statement or section that follows from and supports the information or explanation presented (e.g., articulating implications or the significance of the topic).	**Writing** Lessons: 1, 3, 5, 7, 9, 11, 13, 15, 17, 19, 21

Range of Writing

W.11-12.10	Write routinely over extended time frames (time for research, reflection, and revision) and shorter time frames (a single sitting or a day or two) for a range of tasks, purposes, and audiences.	**Writing** Lessons: 1, 3, 5, 7, 9, 11, 13, 15, 17, 19, 21

Language Standards

Conventions of Standard English

L.11-12.1	Demonstrate command of the conventions of standard English grammar and usage when writing or speaking.	**Identifying Sentence Errors** Lessons: 1, 5, 9, 13, 17, 21 **Improving Sentences** Lessons: 1, 5, 9, 13, 17, 21 **Improving Paragraphs** Lessons: 3, 7, 11, 15, 19 **Writing** Lessons: 1, 3, 5, 7, 9, 11, 13, 15, 17, 19, 21
L.11-12.2	Demonstrate command of the conventions of standard English capitalization, punctuation, and spelling when writing.	**Identifying Sentence Errors** Lessons: 1, 5, 9, 13, 17, 21 **Improving Sentences** Lessons: 1, 5, 9, 13, 17, 21 **Improving Paragraphs** Lessons: 3, 7, 11, 15, 19 **Writing** Lessons: 1, 3, 5, 7, 9, 11, 13, 15, 17, 19, 21

Vocabulary Acquisition and Use	
L.11-12.4	Determine or clarify the meaning of unknown and multiple-meaning words and phrases based on grades 11–12 reading and content, choosing flexibly from a range of strategies.	**Critical Reading** Lessons: 1-21
L.11-12.4a	Use context (e.g., the overall meaning of a sentence, paragraph, or text; a word's position or function in a sentence) as a clue to the meaning of a word or phrase.	**Word in Context** Lessons: 1-21 **Inference** Lessons: 1-21 **Critical Reading** Lessons: 1-21
L.11-12.4b	Identify and correctly use patterns of word changes that indicate different meanings or parts of speech (e.g., analyze, analysis, analytical; advocate, advocacy).	**Roots, Prefixes, and Suffixes** Lessons: 1-21
L.11-12.4d	Verify the preliminary determination of the meaning of a word or phrase (e.g., by checking the inferred meaning in context or in a dictionary).	**Inference** Lessons: 1-3, 4-6, 7-9, 10-12, 13-15, 16-18, 19-21
L.11-12.5	Demonstrate understanding of figurative language, word relationships, and nuances in word meanings.	**Related Words, Deeper Meaning** Lessons: 1-3, 4-6, 7-9, 10-12, 13-15, 16-18, 19-21
L.11-12.5b	Analyze nuances in the meaning of words with similar denotations.	**Critical Reading: Level Four** Lessons: 2, 4, 6, 8, 10, 12, 14, 16, 18, 20
L.11-12.6	Acquire and use accurately general academic and domain-specific words and phrases, sufficient for reading, writing, speaking, and listening at the college and career readiness level; demonstrate independence in gathering vocabulary knowledge when considering a word or phrase important to comprehension or expression.	**Level Four** Lessons: 1-21

History/Social Studies

Key Ideas and Details

RH.11-12.1.	Cite specific textual evidence to support analysis of primary and secondary sources, attending to such features as the date and origin of the information.	**Critical Reading** Lessons: 2, 4, 6, 8, 10, 12, 14, 16, 18, 20

Craft and Structure

RH.11-12.4	Determine the meaning of words and phrases as they are used in a text, including vocabulary describing political, social, or economic aspects of history/social science.	**Critical Reading** Lessons: 2, 4, 6, 8, 10, 12, 14, 16, 18, 20
RH.11-12.6	Compare the point of view of two or more authors for how they treat the same or similar topics, including which details they include and emphasize in their respective accounts.	**Critical Reading** Lessons: 4, 8, 12, 16, 20

Integration of Knowledge and Ideas

RH.11-12.9	Compare and contrast treatments of the same topic in several primary and secondary sources.	**Critical Reading** Lessons: 4, 8, 12, 16, 20